Lying

Lying

An Augustinian
Theology of Duplicity

Paul J. Griffiths

BrazosPress
Grand Rapids, Michigan 49516

Published by Brazos Press
a division of Baker Book House Company
P.O. Box 6287, Grand Rapids, MI 49516-6287
www.brazospress.com

Printed in the United States of America

Library of Congress Cataloging-in-Publication Data
Griffiths, Paul J.
    Lying: an Augustinian theology of duplicity / Paul J. Griffiths.
        p.   cm.
    Includes bibliographical references.
    ISBN 1-58743-086-X (pbk.)
    1. Truthfulness and falsehood—Religious aspects—Christianity. 2. Augustine, Saint, Bishop of Hippo. 3. Truthfulness and falsehood. I. Title.
    BV4627.F3G75 2004
    241'.673—dc22   2003024500

I dedicate this book to Francis George,
Cardinal Archbishop of Chicago;
like Augustine, bishop and teacher

Contents

Acknowledgments

I've had help in writing this book from more people than I can now remember. Those who've helped me by conversing, or by reading and commenting on all or part of this work at various stages, include Margaret Mitchell, Derek Jeffreys, Katherine Tillman, David Hart, Judith Heyhoe, Stanley Hauerwas, Larry Poston, Reinhard Hütter, Del Kiernan-Lewis, Charles Taliaferro, Jeffrey Gibson, Ed Oakes, Rodney Clapp, Thomas Levergood, Mary Beth Rose, Catherine Pickstock, and Stephen Lewis. Those who've helped me by their writings on the subject have been acknowledged in the book's notes. And those who've helped me by providing institutional support and stimulating places in which to work include the faculty, staff, and students of the University of Chicago's Divinity School, where the work was begun (Rick Rosengarten deserves special thanks here); and the faculty, staff, and students of the University of Illinois at Chicago, where it was completed (Stanley Fish deserves special thanks here).

Introduction

Lies bind the fabric of every human life. We lie to our lovers when we whisper sweet nothings; we lie to the glowing screen when we process the words of our novels, poems, and (especially) autobiographies; we lie to the mirror when we smooth on the subtly deceptive unguents that replace our faces with someone else's; we lie to our children when we browbeat them with the image of our imagined rectitude; we lie to our cocktail-party conversation partners when we artfully suggest that someone wittier than ourselves is there, twirling the stemmed glass with implied profundity; we lie to our confessors when, kneeling in the attitude of contrition, we imagine what they'd like to hear in order to think us true athletes of the spirit; we lie to our students when we assume the position of omniscience; and we lie to ourselves when, self-deceived, we obscure our creatively diverse uses of the lie from ourselves and etch the dubious portrait of the truth-teller upon our souls with the acid of the lie denied. We are imaginatively masked, adorned with the lie, bedecked with the elegance of verbal dissimulation. To be so is the very mark of adult humanity.

Or so it may seem.

Children, it is true, have to learn how to lie, but it's not a skill they find difficult to master. Wittgenstein writes, with characteristically careful understatement, that someone who doesn't lie is already original enough. But in fact, adults who don't lie are more than original: they're almost nonexistent. When they are found, they almost always bear the burden of their unremitting honesty together with some clinical psychological disorder: they're retarded, insane, or saintly—or perhaps all three at once. The closer an adult moves to a life free from lies, the more difficult she finds ordinary social life. Wittgenstein's own passion for honesty, evident in his tendency to make formal, face-to-face confessions to friends and casual acquaintances of minor lies he'd told, was among his more difficult personal characteristics; it led those to whom he made such confessions to have reasonable doubts about his sanity.

If the systematic avoidance of lying often goes with pathologies of one sort or another, it's not surprising that all adults are at least occasional liars. It's a little more surprising, perhaps, that most are not quite happy about the fact. There may be some who feel no doubts or perplexities about their mendacities. But most of us wish we lied less frequently than we do, or that our lies didn't cause us the problems they sometimes do, or even that we could manage to do without lies altogether. Our lies, in one way or another, make us uneasy—not all of them all the time, but some of them on some occasions. We're likely to have been told by our parents that we oughtn't to lie; we know that if we lie under oath or about a matter of personal or public delicacy and importance and are found out, there'll be some unpleasant consequences; we understand the extent to which our good reputation depends upon people being able to trust that what we say isn't a lie. We're quite likely to have painted a self-image that includes among its more creatively imaginative orna-ments the delicate colors of honesty, straightforwardness, directness, trustworthiness, and fearless truth-telling. Americans are likely to have folktales about George Washington's cherry tree and Honest Abe lurk-ing deep in mind as they paint their self-portraits. Christians and Jews believe that one of the commandments given by God to Moses forbids false witness, and even if most of them are not quite sure what false witness is, they're likely (rightly) to think that it has something to do with lying. These things tend to make us unhappy about the lies we tell and may even reduce their number and frequency. But it does not stop us from telling them completely and for good. Not even Wittgenstein could manage that. We're left, then, as more or less unhappy liars—but still and always as liars.

We look for ways to decrease our discomfort. We may, as did the sententious and self-righteous serjeant in Anthony Trollope's novel *Lady Anna*, emphasize our negative judgments about the lies told to us, and so attempt to deflect such judgments from the ones we tell to others:

> The Serjeant no doubt hated a lie,—as most of us do hate lies; and had a strong conviction that the devil is the father of them. But then the lies which he hated, and as to the parentage of which he was quite certain, were lies told to him. Who ever yet met a man who did not in his heart of hearts despise an attempt made by others to deceive—himself? They

whom we have found to be gentler in their judgment towards attempts made in another direction have been more than one or two.

But this tactic doesn't comfort many of us for long: it's too transparently self-serving. So also is its kissing cousin, the attempt to excuse all our own lies as benevolent while classifying those of others as self-interested and manipulative.

We may then be driven, if we're unusually troubled by inconsistencies between our convictions and our actions (we think it's wrong to lie but we do it anyway), to think hard about what it is to lie, and why (and indeed whether) it's wrong to do so. These are the two great questions about the lie. Those who do begin to think about these questions may turn to the work of those who've already thought and written about them. This is hard to avoid, for no one can begin to think about anything in a vacuum. There are many conversation partners on the question of the lie, but little agreement among them.

Plato and Aristotle, for example, agreed in damning some lies, excusing others, and recommending yet others (though they did not agree on which lies belong to which category, nor on just what it is to lie); Greek literature is full of significant lies, and one of its heroes, Odysseus, is the very archetype of the mendacious man, the changeable man of tricks and deceits; but Odysseus's lies—and the other pivotal lies of Greek literature—are presented sometimes as evidence of discernment and virtue, and sometimes as evidence of perfidious corruption. Among Christians and Jews there has been and remains deep disagreement about what it is to lie and whether it's ever a good thing to do so—Jerome and Augustine, for example, had an acrimonious correspondence about the matter; the rabbis multiplied cases and interpretations of the lie, disagreeing (as about almost everything) on the circumstances under which the lie is permissible and on which scriptural texts are relevant to the matter; and two of the fathers of modern and postmodern thought, Immanuel Kant and Friedrich Nietzsche, took diametrically opposed positions on the question of the lie, the former arguing that it is never under any circumstances permissible to lie, and the latter that lying is both unavoidable and desirable.

There are surveys and analyses of the history of Western thought on the lie that help to reduce this mass of material to some order. But reading these won't remove the correct impression that there is fundamental disagreement on and considerable confusion about the two great questions concerning the lie: What is it to lie? When, if ever, should or may the lie be told?

I don't intend in this book to answer these questions to everyone's satisfaction. That is an impossible task. I hope, instead, to restate, explore, defend, and apply the answers given to them by one thinker. That thinker is Aurelius Augustinus (A.D. 354–430), more usually and familiarly known as Augustine, a saint and doctor of the Catholic church and one of the few thinkers of late antiquity, Christian or pagan, whose work is still widely read. His answers to the two questions were, in excessively brief summary, that the lie is any duplicitous utterance; and that it is never under any circumstances proper. More on these answers to come, obviously. But first, why Augustine? Three reasons at least.

The first is that what he wrote about the lie has historical importance and remains potent. Augustine was the first in the West to address the two questions about the lie systematically, by which I mean that he was the first to offer a coherent and thought-through definition of the lie (neither Plato nor Aristotle managed that, and neither did any Christian thinker before Augustine), together with a methodical and thoroughgoing position on the question of its acceptability. He was also the first to think about the questions of the lie in specifically and characteristically Christian terms. Christians before him (and many since) had been content to think about lying in general terms, terms that could be shared by Christians and non-Christians alike. Augustine was not content with this. He wanted to find, and thought he found, a position on the lie drawn from and perhaps even entailed by peculiarly Christian convictions about the nature of God and of human persons. In Augustine's thought on the lie, then, we have the first systematic position in the West, as well as the first explicitly and fully Christian position. What he wrote about the two fundamental questions of the lie was immediately controversial: few Christians agreed with him when he wrote, and although his work on the topic has been much quoted and appealed to by Christians (and others) since, very few have fully understood or agreed with it. But his answers have remained potent: they hang like a half-understood shadow over Western thought about the lie—over Christian thought, obviously, but over Western thought more generally, as well. I intend, among other things, to make his position better understood and more accessible.

The second reason for treating Augustine's thought on the lie is that what he wrote about it is extreme, and, to most who have read him on the topic, unacceptable. This has been as true for Christians who claim to be followers of Augustine as for those who think Augustine's work a wrong turn. And of course it has been true almost without exception for non-Christian readers of Augustine. Confusion about how to understand

and constrain our lying hearts, and about the questions of the lie in general, will be bracingly clarified by engaging and fully understanding an extreme position like Augustine's. This is certainly so if the result of reading and thinking about him is conviction that what he says is correct. But even if the result is disagreement, gaining clarity about what's unacceptable in Augustine's position will be a great benefit.

The third reason for engaging his thought is that he is right. Or so I think. I have not come to this conclusion easily, and I remain in many ways unhappy with it; but I am persuaded that Augustine is correct both in his particular answers to the questions of the lie and in his derivation of these answers from other central Christian convictions. My reasons for thinking so will be laid out in what follows, as I restate what Augustine thought, and as I bring his thought into explicit discussion with that of others. I don't expect that what I say will be persuasive to many, any more than what Augustine wrote proved persuasive to many. For those who are not Christians already, such persuasion would require assent to a large number of truths about God's nature and the image of God in us, for Augustine thinks that what he argues about the lie presupposes the truth of such Christian convictions; and it would be profoundly unrealistic to expect non-Christians to come to take such truths as true simply on the basis of an exposition of Augustine's thought on the lie. And, as the history of Christian disagreement with Augustine shows, even for Christians, who share with him some of the Christian convictions he appeals to in his writings about the lie, persuasion that his view of the lie follows from these convictions has not been exactly widespread. It is possible, then, to remain rational, as both a non-Christian and a Christian, in rejecting Augustine's views. If he's right, those who reject his position will of course be wrong; but that it is possible to remain rational in not being persuaded is a function of the disputability and difficulty of any thoroughgoing answers to the questions of the lie.

What did Augustine write about the lie? A good deal—as he did about almost everything. His surviving works extend to many millions of Latin words: few can claim to have read it all (I certainly have not), and anyone who studies Augustine can identify with Isidore of Seville's lament that Augustine wrote so much that it is not only impossible to copy all his works, but even to read them. Fortunately, the main outlines of his position on the questions of lying *(mendacium)* and the liar *(mendax)* can be understood without reading everything he wrote.

Augustine did write two short treatises devoted solely to the topic of the lie: the first, *Lying*, was written in 394 or 395, when he was 40 or 41 and shortly before he was made bishop; the second, *Against Lying*, was written twenty-five years later. In the discussion that follows I'll draw heavily on these works, but reading what I write about Augustine's thought on the lie is no substitute for reading Augustine himself; I hope that this book will persuade some to read at least his treatises on the lie. These are quite easily available in English, and are short enough that they can both be read in a day. But these works are not all that Augustine wrote about the lie. The questions about the lie fascinated and inflamed him, and he returned to the topic often throughout his career, discussing it in his earliest postconversion works, and returning to it in his last systematic works in the years just before his death. He preached on it, mentioned it as an example in works devoted to other topics, and spent a good deal of time and effort on the explanation of scriptural texts that seemed to him relevant to the topic. I shall draw on as much of this material as is known to me that seems relevant; but my goal is not to provide a complete and historically nuanced account of Augustine's thought on the lie; I want, rather, to lay bare the structure of his thought on the topic, its grammar and syntax, and to make constructive use and application of that structure.

The first part of this book expounds Augustine's thought on the lie. His thought on this topic, however, can't be understood by itself: it sounds as a note in the greater harmony of his whole thought, and in order for it to sound clearly some of the other notes in this harmony need to be played along with it. I begin, then, with his definition of the lie ("Lying," ch. 1). This definition requires explanation of what he thinks about the orders of existence and love ("Being," ch. 2)—of, that is, what distinctively human existence is like, and how human desires ought to be ordered. This leads to discussion of how these desires can be disordered ("Sinning," ch. 3), and of the contribution that speech in general and lying speech in particular make to such disorder ("Speaking,'" ch. 4). From all this I derive a picture of what Augustine thinks speech ought to be like: received as gift and returned as praise, without intervening attempts at control and ownership by the speaker ("Disowning," ch. 5). Depiction of speech disowned throws into relief what Augustine thinks wrong with lying speech. A difficulty for his understanding of lying speech is raised by the fabrication of fictions, and this I address at the end of Part One ("Storytelling," ch. 6).

Augustine's position on the lie is neither the only possible nor the obviously best position. Competing positions are taken on any complex question relevant to human nature and the proper conduct of human life, and none is obviously correct—at least, this is so if "obviously correct" means "immediately convincing to all who come to understand it." Augustine's understanding of what it is to lie and of why we should never do it did not prove convincing to most Christians who thought or wrote about the matter, and certainly not to most non-Christians. This is enough to show that it is not the obviously correct position.

But that Augustine's position is not obviously correct does not mean that it is not correct. On the contrary, that it is not obviously correct has nothing at all to do with whether it is correct. To have a theory about what it is to lie and whether it's ever defensible or required to do so involves taking a position on the nature and purpose(s) of human speech, which in turn requires a position on the nature and purpose(s) of human existence as such. Augustine's position on the lie is a case in point: to say that the lie is a sin, a recursively self-defeating action that shatters the image of the Triune God in which we are made, deploys a wide range of disputable (and inevitably disputed) concepts. If you think, for example, that there is no God, or that there is a God but that human beings are not made in his image, you will not be persuaded by Augustine's view of the lie. Rather, you are likely to find it absurd or not worth considering just because it assumes concepts of this sort. But all this is quite irrelevant to the question of whether Augustine is right. It shows only that the rightness of what he thinks about the lie depends upon the rightness of what he thinks about a good many other things. This will be true about any position on the lie. It is not that all such positions require commitments of a Christian sort. But it is the case that they all require commitments of a sort unlikely to be widely shared, commitments as to the nature of human beings, the goal(s) of human life, the principal constraints upon human action, and so on. Disagreements about such matters are, I should think it obvious, not typically capable of resolution by argument. Commentary is likely to do a better job, and that is what I attempt in the second part of this book, "Augustinian Readings."

Why is commentary likely to do a better job than argument? Because it is possible to use commentary to clarify and illuminate the contours of a particular position on the lie by bringing it into close contact with a competing position. One way to do this—the method adopted here—is to read a text presenting a competing view through the spectacles of the Augustinian view. This is what I mean by an "Augustinian reading." The first component in such a reading is exegetical: the concern here is to clarify and restate what the text being read is saying. This will require attention to its particular vocabulary, its characteristic patterns of argument, and the assumptions that inform it but that it does not make explicit or argue for. The second moment in such a reading attends to the clarification of differences: the concern here is to lay bare what separates the chosen text's account of the lie from an Augustinian account, and in so doing to sharpen and clarify understanding of the grammar and syntax of both accounts. The third moment in such a reading suggests, tentatively, what would be required to show which of the competing accounts is to be preferred. Even at this third stage, argumentative resolution is not the goal and will certainly not be the result. The goal is, rather, to suggest how the differences and incompatibilities revealed during the second moment of the Augustinian reading might be pursued, and what is at stake in pursuing them.

An Augustinian reading of non-Augustinian texts on the lie proceeds through each of its three moments (from exegesis to clarification of differences to adumbration of resolution) on the assumption that its own grammar and syntax, together with the concepts that inform them, are the correct ones—that they properly define the lie and that from them a ban on the lie follows. This will be true of the particular Augustinian readings that follow; in them, I shall simply assume the Augustinian view outlined in the first part of this book. I don't make such an assumption out of obscurantism or fear; neither do I make it in order to prevent or short-circuit a genuine disagreement. Instead, I proceed in this way because it is better to be explicit and clear about what is in any case unavoidable, which is that all readings are always and necessarily committed readings, and that the degree to which they are interesting and illuminating is closely indexed to the full-blooded shamelessness of their commitments. To attempt a close look from nowhere at an alien text is to attempt something that cannot be done and that should not be tried. If you try to read and comment upon a text that itself propounds controversial and interestingly complex views about the lie while yourself eschewing assumptions of a controversial sort, you'll inevitably fail and will, in your failure, produce a pallid and platitudinous reading. You'll perhaps deceive yourself into thinking that you're being objective or distanced or judicious; but in fact you won't be because you can't be, and to the extent that you succeed in so deceiving yourself you'll produce a dishonest reading, an anodyne paraphrase that conceals its true distance from what it comments upon.

The readings in part two are not like this, I hope. They are Augustinian in that they assume as true Augustine's account of the lie and its ban, and attempt a reading of nine non-Augustinian texts on the model just sketched: exegesis, clarification of difference, adumbration of resolution. The nine texts are (in chronological order of their composition) (1) Plato's *Hippias Minor* (ch. 7); (2) a section of the fifth book of

Aristotle's *Metaphysics* (ch. 8); (3) the first book of John Chrysostom's *Priesthood* (ch. 9); (4) some letters of Jerome (ch. 10); (5) the seventeenth of John Cassian's *Conferences* (ch. 11); (6) question 110 of the second part of the second part of Thomas Aquinas's *Summa Theologiae* (ch. 12); (7) Immanuel Kant's essay "On a Supposed Philanthropic Right to Lie" (ch. 13); (8) John Henry Newman's notes F and G to the *Apologia Pro Vita Sua* (ch 14); and (9) Friedrich Nietzsche's essay "Truth and Lie in an Extramoral Sense" (ch. 15). I'll say more about each of these texts in the chapter devoted to it, but for now I'll provide a few more notes on the approach taken in each of these readings.

I treat each text simply as it stands, trying, according to the method just sketched, to discern and lay bare what it has to say about the lie. I am not much interested in the relations between the chosen texts and the broader corpus of their authors. I ignore that broader corpus almost entirely, in fact, drawing upon it only when driven to for the clarification of particular technical terms or patterns of thought, and even then doing so only for illustrative purposes. This means that what I say about each text should not be taken to be true of its author's thought on the topic as a whole. Several of the authors of works I've chosen wrote a good deal elsewhere about the lie (Plato, Aristotle, Kant, and Nietzsche all did, for example), and this I shall not address at all. It may be that the patterns of thought evident in the works chosen are emblematic of those in the author's other works. In several cases I think that this is so. But I eschew such questions, and draw upon other works by the authors chosen only where essential clarifications make this unavoidable. My goal is an Augustinian reading of these texts and these texts only.

But why these texts? They are all by figures of considerable importance to the development of European thought, and this is perhaps enough justification for the clarification of differences, which is the main purpose of these readings. But, in addition, the chosen texts provide a representative range of non-Augustinian modes of thinking about the lie. Some are non-Christian, either because they could not have been anything else (Plato, Aristotle), or because they were explicit in their rejection of Christianity (Nietzsche); the rest, in one way or another, are Christian, with perhaps the exception of Kant, who certainly claimed to be Christian but who thinks and writes in general (and certainly in the essay discussed here) as a pagan. An Augustinian reading of the Christian works shows how deep the difference can be between an Augustinian and a non-Augustinian mode of thinking about the lie even when almost all other assumptions are shared. And the presence of non- or anti-Christian works shows how unlikely it is that an Augustinian or quasi-Augustinian account of the lie will come to be offered or will seem anything other than absurd if no Christian assumptions are made.

The upshot of the Augustinian readings offered here is that the difference between Augustine's view and those of his interlocutors will stand starkly forth. Sharply outlined also will be the range of assumptions unshared and the difficulty and extent of the work remaining to do if resolution is to be approached. I hope and intend that it will also be made clear that resolution of the differences from a position other than that held by Augustine or one of his interlocutors is extraordinarily unlikely. With respect to the lie, as also with respect to almost every other question of interest, useful and interesting thinking can only be done upon the basis of controversial assumptions.

If a community were to try living by—or at least taking seriously—Augustine's view of the lie, it would look different, perhaps very different, from any community that now exists. In part three, I sketch, speculatively, the principal points of difference between such a community and those in which we actually live. Since I think Augustine's position on the lie correct, I would naturally be pleased if the number of those convinced of its truth were to increase. Since I am a Christian, I also hope that more Christians come to think him right and attempt to order their uses of speech after his views than appears currently to be the case. And since I am Roman Catholic, I hope most of all that the church comes to listen more attentively to the voice of the most eminent, prolific, and seductively persuasive among its *doctores ecclesiae.* As the postmodern church, together with the West in general, begins to recover its premodern voice (though of course in a new key), Augustine's tones are once again likely to prove compelling. There are signs that this is already happening, and I hope to contribute to it.

This book is argumentative, but it is not an argument. It is instead an attempted seduction. I hope to have presented an Augustinian account of the lie with sufficient clarity and radiance that it will draw to itself some, at least, of those otherwise ignorant of or predisposed against it. I do not think that what I've written is a knock-down, drag-out argument that should convince all who read it of Augustine's rightness. It is not within the power of argument to bring that result about: the fact that a claim is true, and that there are good arguments for it, does not mean that all who come to understand that claim and those arguments will thereby come also to assent to the claim's truth. Such assent is brought about almost always by other means, one among which is being brought face-to-face with the claim in a sufficiently beautiful and interesting guise that it will seem worth entertaining. Entertaining a claim will typically, over time, conform you to it and bring it about that you assent to it. This is assent brought about by seduction into a form of action. Pascal's prescription for the man who would like to have faith but finds himself without it is that he should just do what those who have faith do, whether or not it seems to him that he is being sincere. In that way he will eventually find himself possessed of (or, more likely, by) faith. But what those who have faith do must first look attractive enough that some without faith will want to play that game. It's in this Pascalian spirit that I offer the Augustinian account of the lie that follows.

Part One

Augustine on the Lie

1

Lying

The lie is a verbal act, something we do with words. Augustine calls this act *mendacium*, the lie, and its agent *mendax*, the liar. The characteristic mark of the lie is duplicity, a fissure between thought and utterance that is clearly evident to the speaker as she speaks. Lying words are spoken precisely with the intent to create such a fissure: the liar takes control of her speech, and marks it as her own when she separates it from her thought and grants it autonomy. When this is done, speech becomes the possession and instrument of the speaker. When it is not done, speech comes to birth spontaneously, as an act of gratitude and praise to its giver. Lies require effort; truth none.

Lying speech has nothing to do with the falsehood or truth of what is said:

> No one, certainly, who says something false that he takes to be true should be judged to be lying; for so far as he himself is concerned he does not deceive but is deceived. And neither should someone who has incautiously come to believe to be true what is false be accused of lying; he, rather, is rash. No, so far as the person himself is concerned, he lies who says to be true what he takes to be false.

This means that whether you're lying *(mentiens)* has nothing to do with whether what you say is true or false: if you sincerely say that something is true or false and turn out to be wrong, you're "deceived" *(fallitur)*, but not a liar. The lie has only to do with whether there's a mismatch, a gap, a contradiction, a fissure, between what you think is true and what you claim as true. If you think, wrongly, that Trollope wrote *Vanity Fair* (Thackeray did), and you say, "Trollope wrote *Vanity Fair*," you're not lying: you're just mistaken. But if you say, "Thackeray wrote *Vanity Fair*" while thinking Trollope did, you're lying even though what you say is true, because what you say doesn't match what you think: you're duplicitous. Augustine hammers the point home:

> If you don't pay attention to what someone is speaking about, but only to what the speaker intends, then someone who unknowingly says something false because he thinks it true is better than someone who is knowingly disposed to lie and does not know that what he says is true. For in the case of the former person there isn't one thing in the mind and another in speech; while the latter, by contrast, whatever is the case in itself about what he says, has one thing hidden in the heart and another ready on the tongue. And this is the evil proper to lying.

Malum proprium mentientis—"The evil proper to lying." This is the mismatch between what's in your heart (what you take to be true) and what's on your tongue (what you say to be true). If you intend to lie (to say what you don't think), then even if you accidentally say something true you're worse than someone who intends to speak his mind but mistakenly says something false. Duplicity is the central feature of the lie, of *mendacium*, and the liar, the *mendax*, is precisely the duplicitous one, the one who has "one thing hidden in the heart *(aliud tamen clausum in pectore)* and another ready on the tongue *(aliud in lingua promptum est)*." Augustine here draws upon a tradition of talking about the lie that goes back at least to Homer, who has Achilles say of Odysseus, the archetypal liar, that he keeps one thing in his mind and says another; and Augustine certainly knew and was perhaps consciously referring to the Roman historian Sallust's definition of the lie, given in his work on the Catiline War composed more than four centuries before Augustine turned his attention to the question:

> Ambition led many to become false, to keep one thing concealed in the heart and to have another ready on the tongue, to judge friendships and enmities not as they are but in terms of benefit, to look good rather than to have a good character.

The idea that duplicity is the central feature of the lie is present also in this definition of Augustine's:

He lies who has one thing in his mind and says something else in words or with some other kind of signifying act.

There is an internal fact and an external fact. The internal is what's in the mind (*animus*—Augustine often also uses "heart," *cor,* or "mind," *mens,* for the same purposes), and the external is what's said or communicated in some other way—by gesture or expression or some other nonverbal sign. Lying happens when the two are intentionally separated.

These definitions say that when you lie you're speaking (or communicating in some other way—but for Augustine speech is the clearest case of communication and it'll be simpler to follow him in limiting the discussion mostly to speech), and doing so with intentional duplicity. Duplicitous speech is therefore clearly necessary for the lie. Without it there is no lie: "In fact that which is without the double heart cannot even be called a lie." But it's not clear whether duplicity is also sufficient for the lie. Are all instances of duplicitous speech also lies?

Sometimes Augustine's definitions of the lie include reference to an intention to deceive as well as to duplicity: "The lie is false signification together with an intent to deceive." False signification *(falsa significatio)* here means duplicitous signification. Augustine does sometimes use "false" as shorthand for "duplicitous," but given the passages just discussed it's obvious what he means. The confusion between "false in itself" and "false in the mind of the speaker" is, however, common in both English and Latin, and often causes trouble in discussions of lying. So I emphasize again that whether a claim is true or false in itself is irrelevant to whether it's a lie. The only kind of falsity relevant to this question is what the speaker thinks is false. But the definition just quoted adds to false signification the *fallendi voluntas,* the intent to deceive; it can be read to mean that Augustine thinks that in order to lie you must not only speak duplicitously but must also intend to deceive someone by doing so. This would be an additional necessity because it's clearly possible to speak duplicitously without intending any deceit. You might, for instance, speak duplicitously to someone you had good reason to think wouldn't believe you in any case. If you did, you wouldn't be intending to deceive. Or, you might speak duplicitously to someone you knew couldn't understand you—a preverbal baby, or someone who didn't speak your language, perhaps. The most common reason for speaking duplicitously, no doubt, is the hope or intention to deceive; but it's not the only reason, and so if Augustine does think that the intention to deceive is necessary to the lie (as necessary as duplicitous speech), then something has been added to the definition. But is this what he thinks? Consider the following passage:

> No one doubts that someone who intentionally says something false for the purpose of deceiving is lying. And so it's clear that a false statement together with an intent to deceive is a manifest lie. But it is another question whether only this is a lie.

And:

> The question of whether the lie is altogether absent when there is no intention to deceive needs to be investigated with the greatest subtlety.

These passages raise the question of whether the intention to deceive is necessary to the lie. Augustine does think that when such an intention is present together with duplicity you have the "manifest lie" (*manifestum esse mendacium*), that which "no one doubts" to be a lie. But this by itself doesn't mean that all lies must be accompanied by it. The two passages just quoted bracket Augustine's discussion of a puzzling test case, which helps to explain what he means and why he raises the question. It is the case of the skeptical friend.

Your skeptical friend is someone who always assumes that what you say to her is duplicitous. That is, she thinks that whenever you say anything to her you really take the opposite to be true. Perhaps she's come to think this because you have a long and bad record of speaking duplicitously to her. But whatever the reasons for her skepticism, skeptical she is, and you know it: you know for sure that she'll take anything you say to her as decisive evidence that you think the opposite of what you're saying.

Suppose, then, that your skeptical friend is planning a trip. There are two routes to where she wants to go, and you know that one of them is long and dangerous and the other safe and quick. You have her well-being at heart and you want her to take the safe and quick route. But, of course, you know that if you tell her that route A is safe and quick and route B long and dangerous, she'll assume (because she's deeply and consistently skeptical of what you say) that you think route B is in fact the safe and quick one. So you tell her that route B, the one you know to be long and dangerous, is the short and quick one. Your claim is duplicitous because it says what you take to be false; but it does not intend to deceive your skeptical friend because you don't want to get her to take to be true what you take to be false. Quite the contrary: you want her to take to be true just what you take to be true; it's just that you have to be duplicitous in order to bring this about.

This is an odd case. It shows that it is possible to be duplicitous without intending to deceive, and that it is possible to intend to deceive without being duplicitous. It shows, in short, that duplicity and the intention to deceive are not the same: although they'll usually go together, they need not. Augustine mentions the case (and his discussion of it is quite involved) principally in order to show that there will always be instances in which it's not quite clear whether to say that a lie has been told. Is the one who intends to deceive but who does so by speaking nonduplicitously a liar? Or is the one who does not intend to deceive but who speaks duplicitously a liar? Or both? Or neither? Augustine does not decide, and says that it's not of great importance to decide. Everyone will agree that when you're duplicitous with the intent to deceive you're lying: this is the clear case mentioned. But even if there's doubt about how to classify the odd cases, it's clear that what really counts for Augustine in avoiding the lie is that "the mind is thoroughly aware that it is saying what it knows, judges, or believes to be true." Intentional duplicity, in short, is what really counts about the lie, and its avoidance is what counts in avoiding the lie.

Duplicity is, to say it again, the evil proper to lying, and I read Augustine as claiming that this is both necessary and sufficient for the lie. That the lie is usually also accompanied by an intention to deceive is true and of interest, but it does not pick out what is most deeply characteristic of the lie, and is not relevant to the exceptionless ban on the lie that Augustine advocates. Augustine was not altogether consistent in what he wrote about the relation between the intention to deceive and the lie. He wrote, for instance, that the fault of the liar is to be found in speaking what's in the mind with a desire to deceive, and this suggests that the intent to deceive is necessary or intrinsic or proper to the lie. He also wrote that jokes are not lies because they lack the intention to deceive, which suggests the same. But he also claimed that when someone knowingly says what he takes to be false then it's beyond a doubt that he lies, which suggests that duplicity suffices for the lie.

Is Augustine simply confused about the definitional question? Not exactly—although when he came to catalogue and comment upon his works toward the end of his life, he wrote of his first treatise on lying that he'd have preferred it not to become public because it seemed to him obscure, excessively complex, and altogether annoying. This certainly suggests some awareness on his part that the conceptual questions had not been treated entirely satisfactorily. However, he did certainly understand the lie to have duplicitous speech at its core; and while his search for the clear case of the lie (a case about which there'd be no disagreement) did sometimes lead him to write that a lie should intend to deceive as well as be duplicitous, this narrower definition is not where his interest lay and not what he focused upon when he came to argue that no lie is ever justifiable. The truly Augustinian lie is the intentionally duplicitous utterance, no more and no less; and the true Augustinian liar is the man who knows that he has a double heart, a *duplex cor.* These are the elements always present in his definitions and analyses of *mendacium,* of the lie. The question of the intention to deceive is sometimes present and sometimes absent in his definitions and discussions, but it is not required for a properly Augustinian understanding of the lie.

The intention to deceive is not the only intention with which you may lie. You may speak duplicitously to give yourself pleasure, to deceive yourself by persuading yourself that you are not the kind of person you in fact are, or to give pleasure to others. Augustine often mentions this last: liars may lie because they want to please their interlocutors, not because they want to deceive them. They may, that is, tell them what they'd like to hear, what will please their ears and minds, not because they have any particular desire to deceive but because they want to spread happiness. Your student wants to hear that she has done a good piece of work; your husband would like to be complimented on his appearance in his new suit; your shareholders hope to be reassured that the company will turn a profit this year. But you think that your student's work is mediocre, that your husband's suit is sartorially ill-advised, and that the company has no chance of turning a profit this decade. Nonetheless, you speak duplicitously with the primary intention of giving pleasure: this is to lie *suaviloquio,* with sweetly pleasing speech, as the poets do (or may). *Suaviloquium* is not, however, proper or essential to the lie, and neither is its accompanying motive, which is to give pleasure. Duplicity is what belongs essentially to the lie, and this may or may not be accompanied by a desire to deceive.

But duplicity is not a simple idea. For Augustine, its antonym is sincerity: in discussing the opposite of duplicitous speech he likes to speak of talking *ex animi sententia,* literally "out of the mind's judgment," but better translated "sincerely," or "in all honesty"; he also uses the phrase *corde veracis,* "with a true heart.'" These qualities are what all speech, for him, ought to have; lying speech necessarily lacks them. For Augustine, then, duplicitous speech cannot occur by accident. It happens only when speakers decide to contradict what is in their hearts by what is on their lips.

We now have a working definition: for Augustine, the lie is deliberately duplicitous speech, insincere speech that deliberately contradicts what its speaker takes to be true. Or, in the abstract language of the analytical philosopher: for Augustine, you lie if and only if you speak in such a way as to seem to yourself at the time you speak intentionally to contradict your thought. This is a relatively minimalistic definition: a clear case of it requires two things only. First, the liar must seem to herself to know what she thinks; and second, she must seem to herself to have chosen and spoken words that contradict what she takes herself to think. When both conditions are clearly met there is a clear case of the lie.

Are there such clear cases? Yes. In the second chapter of the book of Joshua, Rahab says to the king of Jericho's men that she doesn't know where the Israelite spies have gone (the Israelites are laying their plans for the invasion of the city). But even as she speaks it seems to her that she does know where they have gone (she's hidden them on her roof), and therefore that the words she's chosen contradict her thought. This is a clear case of the Augustinian lie. Another instance: caught up in the usual academic ecstasy of self-doubt and the desire to impress, I say to a colleague that, yes, I have read Joyce's *Finnegans Wake*, while knowing perfectly well that I haven't. Here too the conditions are clearly met.

Notice that in order for the conditions to be met it doesn't have to be the case that what the liar says does deceive her interlocutor; nor must the words she chooses be appropriate, given local conventions, for the expression of a thought contradictory to hers; nor even need she be accurately aware of what she does take to be the case. It need only seem to her that all these things are so. Augustine's understanding of the lie indexes it very closely to the condition and judgments of the liar. He has almost no interest in the lie's effects external to the liar—or, more precisely, he has a good deal of interest in those matters, but not in such a way as to affect his definition of the lie or his judgment that it can never defensibly be performed. Even the intention to deceive, I've suggested, isn't essential to the lie; and certainly all other intentions (to save from harm, to comfort, to entertain) are irrelevant to it.

Are there unclear cases, cases in which it's not obvious whether what's said falls under Augustine's definition? Yes. Rahab might have chosen a form of words to respond to her interrogators that did not seem to her precisely to contradict or otherwise call into question what she thought. Instead of baldly saying that she didn't know where the spies were, she might have said, "Spies? Are we not all spies in this land of obscurity? Therefore there are many in my house." She might be sure neither whether she thinks this nor even what it means. And as a result it would be unclear whether the conditions for the lie are met. Or, suppose I say to my academic friends that I find Joyce's intentions in *Finnegans Wake* to be a bit obscure, and then I quote a couple of passages by way of illustration—passages I've learned for the occasion. I may intend by all this to deceive the people I'm talking to into thinking that I've read *Finnegans Wake*, but since I'm not clearly saying anything duplicitous (I do in fact find Joyce's intentions puzzling, and I do think the passages I quote illustrate this fact), what I say isn't clearly (and probably clearly isn't) what Augustine calls a lie, an instance of *mendacium*.

But the fact that it's often unclear whether a particular utterance is a lie on Augustine's definition isn't an objection to his enterprise. Augustine is concerned only to interrogate (and ban) utterances that do clearly meet the criteria he states, and all he needs for that enterprise to get under way is that there be such cases. When it is unclear whether some utterance meets the criteria, Augustine usually excludes it from the discussion. This is because he wants to see whether it is possible coherently and convincingly to argue that the clear cases of the lie defined (relatively) minimalistically as duplicitous speech should be banned. If that enterprise fails, arguments aimed at banning or constraining the lie defined more generously will also fail. Many (perhaps most) Christian theorists of his time thought that what Augustine took to be a lie could at times properly be told. Augustine argues that this is not so: that there are clear cases of duplicitous speech, and that these should be placed under an exceptionless ban. He is not interested in defending the application of his definition to ambiguous cases, and to object to his enterprise by saying that there are cases not clearly covered by it is to miss its point.

It also doesn't follow from the fact that a particular utterance doesn't clearly (or clearly doesn't) fall under Augustine's definition of the lie that he takes it to be something you might defensibly say. There might be other reasons that should prevent you from saying it. Perhaps I should not say to my academic colleagues that I find *Finnegans Wake* puzzling if I intend by saying it that they should come to believe (wrongly) that I've read that book. But if there are such reasons (and Augustine thinks there are), they won't be the same as the reasons that ban the lie, for what I've said doesn't belong to that category. It doesn't follow for Augustine (or for common sense) from the fact that some utterance isn't a lie that it should be permitted. It follows only that whatever arguments there are for or against its permissibility won't be the same as those about the propriety of lying. To put this syllogistically: if all lying sentences should be banned and *s* isn't a lying sentence, nothing at all follows about whether *s* should be banned. It might or might not need to be banned, but the discussion about whether it should be will be a different discussion than that about the lie.

Someone, of course, can always be found to doubt anything. But there is in fact no reason to doubt that instances of what Augustine defines as *mendacium* do occur. You may (and do) speak in such a way as to seem to yourself to contradict or otherwise misrepresent what you take to be the case. And so you may (and do) lie. It is speech of this sort, and only speech of this sort, that Augustine wants to categorize as *mendacium*, and so to place under an exceptionless ban.

Augustine's definition of the lie excludes many kinds of speech and action ordinarily—or at least frequently—classified as such by contemporary speakers of English. Among these exclusions the following are especially significant.

Nonverbal actions cannot be lies. It is possible to make public one's thought without words (by gesture or other noverbal sign), and it is therefore also possible to choose to misrepresent what one thinks in these ways. But such cases lie outside Augustine's definition. He is, for the most part, concerned only with speech (or writing). He does say, as already noted, that you can lie with nonverbal signifiers. But once having said so, he scarcely returns to such cases, and I follow him in removing them from further consideration. In discussing the lie I'll be discussing only verbal acts. Whether the definition can be extended to cover nonverbal acts, and what the problems are in doing so—these are interesting questions, but not the questions of this book.

Silence—the refusal of speech—is also excluded. Whether silence can be *mendacium* is another of the matters on which Augustine's thought fluctuates somewhat. But his most mature and consistent position is that it cannot. Silence is not only a nonverbal action, but also, thinks Augustine (perhaps implausibly), one that ought not be taken as making public what you take to be the case. Silence therefore cannot be duplicitous. Augustine emphasizes this even when it is counterintuitive to do so. A good example is to be found in his interpretation of a story found, in its essential elements, three times in the book of Genesis (12: 10–20; 20:1–18; 26:6–11). A man travels to a foreign country with his beautiful wife, who is also (on Augustine's analysis) his half-sister (his father's daughter but not his mother's). The man fears that the country's king will be inflamed with desire when he sees the woman's beauty, and will kill him if he thinks that the woman is his wife so that he may then safely bed her. So the man says that he and the woman are siblings, which the king believes and reasonably takes to imply that they are not spouses. The king therefore thinks that he may take the woman to bed without worrying about what her so-called brother might think or do. The man's statement to the king, "She is my sister," is not duplicitous: the woman is in fact his (half-) sister, and he thinks so. What the man says is therefore not a lie. The man's silence about the fact that the woman is also his wife is also not a lie, says Augustine, because it is not a verbal act, and therefore not an act capable of being a lie. This is so, he says, even though the stories make it clear that the man's silence about the spousal relation is precisely intended (when coupled with the affirmation that the woman is his sister) to deceive the local ruler into thinking that the man and the woman are not married. Augustine says:

> Therefore, he [Abraham] has been silent about something true—that she [Sarah] is his wife—but has not said anything false in saying that she is his sister. . . . It is therefore not a lie when the truth is hidden by silence, but rather when what is false is expressed in speech.

The terms "true" and "false" here must be read as shorthand for "taken by Abraham as true" and "taken by Abraham as false," since these are the relevant categories for analysis of the lie.

Error is excluded from the lie, as well. When I say something false because I take it to be true, I am not duplicitous and will usually not be trying to deceive my interlocutors, from which it follows that I cannot be lying. Sincerity is what counts.

Jokes are not lies, even when they're about people the joker takes never to have existed or events he takes never to have occurred. This is because the joker's utterance is not duplicitous—or if it is, this is not because she's telling a joke: duplicity is not proper or essential to joking speech. Augustine reports a joker as having answered the question of what God was doing before he made heaven and earth by saying that he was preparing hells for those who inquire closely into deep questions. Augustine doesn't endorse this joke himself: he thinks it's an unacceptably devious avoidance of an interesting question. But what the joker says isn't (or need not be) duplicitous, and so also isn't (or need not be) mendacious—and this is true even though the joker does not take it to be the case that God was preparing hells for those who ask such questions. The duplicitous fissure between thought and speech is not present here precisely because the joker takes herself to be joking rather than making a claim that she takes to be false. If I begin a joke by saying, "An Englishman, an Irishman, and a Scotsman went into a pub," I don't think I'm making a claim about some actual event involving a particular pub and some particular natives of the United Kingdom. It does not, therefore, seem to me that what I say is duplicitous with respect to these imaginary characters. I am performing a speech-act of a different sort. It is a complicated matter (and fortunately an unnecessary task) to say in detail just what the contours of the joking speech-act are. All that's necessary is to say what's obvious, which is that the joker typically does not take the imaginary situations about which she speaks to contradict what she takes to be true—and if she does so take them, this is not because she's joking.

The exclusion of the joke from the category of the lie supports the view that a properly Augustinian understanding of the lie has nothing at all to do with whether the hearer is deceived, nor even with whether the speaker intends to deceive. Some jokes depend for their effect upon a temporarily deceptive misleading of the hearer by the speaker. But if, as I speak the words that will produce the needed temporary deceit, I don't think that I'm misrepresenting what I take to be the case, I am not duplicitous and therefore also not mendacious. There may of course be other reasons to avoid joking: I may, by joking, be preferring ridicule to charity (Augustine on the whole does not like jokes, and thinks there will be none in heaven). But whatever is wrong with jokes doesn't have to do with the fact that they're lies.

For much the same reasons that jokes need not be lies, metaphorical and other figurative claims are excluded from the category of the lie—or, more precisely, if they are lies this is not because they are figurative. Augustine is interested in the fact that Scripture is full of figurative language, and since it is axiomatic for him that Scripture does not lie, it follows immediately that figurative language cannot automatically be lying language. It's easy enough to see why figurative language does not meet Augustine's definition of the lie. If I say, "Jesus is a rock," while at the same time not thinking that he is composed of hard inorganic matter, this does not make my claim duplicitous. This is because what I mean by the term "rock" is different from (though related to) its ordinary, literal meaning—I am, as Augustine likes to say, using *petra* (rock) of Christ figurally *(in figura)* rather than in its ordinary sense *(in proprietate)*; and because this is clear to me when I make the claim, there is no mismatch between what I say and what I think, and therefore no duplicity. I don't seem to myself to have chosen and spoken words that contradict what I think. What I intend by the words "Jesus is a rock" is (something like) "Jesus can be relied upon in all eventualities"; and since I also seem to

myself to assent to this claim, I am not duplicitous in making it. It may
of course be that when you hear what I say, you come to think that I
think Jesus really is a rock—perhaps a large granite boulder. If you do
so think, you'll be deceived, but I will not have been duplicitous, and so
will not have lied to you. I may lie with metaphors; but the fact that I
use metaphors does not mean that I have lied. A similar analysis, with
appropriate changes, can be given for other figures of speech, such
as synecdoche. The principle in all cases is that if it is clear to me as I
speak that I am speaking figuratively, and what I take the meaning(s)
of the figure I'm employing to be doesn't contradict what I take to be
the case, then there is no duplicity, no mismatch between thought and
speech, and so no lie.

You might think that this view of figurative language makes duplicity always avoidable. Can't I always specify to myself that the words
I'm using have a meaning that doesn't contradict what I take to be the
case, no matter what the words and no matter what I take to be the
case? Recall Rahab: she duplicitously said, "I don't know where they
went," while thinking she'd just hidden them on her roof. Couldn't she
have avoided duplicity (and so also the lie) by the simple expedient of
specifying to herself that her sentence "I don't know where they went"
meant (something like) "I don't know where they went, but I have a pretty
good idea"? And since that second sentence does represent what she
takes to be the case, she is not being duplicitous. Or so it might seem.
Such moves have sometimes been advocated under the label of mental
reservation: saying *p* while taking *not-p* to be the case can be defended
as nonduplicitous on this view by specifying to yourself as you utter *p*
that what you mean by *p* is something unusual—perhaps even *not-p*.

But such creatively unusual specifications of meaning are not very
much like ordinary figurative utterance. When you specify the meaning
of your utterance to yourself in a creative way in order to avoid duplicity,
you're typically doing something extra, something you don't do when you're
speaking figuratively in the ordinary sense. You're making a second-order
judgment about the meaning of your utterance, a judgment that cancels or
places under erasure the first-order act of uttering it by offering (to yourself)
a radical reconstrual of its meaning. A properly Augustinian response to
this move is to say that the extent to which you have consciously and
effortfully to make such second-order specifications to yourself of what
you mean by your utterance in order to avoid duplicity is closely indexed
to the extent to which your utterance is in fact duplicitous. When I'm
asked to write a check for a good cause and I say, "My checkbook's at
home," while knowing that it's in my pocket, I may specify to myself

that what I mean by "at home" is "in my pocket." But such a specification requires a conscious and fairly elaborate specification of meaning. The utterance is therefore duplicitous. When I say that Jesus is a rock, however, such a second-order specification is not necessary: reliability and durability are ordinarily part of the semantic range of "rock" in my usage to begin with, and so the utterance is not duplicitous. There will be unclear cases, of course; but that this is so is no objection to Augustine's definition, for there are also clear cases.

An implication of this discussion of figurative speech is that what your words seem to you to mean at the moment you speak them is not easily (and perhaps not at all) susceptible to change by act of will. You can't, that is, simply decide what a word will mean for you. You are not, in that sense, master of your speech's meanings. Words have been given to you together with their meanings, and while these meanings are often unclear, vague, fuzzy at the edges, and multiple, they cannot be transformed or rejected by fiat. When Richard M. Nixon said, "I am not a crook," there are many things he might have seemed to himself to mean by those words, but this range of seemings was not under his immediate control. It was a product of many causes, education, acculturation, and idiosyncratic habits of speech no doubt among them. But whatever exactly the correct causal account, the upshot was, as it must have been, that whatever Nixon seemed to himself to mean by his words at the time of utterance was a fact about him not unlike his weight: alterable in the future by effort and change of habit, but simply given in the present. Attempts to alter what you mean by your words through the use of mental reservation or some similar device at or immediately after the time of utterance cannot remove duplicity, and cannot, therefore, remove a lie when one is present. To specify to yourself that what you mean by "at home" is "in my pocket" when in fact it does not seem to you that this is what you mean is very like specifying to yourself that your current weight of 200 pounds is really 150 pounds. Any effects that such specification may have belong firmly in the future.

The speaker is the privileged authority on the question of whether he lies. Since the Augustinian definition of the lie is indexed to the speaker's understanding of the relation between her thought and speech, you will always know better than anyone else whether a particular utterance of yours was duplicitous. This may be put negatively: if, at the time you speak, it does not seem to you that you have one thing on your lips and another in your heart, then you are not lying. Nixon, then, was in a better position than anyone else to know whether, when he said "I am not a crook," he spoke duplicitously.

Augustine's understanding of what it is to lie, I repeat, also excludes by definition any reference to or interest in the results or effects of the lie. Lies, for Augustine, are what they are—deliberately duplicitous verbal claims—no matter what their effects. Some lies will deceive their hearers; others will not. Some lies will be heard and understood; some will not. Some lies will have good effects; others will have bad ones. None of this is relevant to decisions about what is and what is not a lie. Neither is any of it relevant to considering whether the lie is ever appropriate or defensible.

Augustine does categorize lies into kinds according to various criteria. For example, he mentions eight kinds of lie: first, lies about religious doctrine (a classification according to topic); second, lies that unjustly cause injury (a classification according to result); third, lies that benefit some and harm others (result again); fourth, lies told simply for the pleasure of them—these, interestingly, are said to be the real thing, the pure or unmixed lie *(merum mendacium);* fifth, lies told in order to please others with smooth and eloquent talk (a classification according to intention); sixth, lies that harm no one and provide some benefit (result again); seventh and eighth (subtypes of the sixth kind), lies that harm no one and are told with particular benefits in mind, namely, (seventh) protection of someone from capital punishment and (eighth) protection of someone from physical defilement (*inmunditia corporali,* which in Augustine's mind has principally to do with rape). These last two types are also classified according to result. But these classifications are intended mostly to show that although lies can be told in order to bring about good results, and may in fact bring about such results, this has nothing to do with what makes them lies, with the deliberate duplicity that, recall, is the evil proper to lying. That evil is most clearly evident in the fourth kind of lie, the pure or unmixed lie: the fact that this lie is told only for the pleasure of telling it is what makes it pure. The pure lie brings with it its own rewards and its own curses, and in this, so Augustine thinks, it is like all sin. Classifying lies according to topic, intention, or result, then, does not serve to exclude any of them from the category of the lie.

Augustine's definition of the lie, then, excludes in principle nonverbal communication in general and silence in particular; it also rules out the view that jokes or figurative speech are necessarily duplicitous, and makes appeal to the effects of an utterance utterly irrelevant to the question of whether it is a lie.

With these exclusions in mind it should be obvious that the lie, for Augustine, is a matter of interiority, of speaker's intent and decision. It is, he says (commenting on 2 Cor. 4:16), only internally that we set aside the lie and speak the truth. Correspondingly, it is only within, in the sphere of memory, concept-formation, and intention, that we are capable of making the decision to set aside the truth and speak duplicitously. Lying, like all sin, is to begin with a matter of interiority: it depends upon how your thought and utterance seem to you. When your thought is voiced in such a way that its utterance seems to you duplicitous, then you have lied. The decision so to speak is a sin in Augustine's view, and the understanding of sin that makes it reasonable to say this is in turn intimately linked with a particular view of what it is to exist, to be. To this I now turn.

2

Being

Your eyes, says Augustine, are participants in God's light. If you close them you don't decrease the light in which your eyes participate; and if you open them you don't increase the light in which they participate. What he says of the eyes he says of everything that exists, which is to say that for him the characteristic mark of being is participation: to be is to participate, to be a *particeps*, in God. Beings are ordered hierarchically according to the extent of their participation in God: those who participate more *are* more; those who participate less *are* less. But that in which beings participate—God—*is* always to precisely the same extent, which is to say maximally. Ordering beings according to the extent and nature of their participation in God is the fundamental taxonomic principle for Augustine, and taxonomic principles—principles by which we sort things and order them into kinds and hierarchies—are unavoidable tools of thought.

We all order things compulsively and imaginatively. We sort things into kinds and we order the kinds in relation to one another, thinking of some as beautiful and desirable, others as ugly and disgusting, and yet others as puzzling or uninteresting. Most of this we don't do consciously: we receive and inhabit an ordered world as a gift. As we learn to speak we adopt and internalize the ordering of things given by the mother tongue, and we inhabit that order as if it were natural. We learn the taxonomy of medium-sized material objects (books, bodies, kittens, tables, chairs, mountains), of actions (walking, sitting, thinking, hoping, loving), of things we can't see (justice, goodness, God, numbers, electrons), and of things we come to think aren't there (dragons, unicorns, the largest natural number). We also learn a taxonomy of value (loving is good; lying is bad) and of beauty (the burnt umber light of a desert sunset is beautiful; the maggots stripping the flesh from the decayed corpse are ugly), and we write the sighs of appreciation and grimaces of horrified aversion upon our bodies as signs of how thoroughly we've internalized or come to inhabit our taxonomy. By the time we are fluent users of a natural language, we are also accomplished taxonomists, skilled orderers of things into kinds.

Most of the time we inhabit the order of things given to us and internalized by us with ease and grace: the boundaries between the kinds into which we order things seem usually clear, and we can respond to what we happen across with spontaneous naturalness because we know the kind to which it belongs. I offer the dog I haven't met before my hand to smell because that's what you do with dogs whose acquaintance you'd like to make; I embrace my old friend because that's what you do with old friends; I turn in fear from the man who threatens me because that's what you do with such men; I admire the spectacular sunset because that's what you do with sunsets of that kind. All these behaviors depend upon an internalized taxonomy. Conscious and explicit thought about the categories of this taxonomy would hamper these responses, would make them and us stiff and strange.

Sometimes (but quite rarely) our orderings let us down. We happen across something that eludes or questions our taxonomy, and we're not sure how to respond. This person is my enemy, but now she's doing something for my good; this person looks like a man but behaves like a woman; that painting disgusts me, but is being treated with respect and admiration by others; and that . . . what on earth is that? In such cases response is difficult because classification is difficult. Repeated difficulties of this sort usually lead to taxonomic adjustment: I learn, for example, to be less confident that my sorting of people into men and women will always do the job I want it to do (there are drag queens and transsexuals), and so my ordering of people into sexual kinds becomes looser and more complex. But such difficulties may also lead to taxonomic hardening and avoidance of occasions that challenge the order I inhabit.

Orderings differ: the order of things in the world that I inhabit will not be in every respect the same as the order of things in the world that you inhabit. This is true of classifications and categories and judgments about value: of, that is, the entire range of taxonomic acts. Contemporary American psychologists, for example, judge that some states of mind and some behaviors are pathological. They have devoted a good deal of energy to the classification of these pathological states, and the fruits of their work can be seen in the *Diagnostic and Statistical Manual of Mental Disorders*. Browsing in the successive editions of this work provides impressive evidence of the ingenuity of the classificatory impulse and the fluidity of its results. Pathological states of mind appear and disappear with alarming frequency, and the hypochondriac's tendency to think she suffers from a disease as soon as she knows its symptoms is likely to be frustrated by the discovery that what was in one edition presented as a well-established disease with an impressive list of symptoms vanishes without trace from subsequent editions.

It isn't always clear whether such changes result from alterations in the criteria used for classification or from reversals in attributions of value (what was once thought pathological—homosexuality, for example—might later be thought a sign of health); but that they occur is clear evidence, if any were needed, that things may be ordered differently even though they will always be ordered. Still clearer evidence of the same point can be had by comparing the ordering of pathological states of mind presented in the scholastic treatises of the Buddhists with those provided in Christian works of ascetical theology—or either of these with those described and ranked in the various editions of the *Diagnostic and Statistical Manual*.

Not all orderings exhibit the same degree of variation as those given to mental diseases. There is, for example, much less variation in the classifications given at different times and places to colors than to mental diseases; there is much more in the classifications given to literary genres. But the fact that there is variation in the ordering of things at all raises some of the most difficult and interesting questions in philosophy. One is the individuation question with respect to kinds: how are the boundaries between one kind (grasses, let's say) and another (flowering plants) to be determined? Can this ever be done without ambiguity, in such a way that it will be easy to tell to which kind a particular green thing belongs? And even if this is possible, are such criteria invented or discovered, graven into the fabric of the cosmos or brought to birth by human ingenuity? Is it the case that all such divisions are and must remain conceptually fuzzy, like that between tall and short people? Or should more be hoped for in some cases? There is, as well, an individuation question about the members of kinds: what are the criteria that determine where one human being ends and another begins, for example? This is a question of real importance for the framing of laws about abortion, and no answer to it has found wide acceptance (which is not to say that there is no right answer). Or, to move higher up the scale of size, what individuates one galaxy from another? How can we tell where one galaxy ends and another begins? And then, most difficult of all, there are questions about the judgments of value made about the kinds into which things are ordered. How may such judgments be grounded? How may they be defended against competitors? Does either of these things need to be done?

Every ordering of things raises such questions. Most of us, happily, inhabit a deeply ordered world without being troubled by them. They rarely come to mind because the order of things in the world we inhabit is given to us with the grammar of our mother tongue. This grammar we do (and should) use rather than question. This doesn't mean that the order of things given us by our language should be presented in a theoretical way as if it were natural and its alternatives unnatural. That our own ordering of things seems natural to us is itself natural and obvious, but our orderings will not necessarily seem natural to others, just as theirs need not (and usually will not) to us. In the nineteenth century, some French theorists of language liked to argue that the syntax of French follows the order of thought and expresses it ideally, and that French is therefore superior to all other languages. A little thought makes this claim seem ridiculous to all nonnative speakers of French, and probably to most native speakers of that language, as well. That a particular ordering of things appears natural to you does not by itself justify you in arguing (or thinking) that it is natural, much less that everyone who does not find it so is stupid or depraved. Saying this is quite compatible with thinking that the ordered world you inhabit has been rightly ordered, and that those orderings incompatible with yours are, to the extent that they are incompatible, mistaken. Correctness is not the same as obviousness.

Augustine was not much interested in these strictly philosophical questions about the ordering of things. Like most of us, he inherited an ordered world and offered argumentative justification for only those aspects of it he knew to be controversial. But unlike most of us, he was interested in making explicit the ordering of things that seemed natural to him, and in relating its classifications to his thought on particular questions. When he did this it was usually because he thought that showing how a particular controversial claim was derived from a shared understanding of how things are ordered might help to persuade those who did not seem to be convinced by the controversial claim. Suppose, for instance, that someone tells you it's proper to eat fish but not to eat chicken. You do not hold this view (you think that we should eat neither fish nor chicken), but upon discussion you find that you share with your interlocutor an ordering of things into those that can feel pain and those that cannot. It is, moreover, on this basis that you deny the propriety of eating both fish and chicken: you think that they are both pain-feelers, and that it is immoral to kill and eat pain-feelers. Your interlocutor agrees with you about the fundamental distinction between those who feel pain and those who don't, and agrees, too, about the impropriety of eating pain-feelers. But he disagrees with you about which category fish belong to. If he can convince you that they belong to the non–pain-feelers, he'll likely also convince you that you may eat fish. A pattern of thought much like this is evident in Augustine's thought about the lie. He thinks it always improper to lie, and he often explains and defends this view by appealing to a more fundamental ordering of things in order to convince those who share his classificatory commitments that they should also share his exceptionless ban on the lie.

Augustine's ordering of things is of course Christian, which is to say that it is through and through hierarchical. The fundamental division is between God and creatures. These two categories together account for everything: for all particular things (you, me, tables, chairs, stars, numbers), and for what it is that causes them to be the particular thing they are and permits them to continue to be that thing and not another. There is a terminological difficulty here. Augustine typically uses the term *res*, "thing," as a generic term for what there is, and sometimes he subsumes both God and creatures under that generic term. He says, for example, that things *(res)* can be classified without remainder into those which should be enjoyed *(fruendum)* by us, and those which should be used *(utendum)* by us. This is a classification by mode of relation to us, and it is exhaustive: everything comes under one heading or the other, and when Augustine goes on to discuss which things belong to which kind, he says:

> The things to be enjoyed are the Father and the Son and the Holy Spirit, that is, the Trinity, which is a kind of single, greatest thing, to be enjoyed by all in common; if, indeed, it is a thing and not the cause of all things, and if indeed it is a cause.

God—the Holy Trinity—is called a thing, but with modification and reservation: "a kind of single, greatest thing" *(una quaedam summa res)*. Neither the term "thing" nor the term "cause" are adequate to God, and Augustine's worry here is that calling God *res*, "thing," might easily suggest that God is one thing among others, a powerful and unusual one, perhaps, but still of the same fundamental kind as other things, sharing thinghood with them. But this is not Augustine's view. For him, God (he often uses for God the indefinite pronoun *aliquid* rather than *res* when he wants to discuss the sense in which God is different from everything other than God) is the condition of the possibility of there being any thing at all, as well as the condition of the actuality of the things there are. This is what Augustine means when he says that all particular things are creatures: creatures (as the word already suggests) are defined exhaustively in terms of their relation to God. Augustine's ordering of things into two fundamental kinds—God and creatures—is not best understood, then, to say that there is a genus (things) of which both God and creatures are species. It is better understood to say that there is a hierarchy of being according to which God's being is fundamental, and the being of all creatures (everything that is not God) is derivative. This ordering of things is then not only a classification into kinds. To say that every particular *res* is a creature (is related to God by creation and participation) is to hierarchize as well as to categorize: it is to relate everything other than God to God by subordination, creation, and participation. It is, in short, to establish a hierarchy of being in which the very category by which the hierarchy is ordered—being—is what God is. God's nature, then, orders the hierarchy. God is not placed in the hierarchy by his possession of some variable given independently of him. Indeed, all God's apparent qualities or properties—eternality, wisdom, goodness, and so on—are in fact what he is rather than qualities he possesses: they are, as Augustine likes to say, predicated *secundum essentiam* or *secundum substantiam*, not *secundum qualitates*, which is to say according to God's essence or substance rather than according to his qualities or properties. God simply is all the properties he has, and so the relation between God and being is not (for example) like the relation between me and being.

But this sounds mysterious. How can there be a hierarchy of being? Doesn't everything simply exist or not? How, then, can it reasonably be said that beings are ordered by their being? But for Augustine and for his Christian forebears and contemporaries (and not only for them—most Platonists held a view similar in some important respects), there is nothing very mysterious about being *(essentia,* or sometimes *substantia)*. It is, simply, a term to be used for what God is, derived most immediately from God's self-naming to Moses in Exodus 3:14. There, in the Latin version known to Augustine, God responds to Moses' request for God's name by saying "Ego sum qui sum," a phrase most naturally rendered into English as "I AM WHO I AM." This is how Augustine understood it, and the fact that it uses the verb *esse*, "to be" (*sum* is the first person singular present indicative active of that verb), led him to think about the meaning of this verb and the nouns derivable from it by thinking first about God. Being, according to God's own self-description or self-naming, is what God is. It then becomes natural to think that insofar as anything other than God has being, or is, this must be because it derives what it is and that it is from the one who most fully and fundamentally is. Here is a sample of Augustine's way of putting this:

> God is maximal being, which is to say that he maximally is. This means that he is unchangeable, and that he gave it to things to be by creating them out of nothing. He did not, however, give it to them to be maximally as he is himself. To some he gave it to be more amply and to others to be in a lesser way; in this way he ordered natures by grades of being.

"Maximal being" *(summa essentia)* is what God is. Talk about God is therefore unavoidably talk about being *(esse)*, and talk of being is unavoidably talk of God. This means that when the being of particular things—both what they are and that they are—is discussed, the talk must inevitably turn to God if it is to remain Christian talk. Things have being only because it is freely given them (the verb is almost always *dare*), and the being they have is therefore entirely derivative and participatory. They are created out of nothing, as Augustine says again and again: creation is the gift of being, and when this gift is received its recipients are, to the extent that they are, only by participation in and derivation from God. To think of things independently of thinking about God is therefore to fall short of thinking about things as they are, for they are only in terms of God and by gift of God.

This fundamental ordering of things into God and not-God has two important corollaries. The first is that there is and can be nothing (no thing) independent of God. There are no evil forces or beings in the world that came to be by way of anything other than God's free creative act. Insofar as there is evil in the world, then, it is understood by Augustine and those who order the world as he does as nothing (no thing), a privation or absence. And so it is: *malum* is *privatio boni* and also *privatio essentiae*, an absence or privation of both goodness and being—with all the complications and difficulties that such a view brings, complications and difficulties outweighed only by those implicit in any other view.

The second corollary is that being is itself not a quality independent of God. If it were, it would follow that God and creatures would share an identical property (the property of be-ing or exist-ing), and that any difference between them would be one of degree—God, perhaps, would be thought to have more of this independent property than any other thing. This view—which is emphatically not Augustine's—would make God's relation to being like the richest living man's relation to money. The richest living man is not the source or definition of wealth. He isn't maximal wealth. Rather, he and I and all humans have money in just the same way: it's just that he happens to have more of it than I do or than anyone else does. What distinguishes the rich is just that they have more money. Wealth precedes and exceeds the richest man, no matter how rich he is. He could always be richer, and the fact that he is the richest does not prevent him from being just one more wealth-possessor among many. Being and God are not like money and the richest living man: God is, instead, the source and definition of all being. It is what he is, one among his names, and so all being-possessors (all creatures) have what being they have by participation in God-as-being. God is not one more thing among others, not even the most powerful, most benevolent, and most knowing thing. No—rather, each thing is a thing and is the kind of thing it is because of God's creative act, and so God does not belong to the same genus as any-thing else. Augustine's ordering of things makes God's relation to being like the relation Bill Gates would have to money were he the source and definition of all wealth, and were it the case that all wealth was had by participating in Bill-Gates-as-wealth-possessor.

Not all beings participate in God's being to an identical extent, however. Some do so more and some less: what Augustine calls *naturae* or *creaturae*, natures or creatures, a category inclusive of everything other than God, are ranked by the amount of being they have. Some creatures, for example, have free will, which requires an *anima rationalis*, a rational soul. Such creatures can know and choose the good, which is God; they can also deny and refuse the good. Only we and angels are like this. We and they *are* more than those beings that cannot know and choose the good, and so we and they belong to a higher grade of being than all other creatures. Only we and angels are made in the image and likeness of God; this is because we and we alone can come to an explicit understanding of God, and can choose to respond to him with gratitude and love, or to refuse so to respond. Angelic understanding of God is fuller and more direct than human understanding, and so angels are higher in the order of being than we. But we and they participate more closely and more fully in God's being than does any other creature. Other animate creatures—dogs, cats, dolphins—have an irrational soul, which means that they can respond to sensory stimuli and in a limited way make choices and plans for their own benefit. But they cannot know or choose the good, and therefore any knowledge of or response to God they may have remains implicit. This is why they are ranked lower in being than angels or humans: they participate in God less fully. And inanimate objects—what Augustine usually calls simply *corpora*, bodies—participate less fully still. They have no soul of any kind, and they are related to God only because they were created and are sustained by him. Bodies occupy the lowest rank in the hierarchy of being. Augustine describes the hierarchy of being often. Here is one representative example:

> Among those things that exist in any way at all, and which are not what God is, who made them, living things are placed above the nonliving, which means that those that can reproduce (or can want to) are placed above those that cannot; among living things, the sentient are placed above the nonsentient, which means that animals are placed above trees; among sentient things, those with intelligence are placed above those without, which means that humans are above cattle; and among intelligent things, those who cannot die are placed above those who can, which means that angels are above humans.

This fundamental ordering of things into God and creatures is often mapped on to another, which is that between things that can be apprehended by the senses *(sensibilia)* and those that can be apprehended by the intellect *(intellegibilia)*. Creatures that can be sensed take up both space and time: they are always located somewhere, they come into being and pass out of being, and between their origin and cessation they change constantly. This is as true of mountains and seas as it is of human bodies and hot meals. All these are bodies, and all bodies are immersed in time and change. They are also poised on the edge of the void of nonbeing, from which God first brought them into being by the gift of creation. Here is Augustine getting a little overexcited about this aspect of corporeal creatures, of bodies:

> Nothing touched by a physical sense can remain as it is for an instant. Such things slip and slide away; they have no presence, or to say it in [philosophical] Latin, they are not.

He doesn't mean literally that what you can see and touch (and taste and smell and hear) doesn't exist at all (though he does say *non esse*, "they are not"). He means, rather, that nonbeing is that toward which sensible things tend: extension in time and space bears the trace of nonbeing, and this trace can be seen by those with eyes to see on the surface of every corporeal thing. It is written on the body of your beloved, it suffuses the bouquet of your favorite wine, and it scores the heights of the most majestic range of mountains. It is even more deeply interwoven with institutions and artifacts made by us, and this was dramatically evident to Augustine, who was alive when, in A.D. 410, Rome was entered and partly sacked by Alaric's army, the first occurrence of this sort since 390 B.C., when Rome was sacked by the Gauls. Augustine devoted much of the last two decades of his life to interpreting this event for Christians who had thought the Roman Empire eternal, and for pagans who blamed Christians for its decay.

The *intellegibilia* are in every important respect different from the *sensibilia*. They take up no space and no time. They can be known fully only by leaving behind *sensibilia* and approaching more closely to God's mode of knowledge, which is entirely nonspatial and nontemporal. This is not easy to do, and that this is so explains the frequency with which Augustine appeals to the need for purgation and purification on the part of the knower. You can't easily ascend (and this is his standard metaphor) from the temporal to the atemporal: since Adam's and Eve's fall, such an ascent comes neither naturally nor easily. What does come naturally and easily is cognitive distraction by the variety and mutable beauty of what is sensed, and also (partly as cause and partly as result of this cognitive distraction) affective dispersal into the realm of such objects. However, even when we are far gone into such distraction and dispersal, understanding is never completely absent; and to the extent that it remains—to the extent that we understand anything at all rather than merely sense and respond to sensory inputs as do animals—we do so by divine illumination, by God's gift of the capacity to enter into the sphere of the atemporal.

What belongs here? What can be found at this level of being's hierarchy? All truths, including most obviously those whose object is some nontransient state of affairs, such as the truths of mathematics, musical harmony, and the principles of prosody. But even truths whose object is some temporal event (such as that Augustine was born in A.D. 354) or some temporally located person (such as that Paul was a just man) are found here. From the viewpoint of eternity it is atemporally true that Augustine was born when he was born and that Paul was the kind of man he was. The fact that natural languages are irremediably tensed makes this difficult to put with clarity and persuasiveness, and it is not a view without difficulties. But it is Augustine's view, and not only his: some such view is required of anyone who thinks that God is not located in time and yet is related to things that are so located—such as we humans.

God, it might be said, is related identically to all temporal events; and all truths, including those about temporal events, are eternally (atemporally) present to God's mind. Such truths are, in Augustine's terms, inviolable, unshakable, incorruptible, imperturbable, eternal, and so on (these terms are scattered broadside through Augustine's works). Using the Platonist vocabulary, which was his fundamental philosophical vocabulary, Augustine also often calls them forms, species, and reasons. They are, of course, not unrelated to God. They are, in fact, related to God much more intimately than the corporeal things in which the material universe consists. They are, Augustine most often says, thoughts in God's mind. To say anything else would be to suggest that there are eternal things that exist independently of God, and that would be an offense against the grammar of Christian thought. In coming to know truths such as these, we come to know a part of what God knows, and are thereby conformed (though never fully, and in this life not finally) to God's mind.

So much for the hierarchy of being. It reaches from bodies extended in space and time up through the nonrational souls of animals to the rational souls of men and angels; from there to all truths, eternally known to God; and, finally, to the triune being of God. The closer to God's being something is, the more fully it participates in God, the more being it has: God is maximal being, and at the other end of the scale there is minimal being, which is simple nonexistence. Ascent and descent through the hierarchy of being is therefore ascent toward those things with more being and descent toward those with less. Metaphors of distance and motion are important to Augustine: we can be closer to or further from God, and this means that we can ascend and descend the hierarchy of being. But these ways of speaking are always metaphorical: when we move away from God, as we do when we sin, it is not that there is any change of place. There is a change in *similitudo,* in degree of likeness: "To approach *(propinquare)* him is to become like *(similem)* him; to move away *(recedere)* from him is to become unlike *(dissimilem)* him." Nothing that has being—that exists at all—can have it in any other way than by participation in God's being. This, for Augustine, is what the doctrine of creation out of nothing means: nothing exists independently of God, for independently of God there is just nothing. Differently put: being *(esse, essentia, substantia)* is not a quality independent of God in which both he and other beings share: God is, rather, being's measure and origin, and others share in it only by his gift and by way of participation in him.

The order of things is not only a hierarchy of being: it is also, and equally, a hierarchy of goodness. If, as Augustine again and again says, to be is good, then to be more is better, and not to be at all is the complete absence of goodness. Evil, recall, is a no-thing, a privation, an absence; and this explains why it is the worst thing in the world: it is the furthest possible from God's being. The more being you have, the better you are. The less being you have, the worse you are. Goodness is another among God's names, another way of locating and attempting to describe his nature; and since he has being maximally, he must also have goodness maximally. Goodness, just like being, is a quantity of which creatures can have more or less; and, also like being, any possessor of it has it only by gift and participation. God is its measure and origin, the only one who is what he has and has what he is, and so the only one who cannot lose what he has. This is what makes God both supremely good and maximally existent: all other things can lose the goodness and being they have (the soul can lose its wisdom and so become less than it was; the elegant glass vase, its perfect proportions reflecting and imaging the harmony of the cosmos, can be shattered and so cease to be beautiful, and indeed to be at all), but the perfection of God's being—its maximal goodness—is found in part in its simple indefectibility, in the fact that *"non sit aliquid habere quod vel possit amittere"*—that it can lose nothing it has.

Ordering things by being and goodness implies also ordering by love. If some things are better than others, which is the same as to say that some have more being than others, then it follows immediately that some things should be loved more (or at least differently) than others. This is the *ordo amoris*, the order of love, an ordering that parallels those of being and goodness and transposes those orderings into the realm of human affections and desires. If your loves are rightly ordered, thinks Augustine, you will love each creature with the amount and kind of love appropriate to it. This means that each beloved creature, and if you are lucky your world will be overflowingly full of such creatures (your lover, your child, your dog, your ideas, your reputation, the juniper tree you've tended so lovingly in your garden, the silken stuff of your evening shawl, the prose of your favorite novelist), will be loved in the end for the degree and kind of its participation in God. This is the only thing that could make any creature worthy of love, for it is only by participation in God that it has or could have any lovable qualities at all. All love of creatures is, therefore, a form of the love of God. Augustine sometimes puts this by saying that while God and (some) creatures are to be loved, the mode of love proper to God is enjoyment (God is *fruendum*, to be enjoyed), while the mode of love proper to creatures is use (creatures are *utendum*, to be used).

This does not sound good to modern ears. Loving your child (or even your dog) under the sign of use is likely to suggest to most of us making your child an object of self-gratification without paying attention to her intrinsic value. It is likely to appear as, to use the degenerate forms of Kantian language that have entered so deeply into our late-modern forms of political and ethical talk, a morally problematic example of treating the child as means rather than end. And this is indeed partly what Augustine means. But for him, so to treat your child, your lover, and all the other creatures you love is to treat them with the love they merit. They lack and must lack intrinsic value, if "intrinsic" means value belonging to them independently of their relation to anyone or anything else. Your child is, after all, a creature, which means that the value (the being and goodness) she has (and she has much) is without remainder a gift of God and to be understood as a mode of participation in God. To love her, then, cannot mean to enjoy her. To enjoy something is, Augustine says, to hold fast to it in love for its own sake, *"amore inhaerere alicui rei propter seipsam."* Put differently, God is not to be loved as if he were this or that good *("hoc et illud bonum"),* but rather as if he were good itself *("bonum ipsum").* The final good we should seek, then, is not that which can be judged and categorized by us, but rather that to which we adhere, or join ourselves closely, in submissive love *("non cui supervolitet iudicando, sed cui haereat amando").* This can properly be done only for God because only God has intrinsic value—intrinsic lovability—and so only God can be loved for himself alone, for his own sake. Everything else, all creatures, must be loved finally and most fully for what they are, which means for the goodness given them by God, which is precisely not something they possess intrinsically. Loving your child, then, if done well, is love under the sign of use, not love under the sign of enjoyment.

This is not a grimly puritanical rejection of the delight of worldly loves. It is a claim that these loves come to proper fruition and give the full measure of delight possible when they are placed in relation to God, which is to say under the sign of use. Loving something as what it is and for what it is yields delight. Loving something for what it is not—as an idol, lifted up into God's place—puts an unbearable burden upon the act of love and upon the beloved. The inevitable result is loss: loss of the delight proper to creaturely loves and damage to both lover and beloved.

Loss and damage, gain and growth—these oppositions bind together and hold apart, in Augustine's view, those whose loves are well-ordered (the inhabitants of Jerusalem, the city of God) and those whose loves are disordered (those who wander, benighted, in Babylon, the city of the damned). His fascination with this topic, and his endless play with tropes to ornament his thought about it, are evident everywhere in his work. The *City of God* is in the end about nothing else. His descriptions of the two cities constitute yet one more way—the last to which we need pay attention—in which he orders things.

> And so there are two cities, one of the wicked and the other of the holy. They endure from the beginning—the creation of the human race—until the end of time. They are now physically commingled though separate in intention; in the day of judgment they will be separated physically as well. All men who love pride and temporal dominion with empty and arrogant ostentation, together with all spirits who love such things and seek glory in subjecting men [to themselves], are bound together in a single social order. Even though they often fight one another for these things, they are nevertheless thrown into the same abyss by an equal weight of disordered desire. They are united with one another by the similarity of their habits and merits. And, by contrast, all men and spirits who humbly seek God's glory rather than their own and follow him with piety belong to a single social order.

The "weight of disordered desire," the *pondus* of cupidity, is the hallmark of sin. It drags the sinner—the one whose loves are misdirected—from being toward nothing. Liars belong to the single social order of those who are in this sense disordered, and the lie is for Augustine among the clearest examples of sin, the most elegantly transparent instance of what it is to be weighed down, moved toward the nothing from which we came, by an incoherent love. Sin is strange love, weighted toward nothing, consuming itself; and the lie is a paradigm of it. But more needs to be said about sin's strangeness.

3

Sinning

Sin's characteristic mark is self-serving aversion: sinners turn their faces away from God and attempt, narcissistically, to look only at themselves. Sin's result is damage: sinners exchange a free gift of infinite value for a circumscribed piece of low-rent real estate whose freehold they hope to own by their own unaided efforts. The exchange defeats itself: even as sinners make the gesture of aversion and the grab for ownership they know that they have made a strange bargain.

Sin's strangeness is puzzling and almost universal. Augustine's word for it is usually *peccatum*. The Latin word, noun and verb, was often used by non-Christian writers to mean nothing more interesting or precise than error or mistake: grammatical solecisms and inaccuracies in navigation could be called sins, and those who committed them sinners. So too could offenses against sexual norms or against the provisions of civil or criminal law. But for Augustine, as for the New Testament and for most Christian thinkers since, sin has a narrower and more interesting meaning. It is offense against God, offense that finds its first human example and ideal type in what Adam and Eve did in choosing, at the behest of the smoothly subtle serpent, to eat the fruit forbidden them. These two are the first human sinners, and they have almost all humans since then as company. All Christians would except Jesus from the company of sinners, some would except Mary, and some would offer other candidates for sinlessness. But with these few exceptions the generalization holds: sin's strangeness is everywhere, and all the more strange for its universality.

"Sin," says Augustine, "is perversity and lack of order, that is, a turning away from the creator, who is more excellent, and a turning to the creatures, which are inferior." This is sin's attitude: perverted aversion, a turning of the face from what is supremely good toward what is less good, an irrational and disordered *(inordinatio)* exchange. The exchange is a matter of desire, *desiderium,* and will, *voluntas,* rather than one of reason. It is something sinners actively seek and want, an attitude they are desperate to adopt with just the urgency that the lover feels on the way to an assignation with the beloved. The vocabulary of hurried motion is everywhere in Augustine's discussion of the evil will in which sin consists: *peccatum* is an *aversio* best understood as *motus,* motion; when the will moves, it does so feverishly and fast, making a grab for what it moves toward. It is not only that sinners' faces are averted: they are eager for it to be so, decisive and passionate in their turning of the gaze.

Augustine is always the *rhetor,* the master of tropes, and he likes to ornament his depiction of sin's perverted aversion:

> Our good lives always with you, and it is because we are averted from it that we have become perverse. Let us, then, Lord, revert so that we may not be inverted, because our good lives with you without any defect.

English creaks under the strain of this sort of thing. Augustine uses four verbs derived from *vertere,* "to turn" *(avertere, pervertere, revertere, evertere),* and while the first three can be Englished well enough to reflect their common origin (avert, pervert, revert), the fourth is harder, and my Englishing of it (invert) is strained ("evert" is sufficiently archaic that it would now send most native speakers of English to their dictionaries), but "invert" does capture part of the meaning of *evertere*—to cast down, overthrow, destroy. The self-conscious rhetorical play in this passage reflects Augustine's understanding of sin's strangeness in its very language: the act of aversion turns back on itself, making its agent perverse with a perversity whose reversal can only be pleaded for in the knowledge that the plea's failure will leave the sinner not only disordered (perverted), but also inverted—turned inside out and upside down, which is to say so disordered as to be left scarcely recognizable, and certainly beyond its own righting. The damage done by ourselves to ourselves by moving *(vertere)* from God, our fixed center, cannot be repaired by us.

"Sins," then, "are committed only voluntarily." Damage of the sort that sin is can only be self-inflicted, and the infliction of it always involves the will. "The mind can be deposed from the stronghold of domination *(de arce dominandi)* and of right order *(rectoque ordine)* only by the will." When your loves are rightly ordered, you are in a strong place, an *arx* or well-guarded citadel. There you are impregnable, beyond all possibility of defeat by external foes. You can, however, defeat yourself, cast yourself down, damage and mutilate yourself, should you choose to do so. When you do so choose, you sin: you mutilate yourself with an evil will *(mala voluntate)*, and that you do so is a fact about yourself, not a fact about God or about any other agent in the world.

For Augustine, to speak of sin without speaking of the will is a solecism. Sin is by definition willed. He is forced to say this because he thinks the only alternative is that God intends sin, and to say that is to impugn God's goodness, which is a fundamental error in Christian thought. But it does not follow from this that every particular sin could have been refrained from by the unaided exercise of the sinner's will at the time it was undertaken. It might be the case—if Augustine is right, it usually is the case—that a particular sinner's will has become so perversely inverted that he can do nothing other than sin. The weight of disordered loves might be so heavy that it can no longer be lifted without divine help. In such a situation, sin becomes unavoidable by will even though the reason for this unavoidability is precisely a freely willed act that could have been refrained from. Habit becomes immovable:

> The definition of sin I once gave, "Sin is the will to keep or to get what one can freely leave alone that justice forbids," was accurate because it defines sin as such, not the punishing results of sin. When sin and its punishing results have become inseparable, what can the will dominated by passion do, except perhaps, if it is pious, pray for help? One [in such a condition] is free to the extent that he has been freed, and to that extent "will" may be spoken of. Otherwise, all will would better be called passion; this [will-called-passion] is not, as is pretended by the Manichees, an addition to a strange nature; it is, rather, our very own lack, of which we are healed only by the grace of the Savior. And if anyone prefers to say that passion itself is just will, made subject to lack by sin, I have no objection. I don't want to argue about words when the thing is agreed.

Sin, Augustine here tells us, has results and they are punishing *(poena)*. The sinner, once he is subject to these punishing results (and we all are), still has a will, but it is so weighed down that it can do nothing other than implore liberation (freedom, *liberatio*, exactly what it has lost for itself) from the slavery into which it has freely placed itself. Once in this state, the sinner's will has become his very own lack *(nostrae vitium)*: still his, but now present only powerlessly, as an absence. Sin, an act of the will that was free in the sense that it need not have been performed but was, has produced this odd result: in sin the will is freely used to habituate itself in such a way that it can no longer freely be used. It is as if an athlete were to exercise hard to make his muscles unusable. The will has chosen to encumber itself with weights that it cannot by itself remove. The result is that although the will is always involved in sin, it may be involved in such a way that its actions can no longer (without external help: the Savior's grace) be other than they are. The punishing results of sin are seen at their worst when the will has been emptied, vitiated, turned by its own efforts into its very own lack.

The incapacity of our wills to do anything other than sin may some-times be the effect of our own previously willed actions. This is so, for example, when the addict has become thoroughly addicted to a pleasure she once freely chose. But in Augustine's view, things are worse than this: while each of us may be able to avoid a particular kind of sinful action together with the habituation that goes with it (not everyone tries or becomes habituated to any particular pleasure), none of us will be able to avoid sin and its punishing results altogether. This is because he thinks that each of us is subject to the punishing results of Adam and Eve's sin, the *peccatum originale*. Along the gloomily winding paths opened by this line of thought I shall not follow him. It is not that I think him wrong; it is only that a sufficiently full understanding of sin's grammar can be had without doing so. Augustinian talk of sin, it is enough to say here, requires talk of the will.

It is possible to understand Augustine's definitions of sin to be im-plicated with dualism: to suggest, that is, that the sinner's turn from God to the creatures is a turn toward something evil, something with which only sinners would have dealings. But this would be a misreading. For Augustine—and here again his thought shows the pattern of most Christian thinking—the creatures are very good. God made them, and so they must be good insofar as they exist at all. To say anything else would be to accuse God of making something evil, something that could only be an occasion of sin. This is not a possible view for Christians. Every creature in which the sinner might be interested (the bodies and minds of other sinners, the inanimate objects of which the world is so gloriously full, the truths of mathematics and philosophy and music) can and should be loved for what it is: a creature in which God's glory is evident and for the existence of which God is finally responsible. So to love the creatures is not sin. It is a proper response to being rational and capable of love in a world of ordered beauty made by God. Sin lies not in the love of lovable creatures, but rather in the replacement of God by them in the affections and desires of the sinner:

Sin is not a desire for naturally evil things but an abandonment of better things. And this itself is evil, not that nature which the sinner uses evilly.

The desire for creatures becomes sinful only when it requires the abandonment of God. This happens when the creatures are grasped at willfully as if they had goodness or desirability independent of God. To desire or to love another human being in this way is to treat her as if she were not a creature, as if she had the goodness and desirability she has intrinsically, independently of God. This is an error of judgment (your beloved is not in fact like that), which is implicated with the act of will that averts the sinner from God. Sinners turn toward the object of desire as though it were sufficiently succulent to be enjoyed in its own right. In so doing they turn away from God by isolating what is desired from what in fact makes it desirable. Once isolated, the object of desire can be consumed as though owned, and the will so to isolate, possess, and consume is the sinful will, the *mala voluntas*. In this sin properly consists. The juice of the apple so consumed, however, will lie like ash on the tongue.

More flavor is given to an Augustinian syntax of sin by the centrality of it to the idea of *superbia*, pride. Augustine's favorite scriptural text on sin and pride is Sirach 10:13, which read, in the Latin version known to him, *"initium omnis peccati est superbia,"* which is to say that pride is the beginning or point of origin for all sin. What then is pride? Much of what Augustine says about it is just what he says about the act of will in which sin consists: pride, too, is a perverted aversion from God. But whereas the creature toward which the sinful will turns may be anything (another person, a material object, an idea), pride's turn is typically toward the sinner's own self. "The soul is proud," says Augustine, "when it rejoices *(gaudet)* in itself as if it were its own good *(seipso quasi suo bono)*." As with sin in general, the problem lies not in rejoicing (taking ecstatic pleasure) in yourself. Nothing could be wrong with that, for of course you are a great good, just the kind of being in whom ecstatic pleasure-taking is proper. No, the problem is misprision, the mistake of thinking that your glories and goods are your own, without remainder, and that you can rejoice in them without also rejoicing in God from whom they come and without whom they (and you, deceived by pride into thinking otherwise) would not exist at all. Pride, then, is recursive sin, perversion directed upon itself.

If, as Augustine's reading of Sirach 10:13 strongly suggests, *superbia* really is the cause of all sin, then it ought to be possible to trace to it all particular instances of the exchange of the creature for God. One way to do this is by looking back to the first of all sins, which Augustine thought to be that of Satan, the fallen angel who became God's adversary and our tempter. Satan—Augustine most often calls him Diabolus—is an evil angel. But of course he was not and could not have been created as such: God made him and God can make nothing that is not good. The difference between good and evil angels, therefore, is not one of nature or origin. It is a difference of will and passion *(voluntas* and *cupiditas)*. Good angels want and passionately turn to the common good, the good shared by all and freely given to all; bad angels—among whom Diabolus is the first and remains the emblem—want and take delight in *(delectare* is the usual verb) themselves as if they were their own good. Here again is the hallmark of sin: self-seeking and recursively perverse pride, the *initium* of all sin and therefore inevitably present in the initiating sin. Diabolus's sin, like ours, is his very own lack. He sought this lack spontaneously, without a tempter (unlike Eve), and without the inherited weight of another's sin (unlike us). But in every other respect, the structure of the first of all sins is exactly like that of all subsequent sins, from Eve's to ours.

In addition to these originating sins in which sin's syntax is evident with a peculiar starkness, there is in Augustine also a psychological version of the sense in which pride lies at the root of particular sins. Pride is, for example, likened to a many-symptomed sickness of the body. The symptoms (sores, pains, fevers) may be alleviated by treatment, but if the underlying disease is not cured, they will return. The symptoms are particular sins and the underlying disease is pride. Removal of the disease can only be brought about by humility, pride's antonym and antidote, and Augustine often makes that point by emphasizing the medicinal effects of Jesus' embrace of humility by way of the incarnation and the cross. Humility is simply the acknowledgment of who and what we are: creatures whose goods are not their own, but rather free gifts from God. Pride is aversion from this truth by the futile attempt to take ownership and control of one's goods as if they were, without remainder, one's own.

Pride, however, is futile. Those who are proud attempt to own and control themselves without reference to God. This cannot be done. The attempt to be a self-pleaser not only fails to please but, worse, shows and deepens a lack *(vitium)* or deficiency *(defectum)* that is among the conditions of its possibility in the first place:

Only a nature made out of nothing could be depraved by a lack. [The will] derives its existence as a nature from the fact that it was made by God; that it can fall away therefrom is because it was made out of nothing. Men do not, however, fall away so much that they become utterly nothing; they do, however, by turning to themselves become less than they would have been had they clung to the one who supremely is. Therefore, to leave God behind and to be in oneself—to please oneself—is not to be nothing but to approach nothing. This is why Scripture calls proud those who are pleased with themselves.

Pride is made possible by lack and is itself a kind of lack, of absence: it turns from what is to what is not, and in so doing the will, which can be strangely motivated by this lack, falls away from what it was (a creature) toward the only other possibility it has, which is to become nothing. How is this possible? How can what is something want to become nothing? Augustine's suggestion in the text just quoted is striking: the human will, like everything other than God, was created *ex nihilo*, out of nothing; it has, therefore, a tendency to return whence it came. From nothing it came, and toward nothing it may return. The traditional adobe houses and churches of the American Southwest may serve as an emblem: they are raised from the red mud of the ground upon which they stand, and without repeated remudding they lose definition and shape, eventually to be reabsorbed into the ground from which they came. So also for the will: it came from the abyss of what is not, and in pridefully turning from the one who raised it from that abyss, it slips and slides back toward it. In trying to please itself the prideful will begins to remove itself not only from pleasure but from all being.

Augustine makes the same point with respect to the fallen angels, in the following terms:

What else can we call this lack than pride? For "pride is the beginning of all sin" (Sirach 10:13). They [the fallen angels] chose not to preserve their strength for him [that is, for God]; and though they would have been greater if they had clung to him who is the greatest, they chose that which is less by preferring themselves. This is the first defect or fault or lack in that nature which was created not that it might exist supremely but so that it could be happy by enjoying him who does exist supremely. By turning from him, it would not become nothing but would become less, and as a result would be miserable.

Pride's lack initiates all sin, and all sin imitates and is informed by pride's lack. The result of sin is not merely that sinners become less than they otherwise would have been. It is also that they are miserable about it. The attempt to please oneself issues simply in misery, pleasure's dark twin, just as the miserable self-pleasuring of masturbation is the dark twin of the joy of loving sexual intercourse with another.

Augustine also often describes the loss of being that results from sin in terms of an exchange of what is freely given to all for what is privately owned by the sinner:

> The soul, delighting in its own power, slips away from the whole shared by all to the particular, which is private to itself. If it had followed God as guide it would have been able to be ideally governed by God's laws along with all creatures. But by that apostate pride which is called the beginning of sin it wants something more than the whole and schemes to control it with its own law. However, since there is nothing greater than the whole it is thrown into care for the particular. And so the soul decreases by desiring something greater.

Yet again the echo of Sirach: pride originates sin. But pride is here further qualified as "apostate" *(apostatica):* it has turned aside or away from God, obsessed and mesmerized by its own powers and possibilities to the absurd extent that it wants (the verb, *appetere,* is strictly appetitive: the desire is for ownership and consumption) more than everything, more than the *universum.* Everything—all that can be had—has, however, already freely been given to all and is held in common by all. To exchange everything for something *(universum* for *aliquid)* is the incoherent desire of the soul dazzled by itself. The result, inevitable and immediate, is that it is thrown or thrust *(truditur)* from the communal into the private, into a constrained and ever-diminishing care for the particular. And there it is hemmed in, trapped in its self-caused diminution. Augustine likes to connect *privatus* with *privatio*—what is private with privation. This works well in English, too, and it permits us to say that those who seek what is private (who seek to own) deprive themselves of what has been given, and must therefore suffer privation.

But what does Augustine mean by saying that there is nothing greater than what God freely gives to all in common? Just what is it that God so gives? It is the eternal and changeless truth by holding to which we live the *beata vita,* the happy life for which we were made and intended. The happy life consists in large part in seeing things for what they are (God's created goods), and in loving them as they should be loved (for the glorification of God). This is what is the same for everyone, and it is this than which there is nothing greater: "Truth *(veritas)* and wisdom *(sapientia)* are common to all: it is by firmly sticking *(inhaerendo)* to them that everyone becomes happy and wise." Truth and wisdom, to use another favorite Augustinian image, shine freely upon all alike. We participate freely in them unless we attempt to take ownership and control of them. What is freely given cannot be fully owned: the attempt to privatize the common good makes it no longer common and no longer good. Diminution and the attempt to privatize by expropriation go together.

All this can be put in terms of gift-giving and gift-refusal. Sin—apostate pride—refuses God's gift, and does so by asserting the self as its autonomous creator. To accept something (happiness, wisdom) as gift is to acknowledge dependence upon the giver. It is also to acknowledge that the proper use of the gift is not to be woven out of the whole cloth of the desires and intentions of the giver. To attempt this would be to attempt expropriation, which in turn would be to refuse the givenness of the gift, to refuse the fact that you are gifted, and to refuse the importance of the desires and intentions of the giver as relevant to your use of the gift. These refusals, produced by the soul's self-fascination, lie at the heart of sin.

Sin understood in this way is causally and phenomenologically puzzling. There is no good explanation for why it occurs, and when it does occur it is puzzling to the sinner. To the causal question—where do pride, the evil will, and sin itself come from?—Augustine usually returns the answer that he does not know. If these things are all deficiencies, lacks, then it should not be surprising that we cannot give a full causal account of their occurrence. An absence, to use Aristotle's account of causation, has no efficient cause. This sounds more convincing in Latin than in English: the *causa efficiens* must have as its *effectum* that which it effects or brings about, which is something. But the *defectum* that is sin is precisely not something brought about: it is not an *effectum*. It is, rather, a falling or slipping away from all effects toward nothing. So, Augustine thinks, the search for an efficient cause of sin is a mistake. Nothing will be found because nothing is what is sought. The evil will simply occurs, and the chief point of emphasizing its nothingness is to prevent God from being understood as its author.

But the puzzling nature of sin goes beyond the bare fact of its occurrence. The reflective sinner who has come to understand his sin for what it is will also find it hard to account for particular instances. If sin is really a recursively incoherent act of the will, directed toward nothing and issuing in nothing, "a tale told by an idiot, full of sound and fury, signifying nothing," then its very phenomenology—the features of the sinner's experience as it seems to the sinner—will reflect this. It will be difficult to give an account of a particular sin that makes any sense, even to the sinner.

Sin's strange syntax means that its remedy cannot lie with us. Bootstrapping ourselves out of sin is impossible. The instrument we would have to use to do this—the will—is already perversely defective in its aversion from God, and this means that it must necessarily be ineffective as an instrument of its own transformation. What then can we do? We can turn toward God, convert *(con-vertere)* ourselves from sin to praise. *"Non solum non peccemus adorando,"* he says, claiming unsurprisingly that we can avoid sin by adoration or praise of God, but going on to add, more strikingly, *"sed peccemus non adorando,"* which says that only in this way can sin be avoided. Adoration, then, not only suffices for the avoidance of sin; it is also necessary for it. This is because an approach to God in worship necessarily involves acknowledgment of the worshiper's insufficiency and God's all-sufficiency. This is just what it means to worship. Such an acknowledgment is the best possible exercise of humility because it goes beyond the mere judgment that humility is good, and beyond even the thought that humility is the best of which we are capable. No, adoration is humility enacted before the one who gives it sense and makes it possible, the responsive kiss to the one who gave us lips. Adoration's efficacy, like that of the kiss or the promise, is properly and fully performative: just so long as one worships or adores one has left behind the expropriative self-assertiveness of *superbia* and has entered into a right relation with God. Adoration is humility, and both words signify a full and proper reception of the free gift that is everything. Augustine is often lyrical about this, as here in some warm play with the idea of God's water, the water of life, the water of baptism, the water of humility, the water of adoration, and so on:

> This is the water of sin's confession, of heart's humility, of life's salvation. It's for those who abase themselves, who presume nothing of themselves, and who proudly attribute nothing to their own power. This water is in no alien books, not in those of Epicureans, Stoics, Manicheans, or Platonists. Everywhere in them are to be found the best precepts of morals and discipline; but nowhere in them is found this humility. This path of humility comes from nowhere other than Christ. It is from the one who came humbly although he was most high. What else did he teach us by paying a debt he did not owe than to release us from debt? What else did he teach us, he who was baptized though sinless, and crucified though without guilt? What else did he teach us, but this same humility? He had every right to say, "I am the way, and the truth, and the life" (John 14:6). By this humility, then, we draw near to God because the Lord is close to

those who have bruised their hearts; amid the many-watered flood of those who extol themselves against God and who teach arrogance in pieties, no one will draw near to him.

Mary is also used by Augustine as a paradigm of humility's transparency before God and consequent intimacy with God. She accepts the announcement of God's intention to make her the mother of God by faith and without opposition or doubt. Her response to the angel's announcement of what will happen to her is understood by Augustine to be very different in this respect from Zechariah's response to the announcement of the impending birth of John the Baptist to Elizabeth. Mary's words exhibit puzzled confidence; Zechariah's show disbelief and the self-assertion concomitant with it (Luke 1:18, 34). And Mary is rewarded with praise while Zechariah is struck dumb, which Augustine takes as an instance of the loss of being that is produced by sin. Mary's faithful humility is evident in her acceptance of what is given as given without any tincture of an attempt to own or control it. The conception of Jesus in her womb is accepted by Mary entirely on faith, as God's gift:

> [In the conception of Jesus] faith rather than lust came first. Fleshly desire, by which others who carry with them original sin are procreated and conceived, played no part. And because it was completely absent, [Mary's] holy virginity was made fecund by faith rather than by sexual intercourse. . . . For although conjugal chastity can make good use of fleshly desire in the genitals, such desire still has involuntary motions, which show either that it could not have existed in paradise prior to sin's occurrence, or that if it had existed then it would not always have resisted the will.

This passage opens the labyrinth of Augustine's thought about sex, procreation, and original sin. Fortunately we do not need to follow all its twists and turns. We do need to note, though, the important and interesting fact that for Augustine our bodies' lack of responsiveness to our wills is among the signs that we are sinners. *Libido* (lust) and *carnis concupiscentia* (fleshly desire) carry with them movements of the body (erection, secretion, ejaculation, and so on) that are not produced by an act of will, and are not easily checkable or constrainable by such an act. As Augustine often says, such signs resist the will and are opaque to it. They are among the most obvious marks of our subjection to sin, and this explains why he shows at times an endearing interest in the question of which parts of our bodies can now, after the fall, be controlled by our wills. He may be the first and only premodern thinker to have shown an interest in the ability some show to wiggle their ears and to fart musically. Sexual intercourse would not, thinks Augustine, have shown in paradise the body's opaque resistance to the will it now shows, and this partly explains why Mary's conception of Jesus occurred without it—by faith rather than *concumbendo,* by sexual intercourse, or more literally "by lying down with." Her acceptance by faith of God's message to her is a paradigm of what it would be like for the body to be transparent before the will and for the will to be transparent before God. And in being all those things it is also a paradigm of humility and adoration, sin's antidotes.

That sexual desire is opaque to will and understanding (an empirical claim whose truth is close to self-evident: why else would so much human imaginative effort be expended upon attempts to penetrate and illuminate its opacity?) serves to illustrate Augustine's view that sin is mysterious, and especially so to the reflective sinner. But Augustine also likes to illustrate sin's causal and phenomenological opacity by depicting sins of other kinds. And this leads us to his account of an adolescent theft of pears, by way of which an Augustinian view of sin has entered most deeply into the soul of the West. This account has been much read and commented upon, but has more often provoked anger than understanding, and even when it has been admired it has rarely been understood. Nietzsche, for example, wrote to Franz Overbeck in 1885 that he had been reading the *Confessions* for relaxation: "O this old rhetorician! How false and eye-rolling he is! How I laughed—for example about the theft of his youth, nothing more than a student escapade." Forty years later Bertolt Brecht was equally exercised: "For want of some trashy novel I've been reading Augustine's *Confessions.* It's so funny to place his discoveries against the conduct so typical of all students: such pettily envious, greedy, gloating behavior. He treats his religion like a hobby-horse *(Steckenpferd)*." Anyone who reads the episode with American or European students today will encounter similar responses: Doesn't he overdramatize? Isn't it a lot of fuss about nothing much? Well, yes; but the nothing about which he fusses is sin, and his fuss, if carefully read, sheds some light upon the contours of the nothing that it is about.

Augustine writes about the theft as a man in his forties recalling (or imagining) events from his sixteenth year. As always, he addresses himself primarily to God, and he does so in the heated periods of the professional rhetor, using techniques of persuasion learned when, as he dramatically puts it, he sat upon the throne of lies, the *cathedra mendacii,* as someone paid to persuade.

Looking back to his sixteenth year from the perspective of his early forties, Augustine was (he writes) not able to tell the difference between *dilectio* and *libido,* between the serene delight that comes from the love of God and the disturbances that come from sensual desire in general and sexual desire in particular. He was dispersed and lost in the multiplicity of created things, burning with a desire for the pleasures of hell; he was submerged by his desires in a whirlpool of vices, "thrown, spilled, scattered, confounded" by what he calls his fornications—which, again, include but are not limited to specifically sexual acts. This is the condition of the sinner, here connected especially with the sexual sins, but by no means produced only by them. The sinner is dispersed and scattered, entranced by the variety of created things and forgetful of what gives them their unity, which is the fact that they have been created by God. Sin (we have already seen) may constrict and hem in the sinner when he grasps for autonomous ownership of what is freely given; it may also distend him, spreading him out and stretching him thin in his endless desire for particular libidinous (which here does not mean only sexual) enjoyments, in forgetfulness of their origin.

Augustine then had (he continues) time on his hands: he was living at home on a temporary holiday brought about by his family's lack of cash to support him in full-time study. His unoccupied time gave the *vepres libidum,* the thorns of lust, free rein: there was, he says, no one to root them out. He spent time with his peers, boasting of imagined sexual exploits that he had not yet had a chance to undertake. These peers were his *comites,* the companions with whom he wandered the streets of Babylon—the city of exile in which true worship of God is not possible, the archetype of the human city, the city whose human inhabitants' self-interrogation shows that they love not God but themselves, not charity but cupidity, not love but lust—rolling in filth as though bathing in spices and precious unguents. He was seduced by pleasure because he wanted to be (as always, sin is a matter of the will), and God's serene truth was hidden from him by a thick mist.

In this condition he and his companions wander the streets of Babylon, looking for amusement. The amusement they find is a theft:

> I wanted to steal and I did so. I was compelled by no need except the poverty that comes from loathing justice and being stuffed with wickedness. I stole what I already had in abundance and of better quality. I didn't want to enjoy what I hungered to steal, but rather the very fact of having stolen and sinned.

Augustine's theft was not, he thought or retrospectively imagined, for material gain. He was not driven by material needs, by *egestates:* he was poor, subject to *penuria*, only in lacking a sense of justice, of what it means to do right. Instead, his belly was stuffed with wickedness, *iniquitas*, and it was just this that led him to take pleasure in the act of doing something wrong simply because it was wrong. What attracted him, what his appetite turned to, was not pears but theft; and to that only because it was sin. The theft itself followed:

> Close to our vineyard there was a pear tree laden with fruit enticing in neither appearance nor taste. After continuing our outdoor games until dead of night according to our abominable custom, we wayward adolescents set off to shake the fruit down and carry it away. We took a huge quantity, but not to feast on so much as to throw to the pigs. Even though we may have eaten a few, we did it for the pleasure of doing what was not permitted. Such was my heart, O God, such was my heart: you had pity on it when it was in the deepest abyss. Now let my heart tell you what I was looking for there where I freely became evil and where my fault had no cause except itself. It was filthy, and I loved it: I loved my ruin and my defect, not that toward which I was defecting but rather my defection itself. My loathsome soul leaped down from your solidity to destruction; I did not hunger for anything other than shame by acting shamefully.

One matrix for this passage is scriptural. There is an echo of Genesis (3:6), in which Eve is enticed by the beauty and apparent delectability of the fruit she has been forbidden. The Latin of the second book of the *Confessions* resounds to the Latin of this passage from Genesis: Augustine implicitly contrasts the delectable fruit of Genesis with the appearance of the pears he and his friends steal. The latter don't even look good, and so he lacks the excuse Adam and Eve had. His sin recapitulates theirs, but is less excusable and more puzzling: the only thing that entices him is the evil of his action (he is *malus gratis*, evil for nothing, freely evil), and this is the fundamental and endlessly difficult fact about sin. It wants only itself, but its desirability is strange: sin is an absence (how can you want what isn't there?), a defect (how can you want what's less good than what you've already got?). Augustine's rhetorical answer to the puzzle is to say that sin has only itself as cause and only itself as goal. Its defect is recursive, self-directed, tending toward destruction *(exterminium)*.

There are also echoes of the parable of the two sons from Luke's Gospel (15:11–32). The prodigal in that story, like Augustine and his friends, was an adolescent. He demanded from his benevolent father his "substance" *(substantia*, rendering the Greek *ousia*, which occurs only here in the New Testament). For Augustine, substance is something only God has or can have by right; it is God who is three persons in one substance, and Jesus and the Spirit who are *consubstantialis*, of one substance, with God the Father. This language is from the Chalcedonian formula, which had not been formulated or ratified when Augustine composed this passage, but which is entirely in accord with how he thinks about God. God gives *substantia* to us freely, but it is a fundamental defection (falling away, movement toward nonbeing) to ask for it as though it is ours by right, as the prodigal does when he asks his benevolent father for the portion he thinks of as his: "Father, give me the share of your estate *(substantia)* that should come to me" (Luke 15:12). This is precisely to attempt the kind of freehold ownership we cannot have. We can have substance only derivatively, and only when we acknowledge it as gift. It is just such acknowledgment that the prodigal fails to make. Augustine presents the theft of pears as in this respect like the prodigal's request for his inheritance: he and his noxiously adolescent companions are portrayed to Augustine's readers as recapitulating the prodigal's attempted assertion of ownership of what cannot be owned.

The results for the prodigal are disastrous: he dissipates his substance, begins to be in desperate need, and is forced to work as a feeder of pigs, a deeply unclean occupation. At length he is hungry enough that he wants to eat what the pigs eat. Augustine echoes and plays with all this. He denies that the theft of pears is motivated by need *(egestas)*; the prodigal's quasi-theft produces just such need *(coepit egere . . .)*. The prodigal's desperation forces him to want to eat pig-food *(quas porci manducabant)*; Augustine and his friends throw what they have stolen to the pigs *(proicienda porcis)*. The prodigal moves from an arrogant certainty of his rights and of his capacity effectively to own his substance to a desperate understanding that the attempt to own it has led to its waste, and that the only thing left him is to beg forgiveness from the true owner of all substance, the only really substantial one, who is God. The mature Augustine thus imaginatively assimilates the adolescent Augustine's theft to this story with verbal echoes: substance stolen is pig-swill just as pears stolen are fit for the pigs. And those who don't know this are adolescents whose attempted acts of ownership inevitably turn God's gifts into pig-swill.

So much for the scriptural echoes: the literary depiction of the adolescent Augustine assimilates him not only to Adam and Eve in the garden (but without the excuses); it portrays him also as the prodigal who has yet to realize what will come of grasping his inheritance, and who cannot yet say, as the prodigal says by the end of his story, and as Augustine will echo by the end of the eighth book of the *Confessions,*

"Father, I have sinned against heaven and against you; I no longer deserve to be called your son" (Luke 15:18–19).

Augustine's story of the theft of pears also deliberately echoes non-Christian archetypes of gratuitous and incomprehensible wickedness. Catiline is the figure of importance here. He was a Roman patrician killed on the battlefield in 62 B.C. by the armies of the state in the course of attempting a military revolution. This failed revolt is presented by its chief chroniclers, Cicero and Sallust, as motivated by a dubious mixture of idealism and disappointment: Catiline promised the new Roman middle classes relief from crushing debt through a program of debt-forgiveness, but he was also in reaction against his two lost campaigns for election to the office of consul. Catiline's importance for Augustine and Augustine's audience is that he was portrayed by Cicero and Sallust as a man of extreme and depraved appetites: brave and energetic, but also gratuitously and inexplicably depraved and lustful. Augustine's audience would certainly have had Catiline brought to mind by his self-description as *malus gratis,* and to underline the point Augustine makes explicit mention of Catiline later in the second book of the *Confessions.* In comparing himself to Catiline, as with the echoes of the sin of Adam and Eve in the garden, Augustine is at pains to say that his own sins are worse even than Catiline's. Catiline's apparently gratuitous wickednesses are really (says Augustine) motivated by a need to keep the violent skills of the military leader and man of lust in burnished readiness for use on occasions when he might be called on to use them for a reason. Augustine's sins, by contrast, have not even this paltry excuse.

There is (probably) yet another series of echoes in Augustine's confession of the pear-theft: they are of Horace's telling in one of his letters of the proverbial story of the Calabrian host. The *calaber hospes* offers worthless pears to his guest, indeed presses them upon him with phrases that indicate their worthlessness *("at tu quantum vis tolle . . . non invisa feres pueris munuscula parvis"),* and telling him that if he won't take them they'll be thrown to the pigs *("haec porcis hodie comedenda relinques").* Horace comments that the stupidly prodigal *(prodigus)* Calabrian gives in such a way as to ensure a harvest of ingratitude. Augustine's own harvest shares this feature: the sinner is not and cannot be grateful for the fruit of his own sin. What he gives himself guarantees his disappointment.

By echoing these sources Augustine portrays himself and his sin as worse than the worst examples to be had from Christian or pagan sources. But this is not self-flagellation. It is, rather, a presentation of himself and his sins as archetypal. The theft of pears is pictured as starkly as it is because Augustine wants his readers clearly to see in it what is proper to all sin, which is performative self-contradiction. The sinner, as Augustine goes on to say in the latter parts of the second book of the *Confessions,* is a powerless prisoner who parodies divine omnipotence by feverishly asserting ownership of a tiny corner of her prison cell, a cell she has made for herself and that becomes ever more prisonlike as she asserts her title to it with more energy and desperation. Sinners are also like those who exchange God for a shadow, which is how one of Job's laments reads in the Latin version known to Augustine (Job 7:2). In doing this, they abandon substance for its insubstantial counterfeits, an act for which Augustine's paradigm is Adam's futile attempt to hide himself from God in the shade of Eden's trees after eating the forbidden fruit (Gen. 3:8–10). These are recursively self-refuting actions: they are strange failures because they exhibit a love of nothing, "an unsurpassably tortuous and imbricated knottiness" *("tortuosissima et implicatissima nodositas")* of motives and actions whose tangle can neither be understood nor untied by those who made it. This is sin. It makes of the sinner a field of desolate and incomprehensible need, a *regio egestatis,* in yet another phrase echoing the parable of the two sons.

Augustine's account of his youthful theft is very far from unadorned reportage. Its rhetorical adornments and its play with sources make at least that much obvious, and the gorgeous garments in which the account is clothed make questions about what really happened to Augustine in his sixteenth year profoundly beside the point. What we know is what he tells us, and what he tells us is that sin is puzzlingly opaque to the sinner even when it is committed. Sinners want something that is nothing, and they are always half-aware of the strangeness of such a desire even when in its grip and about to act upon it. And so their sins seem mysteriously impenetrable even to them. As her mouth opens to bite the apple Eve knows that its juice will be like ashes on her tongue; she knows, too, that she will take the bite anyway; and she is puzzled by the intensity of her desire to perform an act that guarantees its own disappointment. This, too, is how the lie seems to the liar.

4

Speaking

Speech is the voicing of a concept. It makes thought audible by invocation as the divine word was made visible by incarnation. Duplicitous
speech—the lie—divides speech from thought. It relates speech and
thought inappropriately, improperly, sinfully, and in doing so ruptures
God's image in us. Or so Augustine thinks.

This is not an immediately obvious line to take in thinking about
what's wrong with duplicity. Most contemporary Christians wouldn't
take it, and certainly no non-Christian would. Yet the idea that God is
three persons in one substance is the most characteristically Christian
idea: it divides Christians not only from those who don't think about
God at all and from those who do so only negatively; it divides them
also from Jews and Muslims, who do not think of the God they worship
as triune, and who tend to think of those who do as blasphemers and
idolaters. When he turns his thought to any topic Augustine typically
applies characteristically Christian ideas to it: he wants, first and last,
to think as a Christian, and his trinitarian analysis of speech, thought,
and duplicity shows this desire.

So how does it go? Let's begin with words.

Words, for Augustine, are signs—or, to put this in Latin, *verba* are
signa. Signs, in turn, are such because they bring to mind something
other than themselves, other, that is, than the immediate impressions
they make upon your senses. Smoke is a sign of fire in this way: when
you see smoke (or smell it), the seeing or smelling may bring fire to mind
as well as smoke even when fire is not directly evident to the senses. A
footprint in the snow may bring to mind, and thereby act as a sign of,

the animal that made it; and the smell of a loved one's favorite perfume may bring her physical self to mind, and in so doing be a sign of her. Signs bring to mind something that may be very different from the immediate impressions they make on the senses.

Smoke and footprints are what Augustine calls *signa naturalia*, natural signs. By this he means that the link between the sign and what it signifies is independent of human conventions and habits. The loved one's perfume, by contrast, is a given *(datum)* sign, a product of local and contingent habits. Your loved one need not have chosen that particular perfume, while the deer can do nothing about the shape of the imprint its foot makes in the snow, and fire has no choice about whether it will yield smoke.

All words are, for Augustine, given rather than natural signs, which is to say that they are purely conventional. The fact that *felis*, when spoken to someone who understands Latin, brings the cat to mind is just as contingent as the fact that the term *cat* does the same for speakers of English. What a particular word may signify is therefore a product of local habits. But the kinds of things that words in general are capable of signifying are not: words can signify only two kinds of things. First, things external to the mind, such as pear trees, books, people, and houses. Second, the content of their users' minds, "the motion of the mind, or what has been sensed or understood," or "what's in the mind of the one giving the sign," as Augustine puts it.

When words are used to signify in this second way speech becomes a means to make public what's in the mind. Augustine's vocabulary for what's in the mind is rich and varied, and he often gives special attention to our powerful and pressing need to move what is inside (in the mind) to the outside (the public sphere). Recalling (or, better, imagining) his own preverbal babyhood, he emphasizes the anguish of not being able to make his wants known to his parents and nurses. Acquiring speech makes it possible to bridge this gap: traffic can, when speech is acquired, move from Augustine's mind to those of others.

Augustine sometimes takes externalizing the internal, making public the private by signifying it in words, to be the defining characteristic of speech. When in this mood he'll say that doing this is just what it means to speak—why else would we speak? This suggests that every act of speech is one that establishes a relation of some sort between a set of vibrations in the air and something else, something that he most often calls "thought" *(cogitatio)*. But the exact nature of this relation is not clear. Augustine uses a wide range of terms for it: speech may "show" *(demonstrare)* or "express" *(depromere)*, or (most often) "signify" *(signifi-*

care), or (simply) "give" *(dare)* thought. While Augustine doesn't define
the thought-speech relation with precision or complete consistency, it is
at least clear that thought and speech can be intimately related: speech
can make public what I think (hope for, fear, regret, and so on) in something like the same way that a megaphone can carry my feeble voice to
a distance it would not otherwise reach. The megaphone can provide
what I say to those too far away otherwise to hear it. Similarly, speech
can provide my thought to those who would otherwise have no access to
it. Megaphones always distort, and so too does speech: no perfect vocal
representation of thought is possible (the most fundamental reason for
this is that speech is located in the temporal order—it takes time—while
thought participates in the eternal order). Of course, speech may not
be intimately related to thought in this way: duplicitous speech is not,
and this already suggests that Augustine takes speech and thought to be
capable of being related very intimately. Part of the reason why duplicity
is unacceptable is that it produces speech whose relation to thought is
improper or perverse because insufficiently intimate.

When Augustine says that the lie is a kind of speech or utterance, a
member of the class of signifying acts, he is thinking of speech as signifying what's in your mind—of speaking your mind, as we might say,
using an idiom that has deep roots in an Augustinian (and Platonic)
view of the world. But if you can speak your mind, what is it that you
are speaking about (or expressing, or signifying)? Augustine's answer,
usually, is that you are speaking about your thought, which is what's
in your mind.

Thought as Augustine understands it does not take place in any natural
language. The words of English or Latin are not its tools. When you form
a concept or intention, you do not do so in words. When you mention
the concept or intention you've formed, you'll have to use words. But
this does not mean that the concept or intention mentioned is identical
with the words used to mention it. Augustine often notes that we can, by
introspection, observe ourselves choosing particular words to express our
thoughts, and we could not do this if our thought were simply identical
with some set of words. This is the principal reason why he thinks that
words are not the tools of thought:

> Observe your own heart. When you conceive a word you're going to utter
> . . . there is something you wish to say. The very conception of that thing
> in your heart is already a word: it has not yet come out, but it is already
> born in your heart, waiting so that it may come out. You take note for
> whom it is to come out, which is to say with whom you are talking: if he is

Latin, you search for a Latin utterance; if he is Greek, you think of Greek
words; if Punic, you see whether you know any of the Punic language. You
employ different languages for differences in your audience so that you
might bring out the word you have conceived: but what you had conceived
in your heart was confined to no language.

There's some play here with the verb *concipere*, "to conceive." As in
English, this verb is used to mean both "have an idea" and "bring a baby
into being"—a play that Augustine makes much of. Here, he puts the
argument in terms of the variety of languages and the possibility (for the
multilingual) of choosing which to use in order to say what is thought.
But it could just as well be put in terms of choice among different levels
of diction or different kinds of rhetoric within a single language. I don't
talk about God's love in the same way to a child of five as I would to a
woman of thirty, not even when what I want to say is, so far as I can
tell, just the same in each case. Rather, I choose what to say.

Augustine takes the possibility of choices of these sorts to show that
thought—the word conceived in the heart—is not identical with any
particular set of words. He also, at the end of the quotation just given,
suggests that the same possibility provides support for the view that
thought is not linguistic at all, that "what you had conceived in your
heart was confined to no language." What you think is not in Latin or
Greek (or Punic, the vernacular of Augustine's North Africa): it altogther
precedes these languages. The word in your heart or mind, the *verbum
mentis* or *verbum internum,* is for Augustine a preverbal and entirely
mental thing. It occurs or is brought to birth in the place of thought,
which is not the place of language. It is, he says, "naked to the intelligence
in the bedchamber of the mind," and needs the clothing of language or
gesture in order to be made public.

The inner word, naked of language, is nonphysical, and, in a limited
and partial sense, also nontemporal. That is, while the fact of its being
conceived by a human mind is an event in time, what is conceived is, if
true, eternally so, and if false also eternally so. The mind, in conceiving
such thoughts as "wise people are better than stupid ones" or "the just
person is to be loved" (favorite Augustinian examples), participates in a
limited way in the truths eternally known by God, and does so (as God
also does) in a place free from language. God speaks no language, and
we will have no need of language in heaven, for there our thoughts will
be immediately evident to one another as they already are to God.

So: when you bring a thought into being you do something nonlinguistic and nonphysical. When you speak your thought you enter the realm

of the physical and the linguistic: you move from thought to voice, from *cogitatio* to *vox*. When you've voiced or invoked your thought—clothed your thought with speech—what you think may be understood by those who hear what you say. Their acts of understanding are, because they deal directly with the thought, also purely mental. They too are performed in the hidden place of thought, naked of language, and the principal purpose of hearing someone else's words is to understand what they think, which is not a matter of words.

Augustine is often anxious about speech's capacity adequately to represent thought, and so also about its capacity effectively to communicate:

> It's also true for me that my speaking almost always displeases me. I am greedy for something better, for what I often enjoy inwardly before I begin to express it in audible words. And when I judge this inferior to what I know, I am sad that my language cannot measure up to my heart. For I want the one who hears me to understand everything I have understood, and it seems to me that I cannot so speak as to bring this about. Mainly this is because the understanding that floods the soul is like a rapid flash of lightning, while my discourse is slow and drawn out, and so quite unlike my thought. While the former unfolds, the latter has already retreated into the soul's secret parts. However, in a wonderful way it impresses traces of itself upon the memory; these last for as long as the syllables [which express them]; and so it is from these traces that we can produce audible signs which are called language—Latin, Greek, Hebrew, or what you will.

Speech takes time; thought takes none. Speech belongs to the world of change, which is also the world of imperfection; thought, when it is knowledge, belongs to the world of changelessness and thereby participates in the perfect. Speech, therefore, will always be a problematic and worrying mode of expressing thought. It is at best thought's trace or vestige *(vestigium)*, a decaying trace with a temporal track. God does not need it and neither do angels: they have a daylight knowledge *(in diurna cognitio)*, which they get "not by sounding words . . . but by the very presence of immutable truth." This kind of nonlinguistic knowledge is certitude: it is knowledge of things according to the rational design with which they were made, which is to say according to their very being, what they most essentially are. It is contrasted with "twilight knowledge" *(in vespertina cognitio)*, which is knowledge of particulars in their particularity. In geometry, for example, daylight knowledge (pre- and nonverbal knowledge) might give you knowledge of what, geometrically speaking, a circle is (a two-dimensional figure whose circumference is its radius multiplied by 2π); twilight knowledge would give you acquaintance with particular circles, without necessarily understanding what makes a circle what it is. Augustine likes to put this difference by saying that daylight knowledge is of something *"in ea ratione . . . secundum quam factum est"* (in its rational order according to which it was made), while twilight knowledge knows a particular *"in seipso,"* as it is in itself.

We humans may only have come to need speech as a result of the fall, and we may in the future be able to communicate without need of it (or of any other bodily motions). This is what Augustine's anxiety about speech suggests to him, and this view is intimate with his thought about the lie: speech is unreliable enough as a guide to thought in the best of circumstances, and anything that could deepen this unreliability (as the lie would) should be shunned.

Speaking, it should now be clear, requires a three-tiered progression: from what you think to what you say to what your hearer understands you to think. This progression is fraught with difficulties and dangers. We can't always accurately tell what someone thinks from what they say; we can't be sure that we've got it right even when we have; and we also can't be sure that those speaking to us aren't lying—and if they are it is almost certain that we won't know what they're thinking. But the fact that speech doesn't always reliably catalyze the replication of your thought in the minds of those who hear what you say doesn't, for Augustine, call into question the view that such replication-by-catalysis is among the principal purposes of speech.

For Augustine, then, all mental items (concepts, images, and so on) are stored in the memory. They get there in various ways, and once there they may be brought to birth or conceived, which is to say made active, in the mind. When a thought has been brought to birth in this way it is called an "inner word" or "mental word," and the faculty that uses and presents it is the intelligence. All this—memory as matrix or womb, intelligence as active user, inner word as born from the former and deployed by the latter—is mental. It is only when vocalized words—outer words—are spoken that the changing spatial world of the physical is entered. The word stored in the memory can be understood as a disposition to have certain ideas, assent to certain concepts, hope for certain outcomes, and so on; the word brought to birth by and in the active intelligence is the activation of those ideas or concepts; and the word vocalized is the utterance of those ideas or concepts, typically in an attempt to communicate them to others, to replicate in the minds of others the thought present in the speaker's mind.

All this is deeply trinitarian. It is axiomatic for Augustine that we are created in God's image, and that this image makes us what we are: insofar as we are anything at all, we are that image. The image must in principle be discernible in every aspect of our being, and this means that it must be discernible in the means by which we form thoughts and bring them to utterance. The archetype of Augustine's thinking about thought and language, then, is his understanding of the being of God (which is to say, of the divine Trinity), especially as this is evident in us, who are its image. A full understanding of how words and thoughts are related in us requires and is to be derived from an understanding of the divine Trinity.

But knowledge of the divine Trinity cannot be had by direct contemplation because it is not possible for us directly to gaze upon God. We may, if especially privileged, catch a momentary glimpse of God in a transient flash of awareness; but such things do not and cannot last. The sticky attraction of things that are not God (Augustine likes to call this *cupiditatis visco*, the glue of greed) prevents us from continuously focusing our attention upon him. We can have faith in God as triune, of course. But faith is not knowledge because knowledge is had only of that which can directly be contemplated, and faith is typically based upon authoritative testimony. The vocabulary of knowledge, for Augustine, is shot through with the tropes of sight and vision, and what you see when you know something is always a notion or a concept. For example, when I assent to the claim "Saint Paul was a just man" I do so, Augustine would say, because I find in myself the notions "man" and "just," and know what they amount to. These are notions that apply to many particulars, and I can know them and their relations simply by seeing them in my mind, the place of thought. I can then apply these known notions to the person Paul, and as a result arrive at belief that (though not knowledge that) Paul was just. Belief *(credere)* is the correct category in this case because I do not "see" Paul in the way that I "see" the notions "man" and "just" (at least, this is so if I have no direct acquaintance with Paul, as obviously Augustine had not), and so I can learn what I take to be the case about him only by testimony. What I know is the content of the concepts "man" and "just" and the proper relations between them (so, for instance, I can know the truth of the claim "a just man should be honored" because the truth of this is entailed by the content of the concepts "man" and "just"). But I can only believe that these concepts should be applied to the individual Paul of Tarsus.

This analysis of coming to assent to the claim that Paul is just cannot, however, be applied to coming to assent to the claim that God is triune. This, to repeat, is because there are no general or special notions (no genus or species terms) applicable to God. God is *sui generis* and, therefore, not analyzable in terms of genus and species. We cannot know God in that way. So, if we want to understand better what it means to say (and believe) that God is triune, an important route leads back into ourselves. We can look closely at what we are like, for about that we can know a good deal. And since we are made in God's image, a close look at the image may tell us something about what is imaged. In the order of being (speaking ontologically), God's being-as-triune precedes and exceeds the image of the divine Trinity in us. But in the order of knowing (speaking epistemologically), we must start with the image rather than with what is imaged. The image is the mind, and it is the burden of the second half of Augustine's work *On the Trinity* to look for and at trinities there, traces of the divine Trinity in the human mind.

Augustine finds the least tenuous trace of the divine Trinity in the mind in the relations among memory *(memoria),* intelligence *(intellegentia),* and will *(voluntas).* At any time we know much that we are not thinking about, and this knowledge must be stored somewhere so that it can be accessed when we want it. The place of storage is the memory, where "hidden notions *(arcana notitia)* are stored away." The gaze of thought may then become conformed to these hidden or stored notions, and thus reproduce them in active mode. When this happens, the intelligence is at work. And the force that joins the active intelligence to the memory is the will, which Augustine also often calls love. This set of relations provides us with an inner trinity: memory as store for the concept seen; intelligence as active reproduction of this concept; will as the loving act of intention that makes possible the joining of the two.

We might say (though Augustine does not) that the memory-intelligence-will triad, when gazed at with the appropriate intensity and lack of distraction, serves (or may serve) as an icon of the being of God. An icon participates in what it represents, and because it does so it can displace the gaze from itself to that in which it participates. An icon of my human beloved (a picture of her, say, framed with memories of the occasion upon which she sat for it and of the history of its use) ceases to be a simple representation of her by beginning to participate in her. Similar things occur with physical relics of the saints, and with holy places. Thinking of the memory-intelligence-will triad in this way will help to explain the mix of ontological and epistemological discussion in Augustine's discussion of the enigmatic allegory of the divine Trinity in us.

Augustine often uses sexual imagery for the relations among these three: memory is the begetter *(gignens)*, intelligence the begotten *(genitum)*, and will the love by which the two are joined *(copulantur)*. This sexual imagery is, for Augustine, more fundamentally to be understood as trinitarian imagery. The archetypal begetter is the Father, the archetypal begotten is the Son, and (more obscurely) the archetypal act of loving intent that proceeds from and connects both begetter and begotten is the Spirit. The inner mental trinity of memory-intelligence-will, then, is the mirror in which we see enigmatically the divine Trinity of which it is a created image. Augustine likes to appeal to a text from Paul on this point: *"Videmus tunc per speculum in aenigmate"* (1 Cor. 13:12), which may be nicely rendered as the King James Version does in one of its notes, "Now we see through a glass in a riddle." The enigma or riddle within which we cannot help seeing is classed by Augustine as a kind of allegory—an especially obscure analogy, he says. It, like all allegories when understood as such, displaces the gaze of those who read it from its surface detail to what it allegorizes. And in the instance of interest here, it is the surface detail of the birth of the inner word (the concept) from the memory into the active intelligence, and the clothing of that inner word with sound so that it can be voiced, that points those who can understand it to, first, the eternal begetting of the Son from the Father, and, second, the Son's taking of flesh in the incarnation. Because what goes on in our minds when we think and speak is only an enigmatic allegory of (one aspect of) God's being, we cannot expect anything close to perfect understanding of the latter by way of attention to the former. We can, however, expect to gain some knowledge along the way.

Augustine does not think that attention to enigmatic allegory of this sort is the only way in which we can gain understanding of God's triune being. Far from it. Both Scripture (as he reads it) and the teaching of the church provide us with faith in God's triune being and in many details about the relations among the divine persons. But those resources provide testimony-based belief for us, and because beliefs about God's triune nature cannot become knowledge for us in the ordinary way that testimony-produced beliefs about noncontingent states of affairs would—which is to say, by simply seeing that what we've been informed of is true, as we can do with such claims as "it is better to be clever than stupid" (recall that God's being is not available to us for examination in the way it would have to be if this were to be possible)—trinitarian beliefs would have to remain beliefs and not knowledge were there not open to us the enigmatic allegories of the *imago dei* that we know we are.

The allegory works in two stages. First, there is the production of the inner word from the memory. This is the trace of the eternal begetting of the Son by the Father, and Augustine uses language for it that intentionally echoes Christian credal affirmations about the relation of the Son to the Father. Just as Jesus Christ is "true God from true God" ("*deus verus de deo vero*") according to the Nicene formulation, so the inner word is true word from true thing, as in the following passage:

> Everything, therefore, that human consciousness knows, whether by perceiving through itself, or through its physical senses, or by way of the testimony of others, it holds stored away in the treasure-house of memory. From these [stored] things is begotten a true word when we speak what we know, a word prior to all sound and to all thought of sound. For it is then that the word is most like the things known, begotten from them and in their image. This is because [in such a case] the vision of thought proceeds directly from the vision of knowledge; it is a word that belongs to no language, true word from true thing; it has nothing of its own, but everything from that knowledge from which it is born.

In this first stage of the analogy we remain in the place of thought. The memory is the treasure-filled storehouse, the thesaurus in which all inputs (whether via thought or sensation or testimony) are stored. The active concept is then born directly, as perfect image, from the memory, just as the eternal word is born from the Father. The image contributes nothing of its own: it is at best a copy of what it images. Lying, of course, cannot yet occur because lying requires vocalized speech and nothing has yet been vocalized. (Augustine does use the vocabulary of speech in the passage just quoted, but in an extended or metaphorical sense that does not imply vocalization.) But already it is possible to see that anything less than a perfect imaging of memory by intelligence would be a break, a fissure, in the image of God. Intelligence is supposed to image memory perfectly. When it fails to do so, this is because the divine image has been broken by sin—a point that will be applied, too, to the act of lying.

The second stage of the analogy moves to the incarnation, to the taking of flesh by the divine word as the inner word takes on voice. Augustine understands the second person of the divine Trinity's incarnation (taking flesh, that is, which is what "incarnation" etymologically means) through the category of "assumption," which he typically contrasts with both "transmutation" and "consumption." For you to assume some new state or condition is for you to take it on without losing the properties that make you who you are independently of the new condition.

In this sense I can assume the state of being married or the office of president, for in doing either I remain the person I was before. But if I am transmuted into or consumed by something new, I cease to have any distinctive properties of my own: to lose myself in (be consumed by) the presidential office would be to have no identity other than that provided by the office—and this, it seems reasonable to say, would not be a good thing.

When the second person of the divine Trinity assumes the flesh of a human being, then, he is not transmuted into or consumed by that condition. Similarly, for Augustine my inner word, my thought, can assume voice without being transmuted into voice. It can be invoked without ceasing to be thought. This is how he puts it:

> And so the word vocalized externally is a sign of the word that illuminates internally; this latter more properly deserves the name "word" because what is uttered with the bodily mouth is the voiced word, and this is called "word" in virtue of the one [namely, the inner word] that assumes it so that it may appear outwardly. It is in this way that our word becomes—after a fashion—a bodily word, by assuming that by which it is manifest to the senses of men. In the same way, the word of God became flesh, by assuming that by which it is manifest to the senses of men. Furthermore, just as our word became voice without being transmuted into voice, so the word of God became flesh; but it should not be thought that it was transmuted into the physical.

The application of the second stage of the analogy to vocalized speech is straightforward enough:

> When the [inner] word is vocalized or given by way of some other sign, it is not spoken just as it is, but rather as it can be seen or heard with the body.

There can be no exact replication of the inner word by the vocalized outer word because the former is nonlinguistic and the latter necessarily in some language or other. The same is true of the relation between the second person of the Trinity and the incarnate Son: the latter does not replicate the former in every respect because (among other things) the latter is physical and the former is not. The relationship is no longer one of simple substantive identity. However, Augustine continues,

> But when that which is found in the judgment is also in the [vocalized] word, it is a true word, possessing the kind of truth expected by men.

What is in the concept is also in the vocalized word, and what is lacking
in the concept is also lacking in the vocalized word. Here one recognizes
"yes, yes; no, no."

A vocalized word is true, on this view, when there is in what it says
just and only what is in the concept to which it gives voice. Nothing is
to be subtracted and nothing added. This is how Augustine understands
Matthew 5:37, which he quotes in part in the passage just translated.
Jesus there said, to give the verse more fully in the form in which Augustine would probably have known it: "Let your speech consist of 'yes,
yes' and 'no, no.' Anything more than this comes from the Evil One."
The "yes, yes" indicates the positive relation between inner and vocalized word: the latter says "yes" to the former by giving in vocalized form
what was already provided in concept. And the "no, no" indicates the
negative relation: what was not present in the concept is not added in
the vocalization. This view of what it is for an utterance to be true is
derived from Augustine's view of the relation between the eternal divine
word and the incarnate word. This relation is imaged by the relation
between concept and vocalized word in us. Any change in this relation
is therefore a rupture of the divine image in us.

Not every such rupture will occur by way of the lie, but every lie will
intentionally and knowingly produce such a rupture, and will thereby
be a sin. The fact that duplicitous speech produces this rupture is the
evil proper to the lie.

5

Disowning

Lying speech is owned, controlled, taken charge of, characteristically and idiosyncratically yours. True speech is disowned, relinquished, returned as gift to its giver, definitively and universally not yours. To lie is to reject the gift of speech by attempted expropriation. To speak truly is to accept the gift of speech by adoration. The true antonym of *mendacium*, for Augustine, is *adoratio*, or its close cousin, *confessio;* and the fundamental reason for banning the lie without exception is that when we speak duplicitously, we exclude the possibility of adoration. "It is not only that we avoid sin when we adore," he says, "but also that we sin whenever we are not adoring."

Augustine likes to pursue the idea of the lie as characteristically ours, what we say when we speak as ourselves, with our own voice, by discussing John 8:44–45. In the version most frequently quoted by him, this verse reads: "That one [the Devil] was a murderer from the beginning / he does not stand in the truth / because the truth is not in him / when he speaks the lie he speaks by expropriation / because he is a liar and father of the lie." The Latin phrase *ex propriis* (from the Greek *ek tōn idiōn*) can be nicely calqued with the English "by expropriation." To expropriate, in one of its meanings, is to take to oneself by theft what really belongs to someone else. It may also suggest an act based upon what is—or what one takes to be—one's own (King James's translators rendered the phrase "of his own"). All this, in Augustine's understanding, is what you do when you speak the lie. You take to yourself and make your own what really belongs to God, and you do so out of a misunderstanding of what you are and what you take to be your relation to speech. The thing taken, expropriated, in this case is speech. Diabolus, the devil, is the father of the lie because he is the first to expropriate speech. His is the first theft of language, and all he can do with speech once it has been stolen is to lie. Diabolus is the father of lies, to put the same point slightly differently, because he has chosen to live *secundum se ipsum*, according to himself:

> He [Diabolus] chose to live according to himself when he did not remain in the truth, so that the lie he spoke had to do with himself, not with God. For he is not only a liar but the father of the lie. He was the first to lie, and the lie, like sin, began from him.

Lying is derived from, is a paradigmatic instance of, living according to yourself. If you try to live in this way, you attempt to live autonomously, to take your own nature and desires as your only guides for life and speech. The first result is that you have nothing to speak about but yourself—"had to do with himself" translates *de suo*, which covers object (what you speak about), motive (why you speak about it), and ground (that on which your speech is based). Your speech turns inward toward what you take to be your own (recall the account of sin's movement away from what is universal, shared, given, toward what is individual, proper, owned), and then, inevitably, you lie: what you say has to do with yourself rather than with God. On this account, *peccatum*, sin, and *mendacium*, the lie, are linked very closely. Both begin from the devil, and can be exchanged for one another by synecdoche. Augustine continues:

> And so, when human beings live according to humanity and not according to God they are like Diabolus, because even angels should live according to God and not according to themselves so that they might remain in the truth and speak the truth that has to do with God rather than the lie that has to do with themselves. For the Apostle [Paul] said about human beings elsewhere: "But if God's truth has abounded through my lie" (Romans 3: 7). He spoke of the lie as ours and the truth as God's. And so, when we humans live according to the truth, we do not live according to ourselves but according to God. God is the one who said, "I am the truth" (John 14: 6). On the other hand, when humans live according to themselves, which is to say according to humanity rather than according to God, we clearly live according to the lie. This is not because human beings are themselves a lie: our author and creator is God, who is not the author and creator of lies. Rather, we were made right, so that we might not live according to ourselves but according to the one who made us, which is to say by car-

rying out his will rather than our own. Not to live in the way for which
we were made: that is the lie.

The lie is ours *(nostrum);* the truth is God's. Living according to our
own lights, then, is exactly living according to the lie. Indeed, it is
the lie, because to live in that way is duplicitous. Augustine here extends his understanding of the lie beyond acts of speech to embrace
a mode of life. Just as we can speak duplicitously we can also live
duplicitously, by having our actions represent something (autonomy,
self-directedness, *"secundum se ipsum vivere"*) that we know they
do not in fact represent. The term *mendacium* has now become one
that can be used as synecdoche for sin. The same passage continues,
emphasizing just this point:

> We clearly want to be happy, even when we don't live in such a way as to
> make that possible. What is more of a lie than such a desire? And so we
> can properly say that all sin is a lie. For we can only sin by an act of will,
> and acts of will are aimed either at getting what is good for us or avoiding
> what is bad for us. The lie, then, is what is done for our good but results
> in what is bad for us; or it is that which is done to make things better for
> us but in fact makes them worse. What is good for us comes in fact only
> from God, not from ourselves; we abandon him by our delinquency, and
> we are delinquent in living according to ourselves.

"All sin is a lie" *("omne peccatum esse mendacium").* Or, elsewhere,
"every sin is a lie, because anything opposed to law and truth is rightly
called a lie." Why? Because the definition of both is the same: each is
a distorted act of will, an act aimed at what seems temporarily to be
good for us but is really (and is really known to be) bad for us. The
desire for beatitude, for happiness, is duplicitous (and therefore also
mendacious) when it is coupled with a mode of life that contradicts it.
This is why Augustine says that nothing could be more of a lie than a
desire contradicted—canceled out—by a mode of life that prevents its
fulfilment. Augustine here plays with synecdoche: is sin the more inclusive category and the lie the less inclusive one, which can be used to
represent it? Or is it the other way around? Mostly, I think, Augustine
intends *peccatum* to embrace and include *mendacium;* but that he can
sometimes write as he does in the passage just translated suggests that
the lie has a special place among sins. In its expropriative act can be
seen most clearly (more clearly than in adultery or blasphemy or covet-
ousness or theft) the grammar of sin. This is why, when he categorizes
the lie into kinds according to motive and effect, the paradigmatic and

clearest case of the lie is that told for the sheer joy of telling it. Here, sin's syntax is even clearer than it was in Augustine's narration of the theft of pears in the second book of the *Confessions.*

In the passage just discussed, as also in many other places, Augustine treats John 8:44–45 as though it applied to everyone and not just to Diabolus. He is the paradigmatic liar, the first to attempt expropriation of speech. But when we lie we replicate what he did: we twist and corrupt our speech, so that we cannot speak of or to God, but only of and to ourselves. Augustine recognizes that all of us lie, and even that it is characteristically human to do so. He likes to quote Romans 3:4 on this, which says (echoing Ps. 116:11) that *"omnis homo mendax,"* "everyone is a liar." This, he emphasizes, does not mean that we should relax into the lie's inevitability. It means, rather, that we should acknowledge that abandoning the lie is not something within our capacity. Characteristically human speech is always a lie, and in order to cease speaking duplicitously we must simply recognize that we can learn what it is to be human by observing our own duplicitous speech, and then turn from that to "drink from the truth so that you might be true and so that you might belch it back to God *(de deo ructes)"*—which is to say, to approach God, listen to God, and then return God's words to God in adoration.

"God alone is a truth-teller, while every human being is a liar, so it is written" (Romans 3:4). Therefore, if only God is a truth-teller "while every human being is a liar," how will a human being become a truth-teller without approaching the one who is not a liar? In this connection it's said to human beings, "once you were darkness" (Ephesians 5:8), which is to say "every human being is a liar." To God it's said, "with you is the spring of life, and in your light we shall see light" (Psalm 36:10). And because God alone is a truth-teller "since God is light and there is no darkness in him" (1 John 1:5), human beings are darkness while God is light. Human beings are liars; God is a truth-teller. When will human beings become truth-tellers? "Approach him and you will be illuminated" (Psalm 34:6). Scripture thus wants to show that everyone without exception, so far as he is merely human, is a liar. . . . He has nothing of his own except to be a liar. This is not because he can't be a truth-teller, but because he won't by himself be a truth-teller. And so, in order to be a truth-teller, "I spoke because I believed" (Psalm 116:10). In the absence of believing, "every human being is a liar." For when you have moved away from God's truth you'll remain in your lie, because "the one who utters a lie speaks about himself" (John 8:44). If, then, you have become a truth-teller, understand how this happened so that you don't become a liar about that very matter. O truth-telling man, when you've said, "I am a truth-teller by myself," you'll be a liar in saying that. If, therefore, you are a truth-teller, you're filled up from outside, you've become a participant in the truth.

Here, God is the radiant truth-teller: we are liars shrouded in shadow. Approaching God makes truth-telling possible for us by shedding light on our darkness: moving away from God guarantees that we lie by leaving us in the shadows. The liar speaks always and only *de suo*. This pregnantly brief phrase occurs three times in this passage, and it indicates all at once what the liar speaks about (himself), where his speech comes from (himself), and who owns what he says (himself). To speak by expropriation is the same as to speak *de suo*. It is also the same as to speak *secundum se* (according to oneself) or *secundum hominem* (according to humanity, humanly). All this is contrasted with using speech as gift, being filled up *(impletus)* from outside oneself—from God—and as a result becoming a participant *(particeps)* in God, who is, once again, the radiant and only source of truth. Abandoning the lie, then, requires acknowledgment of the fact that speech is a gift, something with which we are filled and by means of which we participate in the truth that is not ours. We cannot, when acting expropriatively (by theft, in an attempt to own), do anything but lie.

We must, then, in order to cease lying, disown speech. And in order further to explain this idea, Augustine often distinguishes between having *(habere)* and controlling *(dominari)*, as in the following anti-Donatist discussion of baptism:

So what do they [the Donatists] say? "We've got baptism." You have got it, but it's not yours. It's one thing to have and another to control. You have baptism because you accepted that you should be baptized; you accepted this to the extent that you've been illuminated, which is also the extent to which you have not darkened yourselves. And when you give, you give as a servant, not as an owner. The herald announces, not the judge; but the judge speaks through the herald, and the written record says that it is the judge who speaks, not the herald. So you should look closely at whether what you give is yours by your own power. If, by contrast, you've accepted it, confess with the bridegroom's friend that "no one can receive anything unless it's been given to him from heaven" (John 3:27). Confess with the bridegroom's friend that "the one who has the bride is the bridegroom; the bridegroom's friend stands and listens to the bridegroom" (John 3:29). If only you were to stand and listen to him, and not fall down so that you might listen to yourself! It's by listening to him that you can stand and hear; if you speak, then your head swells.

Augustine here comments on John 3:22–30, a passage in which the Jews dispute with John the Baptist. They tell him that Jesus is baptizing and attracting crowds; John replies that no one can accept *(accipere)* anything unless it's been given *(datum)* to him out of heaven. Augustine glosses *accipere* with *habere*, "to have": having something (in this case baptism) means having received it as gift. Giving what you've received as gift can then only be done as a servant (Latin *minister*) or a herald *(praeco)*: in these roles you pass on the master's goods or the judge's words to others. The goods and the words aren't yours: you didn't make them and you don't control them. You have them only in the sense that you can pass them on to others. The image of the bridegroom and the bridegroom's friend makes the same point: the bridegroom speaks and the bridegroom's friend listens. The words are the bridegroom's and they are given to his friend by speech. The friend's task is to listen *(audire):* this is how he can "have" the words. He must receive them as gift, he can "stand" *(stare),* which is to say adopt the true posture of a human being, the attitude of the listener. If listening is refused, that posture is also abandoned, and then he "falls" *(cadere)*—as, by implication, Diabolus also did. The fall that comes from refusing the gift of speech is listening to yourself, and since what you say from yourself, after expropriation, is nothing but the lie, this will not be very edifying. As for baptism, so also for speech: attempted expropriation leads to loss, a decrease in being.

Speech, properly used, abjures or disowns itself, abnegates itself by returning itself to its giver. The speech-act that does this most fully and perfectly is the act of confession, which is also the act of adoration. To confess with (in) speech is to consume speech with itself, to make of it an offering burnt to ash with its own fire. To adore God with words is to remove words by means of words: adoration is not only sufficient for the removal of sin, but also necessary. All nonconfessing, nonadoring speech is sinful because it does not return itself to its giver. Instead, it appropriates itself, becomes owner of itself, and in so doing distends and extends itself to infinity, replicating and reproducing itself until the libraries of the world, virtual and material, can no longer hold the proliferation of the verbal idols produced by it.

The verbal idol is curved in upon itself, a window upon nothing. The verbal idol is all rhetoric, an elaborately ornamented persuasion of those who contemplate it to gaze upon nothing, and in so doing to themselves become less, to tend asymptotically toward nothing. So to use language is to sit upon the *cathedra mendacii,* the throne of the lie, to own one's speech and thus become a liar.

Adoration's antonym is rhetoric, which is of course the lie. Where rhetoric produces the verbal idol, adoration produces the verbal icon, the invoked form of the only finally coherent thought, which is the thought that moves into silence by participating in God. When we confess and adore we invoke the only thought that can participate in God—the self-abnegatory thought. To speak the word of adoration is to speak Christ: just as God incarnate returns God's gift by way of the self-abnegation on the cross, so thought invoked returns God's gift by way of the self-abnegation that is adoration. Hard upon the cross follows resurrection: life is returned with abundance. Hard upon adoration—the invoked truth—comes the silence in which we know and are known, the silence in which the enigmatic riddle of speech is resolved and answered. Adoration removes speech's necessity by being taken up into participation; crucifixion removes its necessity by being taken up into resurrection. All this is prevented, cut short, by the lie, the rhetor's use of speech. Each lie replicates the fall and imprisons us more closely in what is our own, our adorned and persuasive verbal idols. This, most fundamentally, is why the lie must be repudiated.

The only coherent speech-act, therefore, is confession. Augustine meditates upon what it is to confess in the tenth book of the work to which he gave that name. He asks himself there why he has written a book of confessions. The first answer is that the act of composing such a book must itself be understood as an instance of what the book is about. The book is about a man becoming fit *(coapta)* for God, and the book itself is a performative speech-act that helps to make the one composing it fit for God. The book is about learning to confess, and is itself an instance of what it is about. But what is it to confess? First, it is to say that one is displeased with oneself *(displicere sibi,* echoing and reversing 2 Peter 2:10, in the version known to Augustine) because and to the extent that one is evil. Second, it is to say that when and to the extent that one is good one takes no credit for this, allocates no merit to oneself, but instead returns praise for it to God. The act of confession, so understood, need not be in words, but when it is it says only that *secundum se* one is nothing and can do nothing, and that what one does and is can only be understood as sheer gift, returned to God alone *(soli deo)* as praise. There is, then, a confession of praise to God as source of all and a confession of sin, which is the nothing, the performative contradiction, that opposes itself to God.

But the act of confession doesn't just say these things. It performatively instantiates them. It is a speech-act that simultaneously presents and enacts the grammar of the faith with respect to the categories of grace and free will. It is only in saying what confession says that the one who confesses is rightly related to God. Confession is the only speech-act not performatively incoherent in the mode of the lie, and so confession is the ideal type of truthful speech. It is in fact, says Augustine, what is meant by "doing the truth *(veritatem facere)*" in John 3:21:

> Confession of evil actions is the beginning of good actions. You do the truth and come to the light. What do you do when you do the truth? You don't praise yourself or give yourself blandishments and adulation. You don't say, "I'm just," when in fact you're unjust. This is when you begin to do the truth. You come to the light so that it might be clear that your actions were made in God. This is because the very sin of yours that displeased you would not have displeased you unless God had illuminated you and showed his truth to you. The one who loves the sins against which he has been warned hates the light warning him and runs from it so that the actions he loves might not be shown to be evil. But the one who does the truth accuses his own evils to himself.

The confession of sin as presented here is one element of doing the truth. It averts gaze and speech from the one who looks and the one who speaks: it disowns self and speech by self-accusation, and in so doing it approaches the light that is God, to whom the only possible response is praise, confessional adoration. The extent to which speech-acts diverge from confessional adoration is just the extent to which they approach the lie and lose coherence. This suggests that all nonmendacious speech will circle about and reprise a single theme, which is precisely its own inadequacy for anything except confession of its own inadequacy. Christian poetry, drama, and the novel will be, to the extent that they remain Christian, filigreed and repetitive self-consuming artifacts that offer themselves to God—which is a pretty good description of Augustine's *Confessions* as a literary artifact. This is certainly the way in which he presents his own self-understanding of that work. For such literature, there is only one drama: will the text become an idol by attempting to take possession of itself, and in so doing repeat the fall and tend toward nothingness? Or will it repeat, textually, the drama of redemption as the liturgy does, as Augustine's *Confessions* do, and as, arguably, the entire corpus of Scripture does? If the latter, it has disowned itself; if the former, it is a lie.

A possible misunderstanding needs to be guarded against here. To say, as Augustine says and as I have frequently repeated, that to be a practitioner of rhetoric is also to be a liar does not imply that literary elegance and ornament are to be renounced. Augustine certainly does not renounce them: his own work is full of them, not least in the places where he offers a critique of rhetoric. Mendacious rhetoric and ornamented confession, then, may be formally indistinguishable from one another. The difference lies not in the extent to which or the skill with which they use the techniques of the literary trade. It lies in what they performatively enact. Mendacious rhetoric performs possession of what it says, and is to that extent a lie; ornamented confession performs disowning of what it says, and is to that extent a doing of the truth.

Any lie, any duplicitous speech intended to deceive, is for Augustine precisely a perverse attempt to own and manipulate at will what can only be used coherently if treated as something not possessed, something whose freehold is not subject to human title. Speech is given as a gift to invoke thought, just as (analogically) the incarnate son is given as gift to enflesh the eternal word. The lie grasps the gift, owning it in imagination, and, so, sinning. And since Augustine thinks that no sin ought ever be committed, the conclusion that no lie ought ever be told is unavoidable. Augustine's exceptionless ban on the lie is simply an instance of his exceptionless ban on sin in general. Augustine thinks of the lie, to borrow later terms, as *malum in se*, something intrinsically evil, not under any circumstance or for any reason to be done.

Words are, for Augustine, instruments to be used "so that each person may transfer his thoughts *(cogitationes)* to the understanding *(notitiam)* of another." To use words instead in such a way as deliberately to obscure one's thoughts is exactly the same sort of act as using one's sexuality outside the bonds of marriage; he often likens the lie to an unchaste sexual act. In both cases, one sins by deciding to appropriate a gift (words, sex) for purposes contradictory to those for which it was given. Such a decision, together with the actions that flow from it, cannot be defended and will have the disastrous consequences that follow upon all sin.

Augustine's ban on the lie is then an instance of his broader ban upon attempts to reject the divine gift. He objects to such attempts in whatever sphere of human action they occur because they all share a common feature: they are performatively incoherent. That is, they deploy, and thus implicitly affirm, something that at the same time they explicitly reject and deny. Speech is a gift given, and a condition of its use is that it is received as such. But the lie is a use of speech that rejects precisely this condition by attempting, incoherently, to own speech as if it had been created from nothing by and for the speaker. This is performative contradiction. What issues from it is an act that appears to be an act of speech but is really something else, really an absence of speech cloaked in words.

This analysis applies Augustine's understanding of evil to the particular case of the lie. Evil is for Augustine *privatio boni,* an absence of the good. It has and can have no independent existence as a power over against God because such a state of affairs would imply either that God created evil, or that something exists that God did not create. Neither conclusion is acceptable. Evil, therefore, is simple absence. This is not to say, of course, that it is impossible for particular actions or utterances to bring about results such as the death of the innocent. It is only to say that when such results occur, they do so because of the misuse of something good, not because of the deployment of evil. When a created good (speech, sex, material objects) is used for evil ends (lying, adultery, killing), the good in question is placed under the sign of contradiction—precisely the kind of performative contradiction just mentioned—which in part erases it, reduces it to nothing, but which also permits it to have effects not implied in its existence or intended by its creator. The sword's steel is a created good. This good may be used to chop off the head of an innocent person, but when this is done the evil lies in the performatively self-contradictory intentions of the wielder, not in the steel or the muscles and sinews that do the wielding. Evil *(malum)* for Augustine is found always and only in the self-contradictory acts of the will by which the gift given is used in its own rejection. It is only these acts that can recursively remove themselves by repudiating the conditions of their possibility in the very act of implicitly affirming those conditions. The term "evil" may of course be used by extension to label the effects of such actions (and indeed many other things too). But this is not the term's proper or primary use in Augustine's thought.

It follows directly from this analysis that a decision to lie cannot coherently be made. And since no lie can be told without a decision to tell it, it follows that no lie can coherently be told. Hence the exceptionless ban on the lie.

Augustine is aware that such a position is deeply counterintuitive for almost everyone, whether Christian or not. He is also aware of how easily and naturally we lie, with ease of heart and good conscience, when it seems to us that by so doing we can save the life of those who have done no wrong, protect an innocent from rape, comfort a dying man—or, we might add, assuage the doubts of someone unsure about the attractiveness of a new hairstyle. Augustine says that he has frequently himself been tempted to lie in such cases, and has sometimes succumbed. But he thinks that all attempts to defend well-intentioned lies that produce good effects fail because they all, in the end, deploy the same indefensible principle.

The principle in question is a consequentialist one: a lie is defensible (perhaps even required) only when a greater harm than that involved in the lie is prevented by it. There are, in Augustine's view, only two kinds of harm: sinful harms (like adultery or idolatry or lying), and nonsinful harms (like physical suffering). The consequentialist principle mentioned might be taken by those who want to defend it to apply to either or both kinds of harm. Augustine thinks that it cannot be successfully defended with respect to either, but his reasons for thinking that it fails differ in each case, so it will be useful to treat them separately.

Consider the case of sinful harms. It might be argued that a sin is defensible (perhaps even required) if and only if performing it prevents a greater sin. Sins that do this we might call countervailing sins: I commit a countervailing sin if and only if as I commit it (or decide to commit it), it seems to me that doing so will prevent a weightier sin from being committed, either by me or by someone else. A weak consequentialist principle deploying this notion would then be *countervailing sins are permitted;* a stronger one would be *countervailing sins are required.* Both principles require that there be a hierarchy of sin, and that such a hierarchy be accurately understood by someone who uses either.

Augustine accepts that there is a hierarchy of sin in the sense that some sins produce more nonsinful harms than others. But the repudiation of the gift is the same in all sins (and *a fortiori* in all lies), and in this fundamental sense there is no hierarchy of sin. He therefore rejects both the weak and the strong versions of the consequentialist principle just mentioned. He thinks it obviously improper to say that you are responsible for sins that could be or have been committed by others just because you could have prevented them by sinning yourself. This view, he says, rapidly leads to absurdities. Will we not have to say, if we adopt it, that you are responsible for an adulterer's adultery if you could have prevented it by committing adultery with the proposed partner yourself? Or that if someone declares to you his intention to kill his father and then goes ahead and does it, you are responsible for the death of his father because you did not first kill the murderer (assuming that we could have prevented the murder in no other way)? Or, worse yet, that you are responsible for the murderer's sin if you could have prevented it by committing the identical sin yourself before the murderer could get to it?

In these and like cases, says Augustine, it is not the case that if you refuse to sin in order to prevent someone else sinning you thereby approve of or become responsible for the sin you might have prevented by sinning yourself. Such a refusal might entail a kind of assent to another's sin, but it is a weak assent, the kind produced by a dilemma, and not one that is culpable. It is like that of the wise judge who sins by ordering the torture and execution of those of whose guilt he cannot be sure. He is constrained to do this by his unavoidable ignorance of the details of each case, and by the nature of his office as judge. But this kind of sin, like the weak assent to another's sin involved in refusing to commit countervailing sins, is nonculpable, and for the same reason: it involves neither the intention to sin, nor the conscious approbation of another's sin. The judge does what he does without intending to cause unjustifiable harms (even though such harms result from what he does, and even though he knows that they will, without knowing in which particular cases this will be so), just as truth-speakers refuse to lie without intending to bring about the harms that may result from their refusals.

Therefore, rather than committing countervailing sins you should always avoid sin, even if such avoidance means that another will commit a worse sin than you would have committed yourself had you sinned countervailingly.

If countervailing sin is indefensible, it follows rapidly that lying to prevent nonsinful harms is even more clearly unjustifiable. This is because for Augustine nonsinful harms are transient: they have to do only with life in time and the goods that go with it, and are as a result vastly less significant than harms that threaten the goods belonging to eternal life. These latter can be damaged only by sin, which involves the consent of the will and the engagement of the passions. They cannot be touched by, for instance, physical suffering. Augustine takes it to be clear as a result that no temporal good, not even the saving of life or protection from rape, can warrant the lie. He does not like this conclusion, and shows most uneasiness in the case of a lie that might save an innocent from rape. But he sticks by it nonetheless, comforting himself with the conclusion that chastity cannot be taken by force since its loss requires an assent of the will and this cannot be brought about by force. The same is true, for him, of all material and temporal goods: their loss can do no deep or final harm, and so he is willing to say that Christians should not be unduly concerned about when or how they die, nor about the suffering connected with death. One of the chapter titles in *The City of God* reads: "On the end of temporal life: whether it is far away or close at hand." The answer is that it doesn't much matter so far as eternal life is concerned. Sinning to preserve temporal goods, whether your own or another's, therefore makes no sense. It would be like sinning to preserve physical beauty or youthful energy.

Further, all consequentialist defenses of lying, whether they envisage the prevention of sin or the prevention of nonsinful harms, require the ability to calculate the relative weight of sins and their effects in such a way that you could reasonably judge that the sin you might commit is less grievous than the sin or nonsinful harm it might prevent. Augustine takes this to be difficult to do even with the best will in the world, and since the will of the liar (or of any sinner) is by definition not the best in the world, sinners have even less chance of success at the enterprise. It will almost inevitably happen, Augustine says, that when sinners begin to measure and weigh evils one against another (as they must when considering whether to commit sins) they will do so by consulting their desires rather than the truth, and that these desires will be directed to temporal and physical goods rather than toward eternal ones. The whole enterprise of calculation will therefore be vitiated because of the perversity of the desires involved in it, a perversity in part produced by the very attempt to perform such calculations.

The upshot is that consequentialist defenses of the lie are utterly unpersuasive for Augustine, and that he considers them the only ones available. Lying, or even considering whether to lie, is evidence of disordered desires. No supposed good that might come from a lie can, therefore, justify either lying or considering whether to lie: calculating consequence moves on an entirely different level of significance than the assessment of whether a particular action is a sin, and therefore cannot override the ban placed upon an action by deciding that it is indeed a sin. This position requires the theological anthropology and the theology sketched above. With them it is at least coherent and possibly persuasive. Without them it is likely to remain profoundly unpersuasive and may also seem incoherent.

In 410 or 411, at his home church in Hippo, Augustine preached a sermon on a text from Matthew 18 about the danger of scandals *("vae mundo ab scandalis!")*. The defense, the *murus munitus* or well-fortified wall, against the scandals mentioned in Matthew's Gospel, he says, is loving observance of God's law; only this can bring peace and avoid scandal. He weaves a tapestry of psalm texts to illustrate the connections: "Much peace comes to those who love your law; there is no scandal for them" (Ps. 119:65); "The meek *(mites)* shall possess the earth as an inheritance, and shall delight in an abundance of peace" (Ps. 37:11—this one sung as part of that day's service); "Blessed is the man whom you instruct, Lord, whom you teach from your law in order to make him meek *(ut mitiges eum)* in evil days" (Ps. 94:12–13). Verbal echoes connect these texts: peace brought by loving and doing the law; meekness (softness, malleability) produced by instruction in the law; and avoidance of scandal as concomitant of both. The words of Scripture seem diverse, says Augustine, but in fact they concur and flow together into a single truth *(una sententia)* for those who can see them whole. The tapestry he weaves is evidence of how Scripture is read on this view.

Given this tapestry of connections, how can we be meek? What does it mean to be meek, and what are the scandals avoided by meekness? Augustine takes Job as an instance: he avoided the scandal of cursing God by remaining meek, malleable to and well-instructed in God's law, and in this Job was like all the meek, who when they do good things take pleasure only in God *("non placet nisi deus")* rather than in their own achievement, and when evil things happen to them do not displease God by abandoning meekness, becoming hard and resistant to what God requires of them. To be meek in this sense is exactly to love and observe the law of God, and so to avoid scandal. There can, for Augustine, be no good reason for abandoning meekness.

An instance: suppose an influential rich man wants you to tell a lie to help him in his looting and pillaging *("propter praedam suam, propter rapinam suam")*. Suppose, too, that he threatens you with dire consequences if you refuse. And suppose, finally, that a Christian friend of yours tries to persuade you to comply in this small thing *(quid magnum est?)* so that you might avoid unnecessary suffering. This Christian friend quotes a psalm to you: "Everyone is a liar" *(omnis homo mendax*, Ps. 116:11): why, says your Christian friend, should you be any different? Who are you to set yourself up against what Scripture says everyone does? This friend, says Augustine, is a scandal to you. What should you do? You should "amputate him and throw him away" (Matt. 18:9, returning to the Gospel text for the day) and the best method of doing this is to quote Scripture back at him, especially "a lying mouth kills the soul" *("os quod mentitur occidit animam,"* Wis. 1:11). The powerful man who wants you to lie threatens the body when he depicts the bad things that will happen to you if you don't lie for him. But your Christian friend threatens the soul when he tries to persuade you to lie: "He—the angry powerful one—kills my body, whereas a lying mouth kills the soul; he kills the body, which will die in any case, even if it is not killed; but the soul that is not killed by iniquity is received by truth into eternity." The truth that receives your soul into eternity (if you don't kill it first by lying) is Christ. Why, then, would you lie simply to preserve the mortal and perishable body? Augustine means this as a reductio: no one, he thinks, can reasonably argue that it is right to abandon an eternal good in favor of a transient one.

And there are other scriptural texts to bring to bear. God says that he will "destroy everyone who lies" *("perdes omnes qui loquuntur mendacium,"* Ps. 5:7), and God forbade false witness *(falsum testimonium)* when he gave the law to Moses (Deut. 5:20). The psalm that says that everyone is a liar, therefore, means only that lying is characteristic of human behavior prior to the grace given by God in Christ. To use such a text to justify lying is like using the text "there is no one who does good" (Ps. 14:3) to justify the doing of evil. Such texts indicate only what people are like without and before Christ's coming. Meekness, then, requires loving observance of God's law. This is what it means to avoid scandal, and only by such avoidance is peace attainable. Acceding to a friend's request to lie would be to fall into scandal, and there can never be a good reason for doing this.

This sermonic exhortation of Augustine's shows how he approaches the exceptionless ban on the lie when he is speaking to his congregation rather than doing philosophy for his intellectual peers. He advocates the ban in just the same way and for just the same reasons that he advocates a ban on all sin. Enacting sin makes no sense: it is a performatively self-contradictory act, and the only good reason for doing it is to prevent suffering, which is a nonsinful harm. While this is a good reason (suffering is a real harm that ought when possible to be minimized—Augustine does not think it can ever be finally and completely removed in this life), it is not a good enough reason, and to think that it is exhibits confusion. It is also to abandon meekness, malleable submission to God's will, for the rigidity of self-assertion: in order to decide to sin, you would have to think that you know better than God in what your good consists. And such thought is, once again, evidence of a desire for autonomy that guarantees the failure of its own ambition. The instance given in Augustine's sermon couches all this in terms of potential harm to the liar. You might think that things would turn out differently if you were asked to lie to protect someone other than yourself, some innocent, from suffering. But here too Augustine maintains his position: even in the hard cases, the evildoer at the door seeking to kill your innocent children, the rapist in the street seeking to rape your beloved, he says that the lie is not and cannot be justified.

The lie, then, is performatively incompatible with the love of God:

> When I place before the eyes of my heart the intelligible beauty of the
> one from whose mouth no falsehood has come, although my trembling
> weakness shudders before the radiant truth that shines with more and
> more clarity so that I burn for love of such beauty, I nonetheless condemn
> all human things which call me back from there.

The "human things" *(humana)* include the lie's performance and justification. The decision to abandon "intelligible beauty" *(intelligibilem
pulchritudinem)*, God's eternal and changeless beauty, for such things is
beyond coherent justification, from which it follows that the lie ought
never to be told.

A final text (Augustine is retrospectively lamenting his sins, and the
addressee is God) to illustrate the point that loving God and lying are
performatively incompatible:

> You are the truth, presiding over everything. I, in my avarice, wanted not
> to lose you but to have you along with the lie—in much the same way that
> no one wants to say what is false in such as way as to become unable to
> know what is true. In this way I lost you because you do not deign to be
> possessed along with a lie.

Continuing to lie and "possessing"—being lovingly intimate with—God
are not compatible. To want both at the same time is to have contradictory desires. No one, once he understands what it is to be lovingly
intimate with God, willingly abandons that intimacy. But many (all?) of
us make the mistake of thinking that we can have it while continuing
to lie—and this is the contradiction at the heart of the lie, the reason
why it cannot coherently be told. All possession and all control must be
disowned if the lie is to be abandoned.

6

Storytelling

In 1911, A. E. Housman spoke the following words in his inaugural lecture as Kennedy Professor of Latin in the University of Cambridge:

> The aim of science is the discovery of the truth, while the aim of literature is the production of pleasure; and the two aims are not merely distinct but often incompatible, so that large departments of literature are also departments of lying.

Augustine would not have agreed. Housman was perhaps entitled to the view: he was not only an accomplished classicist of scientific bent, but also a notable poet; and although poetic tastes have changed since he published *A Shropshire Lad* in 1896, the poems in that volume—and especially "When I was One–and–Twenty"—brought much pleasure to many in the half-century following its publication. Augustine, nonetheless, would have found the view too crude. He would have agreed that poets and littérateurs often aim at pleasure—they use *suaviloquium*, sweetly elegant speech, and they are concerned with *verborum integritas*, the unadulterated purity of words. But he would not have thought the production of pleasure the only purpose of poets, nor all literature duplicitous even if it had been.

What then did he think? For it is clear that poetry and novels and plays (fictions in general) are often about people and places who never were and events that never happened, that this is clear to those who fabricate them, and that they are nonetheless presented as if they were real. And unless the storyteller is deceived about the reality of the people

101

and events in their stories, this approaches duplicity. Fictions, are, etymologically speaking, *figmenta*, things that are not what they seem, artifacts fabricated (made, molded, formed, constructed, ornamented) out of the imaginations of their makers. The Latin verb is *fingere*, from which both *fictio* and *figmentum* come. Sometimes Augustine does write of these things as if they were lies, as these remarks from the *Soliloquies* show: "For mimes and comedies and many poems are full of lies, but they are there from a desire to provide delight rather than to deceive"; and "a story *(fabula)* is a lie composed for usefulness or delight." But these quotations are from an early work, composed when Augustine had not yet arrived at a clear distinction between falsehood and lie. He calls poetry and dramatic performance instances of the lie in this work because they are false (they depict what didn't happen), but he is not thereby saying that those who make these artifacts are necessarily and always duplicitous.

Storytelling, let's say, is the act of fabricating a fiction and making it public. A fiction is a collection of words, spoken or written, that depicts a sequence of states of affairs (actions, speeches, landscapes) that did not and do not exist as they are portrayed. And the storyteller is the fabricator of fictions. For Augustine, the paradigmatic storyteller is Vergil, and so when he considers the question of storytelling he usually does so by discussing that poet and his *figmenta*, his fictional creations.

Some poets make their fictions under the impression that what they depict is true, that the events about which they write happened and the people whose doings they describe were real. This of course is not lying, though it is error, the error of taking as true what is not. When, for example, Vergil wrote in the sixth book of the *Aeneid* about what Aeneas saw in the underworld, he may or may not have taken what he described to have happened. Augustine is clear that what is described did not happen: there is no underworld of that sort, and probably no such person as Aeneas who could have visited it. It follows that what Vergil wrote about these events must be understood as a poetical falsehood, but it does not follow that Vergil lied in writing about them. In order to know whether he did, one would have to know what he thought about the events he depicted, and such knowledge is not easily available to us, as it also was not to Augustine. Augustine is very alive to the difficulties of knowing what a particular writer took to be the case if all we have available to us is what he wrote, and he usually prefers to portray Vergil as the transmitter of false ideas and traditions rather than as their fabricator. For Augustine, Vergil may sometimes be in error and his readers may often find themselves in error as a result of reading him. But he is not himself to be understood as a liar.

Poets, however, may also know their fictions to be such. In this case, too, the poet need not be a liar. Everything will depend upon the storyteller's understanding of what she is doing. As with the case of figurative language in general, speaking poetically of fictional characters for didactic purposes need not be a lie. It will not be if the act of so speaking does not seem to its speaker to be duplicitous. Jesus, for example, spoke parables about people (the good Samaritan, the prodigal son) who never existed. Jesus knew they never existed, and so when he began a story, "There was a man who had two sons . . ." (Luke 15:11), he did not seem to himself to be speaking duplicitously, to be thinking one thing and saying another. Instead, says Augustine, he seemed to himself to be fictionalizing in order to express something true, and this suffices to make what he says not a lie:

> After his resurrection, our Lord Jesus was walking along the road with two disciples. When he approached the village where they lived, he pretended that he was going on. The Evangelist says, "he pretended to go on" (Luke 24:28). These are words in which liars delight excessively, taking everything pretended to be like a lie so that they might lie with impunity. But in fact many pretenses are undertaken in order truly to signify one thing by means of another. If therefore Jesus had intended to signify nothing else by pretending to go on, it would have been proper to judge it a lie; if, on the other hand, what he did is properly understood and referred to what he wanted to signify by it, it is found to be a mystery. Otherwise, all those things will be lies that, because of a certain resemblance to things signified, are narrated as if they'd happened when in fact they haven't. Of exactly this kind is the long story about the man who had two sons, the elder of whom stayed at home with his father and the younger of whom went on a long journey.

"To pretend" in this passage renders various forms of *fingere*. Augustine here rejects the view that *omne fingitur*, everything pretended or fictional, is like a lie. If a fiction is told by a storyteller in order figuratively to express something the storyteller takes to be true—*"veraciter aliud ex alio significandi causa,"* for the purpose of truly signifying one thing by another—it is not a lie because it is not duplicitous. In Jesus' case, of course, there is no error, and so what he intends to signify by his fictions is true in addition to not being a lie. When Horace or Aesop tells stories about talking animals and walking trees, and when Vergil tells stories about Dido and Aeneas, what they intend to signify may or may not be true (and may or may not be taken to be true by the poets), but in every other respect the fictions of the poets are just like the fictions or pretenses of the prophets and of God himself.

Stories that are straightforwardly lies, then, will have the following features: they will seem fictional to those who tell them; and they will seem to their tellers to signify nothing other than what they say. Any story that meets these criteria will be a lie, and will, *ipso facto*, be unacceptable. But it will typically be difficult to decide in particular cases whether a story is a lie. We are unlikely to have access to what we'd need to know about the story's author in order to decide. This comports well with Augustine's definition of the lie: if the lie is something decided upon and intended internally, an act of grasping and owning one's speech, the best witness to its being a lie will be the speaker, not the hearer. Augustine is not to be numbered among those who would in principle ban fiction to Christians—not, at least, if the reason for the ban is that all fictions are lies.

There are, in Augustine's mind, reasons to worry about reading pagan fictions and attending performances of pagan dramas other than that they might be lies. Christians might be led into conceptual error by such reading, either because its authors were themselves in error, or because they intended to deceive. Christian emotions and appetites might also be stimulated or aroused in vicious ways: Augustine relates in the *Confessions* the grief aroused in him by reading Vergil's account of Dido's self-immolation, and calls it a kind of dementia. Why, he wonders, did he weep for Dido's suicide from disappointed love while not weeping over his own loveless dying to God? Why would he have grieved if he had not been permitted to read something that brought him grief? The vain spectacles of pagan poetry are the occasion and stimulus for much sin in Augustine's mind, but the reading of such poetry need not always have such results, and when it does this is not because the poets are liars. Augustine's usual vocabulary for the criticism of the poets is that of error and falsehood rather than that of the lie.

It is also important to see that there is nothing in principle wrong with the pathos of poetry, with its capacity to engage and arouse the reader's passions. Augustine's sermons are designed to arouse his hearers, and his *Confessions*, he notes on reconsidering that book toward the end of his life, might well excite its readers' passions in a positive way, encouraging them to feel remorse for their sins and to offer praise to God. And, most strikingly, he says that the passions (anger, fear, sadness, and so on) of the *pius animus*, the wise mind, should be analyzed and judged good or bad in terms of their cause and result, not simply in terms of their occurrence. If you're sad because someone you know is unhappy or distressed and you want to comfort them, that is good. If you're angry because a sinner has acted wrongly and you'd like to reform him, that too is good. And insofar as pagan poetry can arouse these passions, reading it is good. Augustine is also (usually) entirely positive about good literary style: he praises the polished and elegant style of a correspondent, and says that among the goods of poetry is the dignity and beauty of metrical form. Good style is good intrinsically and is to be criticized only when it serves bad purposes or has bad results.

Storytelling's goodness depends, from the perspective of the storyteller, upon how her activity seems to her. If it seems duplicitous, it's a lie and is placed under the ban; if it seems sincere, told *ex animi sententia*, then it escapes that ban. But in this respect it is no different from nonfictional speech. From the perspective of the story told, the work produced by the storyteller, goodness depends upon the degree to which the work is beautiful: the greater its ordered harmony, the deeper its participation in God's ordered harmony and the greater its merit. Vergil scores very high here. From the perspective of the reader, goodness depends upon result: if, by reading, you come to recognize a particular truth or in some other way to have the setting of human life illuminated, this is good, indeed the highest good to be gained from reading. And if you are moved to do what you ought, that too is a great good. But neither of these goods is dependent upon what the poet intends. You can come to understand a truth as well (perhaps better) by misunderstanding a falsehood an author means to communicate as you can by accurately understanding and assenting to a truth an author intends. Of course, in the latter case you gain understanding of an extra truth not had in the first case: that about what the author intends. But this, thinks Augustine, is vastly less important than eternal truths about the order of things. Comprehension of those may be had by way of reading, quite independently of authorial intent.

Augustine was a literary artist of a high order and was capable of recognizing and appreciating literary artistry in others, whether pagan or Christian. His ban upon the lie does not call this into question. He was, however, also alive to the dangers of reading (and writing): this, like all other human activities, may be corrupted and corrupting, an instance of taking possession rather than relinquishing. The ideal story, for Augustine, is a ceaseless act of praise, ornamented, burnished, filigreed, and harmoniously glowing with the light it reflects and returns to its giver. This act runs out finally into silence by consuming its own words, for there are no acts of speech in heaven. But before this goal is reached, the story can shed light upon the setting of human life: it can suggest to the Christian reader truths about that setting; it can engage that reader's passions in the direction of encouraging her to act appropriately (as tax-collector rather than Pharisee) in that setting; and it can itself embody, represent, and instantiate a proper response to the human scene.

Pagan literature can do this as well as Christian. God does not give rhetorical gifts only to Christians, the gift of fictionally depicting the setting of human life with pathos and profundity is not restricted to Christians, and it is not even the case that the Augustinian literary act of confession is performed only by Christians. Christians, it is true, will have an explicit understanding of humanity and of human speech (fictional or otherwise) not granted or available to pagans. Christians will know, for example, that the shape and order of each human existence, of all human history, and of every human utterance is given by the cross. But such knowledge, while a great gift, may not foster and may sometimes work against the writing of great literature. It tempts to didactic allegory, to the stiltedly serious stiffness of a Bunyan or (at his worst) a C. S. Lewis. Knowing what your fictions are really about, understanding the human scene they depict, may make it more rather than less difficult to write them as true confessions in Augustinian mode. Not knowing—or knowing less—may make it easier to listen to the word spoken in creation and evident in the affairs of men, and to return it in praise. It is certain, in any case, that Christian knowledge permits a reading of pagan fictions more profound than any possible for pagan readers of the same works.

Consider, for example, Sophocles' play *Philoctetes,* a work that could have been known to Augustine but that is not, to my knowledge, mentioned by him anywhere (he is remarkably silent about Greek tragedy and comedy; the few and very critical remarks he makes about the theatre seem to have burlesque and low comedy in mind, not Sophocles or Euripides). The play's scene is Lemnos, an almost uninhabited and largely barren island of misty rock where the ceaseless crash of the waves is deadened only by omnipresent fogs and drizzling rains. There is little light and no comfort on Lemnos. The island's sole unwilling inhabitant is Philoctetes: he lives there in constant pain from a foot wounded by snakebite. The wound will not heal. It drips pus and blood; it stinks of rotten flesh; and its pain reduces Philoctetes often to incoherent screams, which abate only when he is beaten down by pain into a shallow unconciousness from which he is woken, unrefreshed, by yet more pain. The rhythm of the waves and the fogs provide counterpoint to the rhythm of his agony. He lives in a cave open to the air, surrounded by the scattered bones and half-eaten bodies of the beasts he kills for food. He survives only because he has the bow of Herakles, a magical weapon whose arrows always hit their mark.

Sophocles depicts the grimness of Philoctetes' life through the speeches of those who wish him harm (Odysseus), those who observe him compassionately (the chorus), and Neoptolemus, the drama's pivotal character. Neoptolemus moves from being a grudging cooperator with Odysseus's devious and duplicitous schemes to harm Philoctetes to being the latter's advocate and helper. All of Sophocles' depictions of Philoctetes' plight arouse the reader's passions, as they do even more strongly when the play is well presented on stage. For the Christian, Philoctetes' situation (solitude, unremitting pain, an environment without care or warmth or beauty) dramatizes the setting of human life, the human scene without God and after the fall: a desert of pain without hope. Its gloom is heightened by the fact that Philoctetes was marooned on Lemnos by his friends and allies: he had been one of a party of Greeks on their way to the war at Troy, and was put ashore in a wild place because his companions could no longer put up with his screams and the stink of his wound. Philoctetes' situation makes Job's seem almost enviable. Job at least had his comforters.

Sophocles' attentiveness to the human scene rivals that of any scriptural or Christian author. Christians can and should be moved by it to fear, repentance, and a deep sadness at what we, God's images and children, have become and are capable of doing. In this sense, at least, Sophocles' words can serve as *confessio* by doing what Augustine hoped his confessions might do: inculcate pity and terror, not only at the bleakness of the human scene but also at our agency in deepening and intensifying that bleakness by violent betrayal and manipulative cunning.

Philoctetes' abandonment on Lemnos is (or can be read as) a confession of the truth of the human scene. But the marooning is not the story of the play. It is mentioned only as an element in the back-story. The real story is the attempted corruption of Neoptolemus, the upright and noble son of the (now dead) Achilles, by Odysseus, the man of guile and tricks. Odysseus wants to subvert someone truthful by nature into a liar, someone who will use deceit to trick Philoctetes out of his bow, which is the only thing that keeps him alive. Odysseus tells Neoptolemus to beguile Philoctetes, to steal away his mind with lies so that Herakles' bow might be taken to Troy, there to be used to help the Greeks win the war. The lie's purpose, says Odysseus, is a good one: it's a trick, a *dolos*, preceded by good intentions and followed by good results. Odysseus acknowledges that it's disgraceful to speak the lie, *pseudē legein;* but he defends doing so by appeal to consequences. Neoptolemus is temporarily persuaded: he does lie to Philoctetes, going against his nature to do so, and succeeds in convincing him to hand over the bow. But then he repents, seeing that the lie to which he'd been persuaded was not defensible and that it ran counter to his own nature. Things end well enough (though not for Odysseus, who in this play is beyond redemption): the bow is returned to Philoctetes and he goes with Neoptolemus to join the war at Troy, persuaded in part by an appearance by Herakles himself, and in part by the promise of a cure for his suppurating wound.

Here too Sophocles effectively depicts the human scene, so effectively that the playgoer may need to avert her gaze and will certainly shudder: sin, with its attendant corruption, couches always at the door of even the most righteous and just person, which is to say even of a Neoptolemus, upright by nature. Apparently reasonable justifications for sin are always with us, and it is not hard for the Christian reader to see Satan's temptations of Jesus as a palimpsest beneath Odysseus's twisted advocacy of the lie. It is interesting, too, that the dramatic tension of the play is provided by a debate over the lie. Sophocles is more critical of consequentialist attempts to justify the lie than are some of Augustine's Christian contemporaries, as we shall see. But it is not the play's rejection of the lie (which is in any case not a clear and consistent exceptionless ban) that makes its reading potentially transformative for Christians. It is, rather, Sophocles' rhetorically elegant and powerful depiction of loneliness, betrayal, abandonment, temptation, and (partial) redemption. To have Christian passions aroused by this would be, to use a scriptural image beloved by Augustine, like stealing gold from the Egyptians (Exod. 3: 22)—which is to say, taking truth from the Greeks.

The words of the *Philoctetes* can be read by Christians as those of a careful participatory listener (Sophocles) to the revelation of what it is like to be human before God and in the grip of sin's incomprehensibility. This is not to say that Sophocles would have described what he was doing in these terms. Far from it. But for a Christian, this is what all those who write good literature are doing whether they know it or not. All literature can be so read because to the extent that a literary work has form at all it has and must have it as a result precisely of such participatory listening. But authors can refuse to listen, to observe, to taste, to touch. When they do, the story's participation in the order of things is to that extent occluded. When authors refuse to listen, refuse to recapitulate the confessional act in their own storytellings, and instead attempt possession of the story, owning it and ornamenting it with their own self-fascinated wit—when confession is obscured by the obsessive loquaciousness of the author—literature approaches the lie, and then Housman, with whom we began this chapter, is right: departments of literature are indeed departments of lying, not because literature aims at pleasure but because literature has taken possession of itself.

Here, for contrast, is Geoffrey Hill, a poet who knows what he does, who understands confession's recursivity and the inevitability of story-telling's self-consumption:

> I desire so not to deny desire's
> intransigence. To you I stand
> answerable. Correction: must once have stood.
> What's this thing, like a clown's eyebrow-brush?
> O my lady, it is the fool's confession,
> weeping greasepaint, all paint and rhetoric.

Iconic poetry, when it represents its own iconicity, must gesture at its own self-consuming recursivity. Not only does poetry make nothing happen, as W. H. Auden wrote; the best poetry also represents its own unhappening. Consider, for example, George Herbert's profoundly Augustinian "Sinnes Round":

> Sorrie I am, my God, sorrie I am,
> That my offences course it in a ring.
> My thoughts are working like a busie flame,
> Until their cockatrice they hatch and bring:
> And when they once have perfected their draughts,
> My words take fire from my inflamed thoughts.
>
> My words take fire from my inflamed thoughts,
> Which spit it forth like the Sicilian Hill.
> They vent the wares, and passe them with their faults,
> And by their breathing ventilate the ill.
> But words suffice not, where are lewd intentions:
> My hands do joyn to finish the inventions.
>
> My hands do joyn to finish the inventions:
> And so my sinnes ascend three stories high,
> As Babel grew, before there were dissensions.
> Yet ill deeds loyter not: for they supplie
> New thoughts of sinning: wherefore, to my shame,
> Sorrie I am, my God, sorrie I am.

The first line of the poem is the last: its recital can never end. In this the poem is an icon of its topic, which is sin, itself a never-ending cycle: flaming thoughts beget the cockatrice, the fire-breathing death-dealing serpent (Herbert plays here with Isa. 59:5) of words; these words are spat forth, magma-like, from Etna, the "Sicilian Hill"; and then they issue in actions that beget "new thoughts of sinning" . . . and so on, without end. But the poem brings the cycle to an end: writing, reading, and speaking the poem displaces the cycle it represents and also consumes itself. It does this because the poem is an act of Augustinian *confessio,* a returning of the gift of speech to its giver. It is a properly liturgical act, and is therefore the ideal act of storytelling.

Part Two

Augustinian Readings

7

Plato

My Platonic text is the *Hippias elattōn*, or *Hippias Minor*, a short Socratic dialogue by Plato with no useful indications, external or internal, as to its date. The dialogue's argument revolves around a set of terms derived from the root *pseud-* (*pseudos*, *pseudēs*, *pseudō*, and so on), whose meaning fluctuates alarmingly: sometimes these terms seem to indicate an intentionally duplicitous act, which is to say an Augustinian lie; but more often they mean the act of saying something false, whether or not the speaker so intends. This lack of clarity about terms and meanings leads to some conceptual difficulties. For the sake of consistency I'll translate these terms always with "false" and derivatives ("falsehood," "false (man)," "to be false/speak falsely," and so on), though this will raise difficulties. Since the main speaker in the dialogue is Socrates, I'll usually write as though the arguments offered and opinions expressed are his; but I also attribute those arguments and opinions to Plato, without distinction or remainder. For my purposes, nothing hinges upon how Plato's thoughts relate to those of Socrates in this dialogue.

The dialogue's two important speakers are Socrates and Hippias. The conversation opens as Hippias, a man of surpassing arrogance—"I've never met a man better than me at anything at all," he says, without a trace of irony, though Plato's lack of explicit comment on Hippias's claim drips with it—has just finished an oration on some unspecified Homeric theme. Socrates pretends not to have understood some things in Hippias's speech and asks for clarification: Does Hippias think Achilles or Odysseus the better man, and in what respect? How does Hippias distinguish and discriminate between the two heroic Homeric characters? Hippias answers with a rhetorician's move: Homer, he says, depicts Achilles as the best *(aristos)* of the Greeks who went to the war at Troy, Nestor as the wisest *(sophōtatos)* of that company, and Odysseus as the most changeable, tricky, or wily *(polutropōtatos)*. This last epithet means, literally, "one who turns or faces many ways"—one to whom it is applied is not just two-faced but many-faced, someone who is prepared to appear in any guise in order to achieve his ends. Odysseus, then, is the maximally many-faced one. Socrates confesses himself puzzled by this last epithet: he knows what it means to say of someone that they are good or the best; he understands, too, what it is to be wise; but he does not understand very well what it is to be changeable, tricky, wily, many-faced. After all, he asks, hasn't Homer represented Achilles as *polutropos*, as well? And if so, how can Achilles and Odysseus be differentiated by appeal to this epithet?

No, says Hippias. Homer consistently depicts Achilles as straightforward and simple *(haplous)*, which is the same as being "true" *(alēthēs)*; and he consistently depicts Odysseus as many-faced, which is the same as being "false" *(pseudēs)*. Achilles says what he thinks and does what he says, while Odysseus is a man of many inventions and resources *(polumēkhanēs)*, who (it's implied) is very likely to say one thing and do another with wit, artistry, and imagination.

Socrates then suggests that since Homer is no longer available to consult about what he meant by his depictions of these two heroes, he and Hippias had better leave exegetical questions aside and talk directly to one another rather than through or about Homer's text. The two agree that Hippias's view amounts to the claim that there is a deep difference between the "true man" *(anēr alēthēs)* and the "false man" *(anēr pseudēs)*, so deep, in fact, that the two cannot be the same person. They also agree (implicitly) that these terms *(alēthēs/pseudēs)* can do duty for the other contrastive pairs (straightforward/many-faced; simple/multiple; and so on) they'd also mentioned. And with these preliminary clarifications in mind, the train of the Socratic dialectic chugs slowly out of the station, with Hippias as an increasingly unwilling passenger on board.

Socrates gets Hippias to agree that false men must be capable (they are *dunatos*), maliciously shrewd (they have *panourgia*), practically intelligent (they have *phronēsis*), and, therefore, wise *(sophos)*. They are capable of doing what false men do, which is to trick or deceive *(exapataō)*; they are maliciously shrewd and practically intelligent in knowing just what to do to succeed in their tricky deceits; and they are wise (rather than ignorant) with respect to all these matters. Hippias agrees, as well, to the strong claim that "those who speak truly and those who speak falsely are in two completely opposed categories," which I take to mean that no one can belong to both. These terms provide Plato with the raw materials for an *elenchus,* an argument in which the opponent is persuaded to assent to a claim (in this case that false men are capable, and so on) that contradicts some other claim or claims he also wishes to hold. The task of the presenter of the *elenchus* (in this case, as usual, Socrates) is initially just to present this difficulty. It may also then be to argue for (or suggest the acceptance of) the contradictory of the thesis to which the opponent has initially been led.

Being false, a speaker of falsehoods, requires the capacity (the power) to tell the difference between what's true and what's false: "An ignorant *(amathēs)* man incapable *(adunatos)* of speaking falsely cannot be false." Socrates deploys a mathematical analogy: someone skilled in arithmetic can quickly give the right answer to a question of calculation—Socrates calls this telling the truth about such a question; but the same skilled person can choose to give the wrong answer, and in so doing to speak falsely. Those with the greatest power and wisdom in arithmetic are therefore the most capable of being liars, for only they can consistently and correctly give the wrong answers. Those not very good at arithmetic will sometimes speak truly when they intend to speak falsely—and that he can say this shows with great clarity that Plato does not have duplicity in mind as the central characteristic of false speech. A "man false with respect to arithmetic" is a man who gives the wrong answer deliberately, which requires him to know what the right answer is and to choose not to give it.

The understanding of *pseudesthai* implied (though never clearly stated) here is: you speak falsely if and only if you know what the truth is and you choose not to tell it. Such an act will always be an Augustinian lie because it will always involve duplicity. But not every Augustinian lie will be an instance of Platonic false speech because it's possible to speak duplicitously without saying anything false (and, of course, without knowing what's true). Plato's arithmetically skilled speaker of falsehoods is a liar because he's duplicitous. But so might an arithmetical dunce be, because the Augustinian lie doesn't require that you know what the truth is: it requires only that you know what seems to you to be the case, and the arithmetical dunce is quite capable of that. Plato, by contrast, needs an understanding of false speech that requires its practitioners to be knowledgeable and clever. Only this will permit him to convict Hippias of inconsistency. This means that much of what he has Socrates say about falsehood has nothing much to do with the lie.

To return to the remorseless Socratic assertion-disguised-as-question: to be capable of falsehood (and of truth) in arithmetic is "just the same as to be good *(agathos)* with respect to arithmetic." And so, Hippias is forced to agree (he is by this time monosyllabically reluctant to commit himself to more than grunts of assent), the same person may be both false and true. Which means that Hippias's earlier claim that no man can be both false and true—that no individual belongs both to the set of true and to the set of false men—is refuted. Not only this: being false and being true are equally good, for to be good with respect to some skill is just to have the capacities and knowledge intrinsic to the practice of that skill—and the false and true man are indistinguishable in this respect. To be good *(agathos)* at something is to be able *(dunatos)* to do it; to be bad *(kakos)* at something is to be unable to do it, and since to be truthful and to be false require the same capacities, it must also be that they require the same goodness. It is, then, not the case that "the true and the false [person] are separate, not the same." The same point applies, Socrates urges (and Hippias glumly agrees), to all the arts and sciences. It applies, as well, to the example of Achilles and Odysseus, with which the discussion began: if the same man is false and true, then both Achilles and Odysseus are indistinguishably false and true.

Hippias protests. Socrates has missed the point, he says, which is that Homer depicts Achilles as better than Odysseus and Odysseus as worse than Achilles, and this exactly in the fact that Achilles is true and Odysseus false, a trickster. Hippias offers to prove this. But before he gets a chance, Socrates returns to the text of the *Iliad,* and says that as far as he can see Achilles is there shown to be at least as false as Odysseus, and perhaps more so. He quotes again Achilles' criticism of Odysseus as the one who hides one thing in his heart and says another; and he then goes on to quote episodes in which Achilles is shown claiming that he will shortly put to sea but then failing to do so. These are clear instances, as Socrates reads Homer, of Achilles claiming that he will do something while at the same time having no intention whatever of doing it—and, later, of fulfilling that intention by failing to do it. It follows from this reading that Achilles fits the definition of the many-faced just as well as Odysseus.

The *Iliad* is not in fact as clear as Socrates makes it on this point. It is interesting, though, that Socrates here uses an understanding of speaking falsely to which duplicity does appear central. On his reading, Achilles does in these Homeric episodes speak the Augustinian lie, and this means that for Socrates it's reasonable to say, in accord with his earlier argument, that Achilles and Odysseus are identical with respect to truths and falsehoods and with respect to virtue *(aretē)* in general.

Hippias objects to this reading on the principal ground that even if Achilles does on occasion speak what is not true, he does it because he is "moved by compassion" *(hupo eunoias anapeistheis)*, whereas Odysseus does it intentionally *(hekontes)*. But this gives Socrates just what he wants: as the argument earlier given already shows, his view is that "those who intentionally hurt and injure people, speak falsely, play tricks, and do what is wrong are better *(beltious)* than those who do these things unintentionally." Socrates does not think that voluntary or intentional wrongdoing is always better than involuntary or unintentional wrongdoing. But he does think that those who do wrong (that is, do what they should not do and what they know they should not do) voluntarily or intentionally have some good qualities necessarily lacking in those who do wrong involuntarily or unintentionally. He says (ironically) that he is unhappy with this conclusion, and he begs Hippias for help in disabusing him of it.

Hippias, however, does not get the chance to provide any such help. Instead, Socrates provides him with examples of voluntary and involuntary imperfection in the body in order to drive the point home. Consider the man who limps voluntarily and the man who does so because he can't help it. Whose feet, Socrates wants to know, are better? The answer is obvious, and Hippias finds that he can't avoid it: the feet of the voluntary limper are better than those of the involuntary limper, because the former have a good or a perfection missing in the latter, which is that they can be made to walk without a limp. Voluntary limping, then, is better than involuntary limping for just the same reason. The same point is made of the archer who voluntarily or intentionally misses the mark in comparison with the one who misses because he can't help it. And, most dramatically, the same point is made of the *psukhē*, the soul: the more capacity for deliberation and understanding it has, the more *dikaiosunē* and *epistēmē*, the greater its capacity for doing disgraceful things *(ta aiskhra)*.

The final argument is an application of the general principle to the goodness of the soul. The extent to which a person's soul is replete with power *(dunamis)* and knowledge *(epistēmē)* is the extent to which that person's soul is good; the extent to which a person's soul is good is the extent to which that person is good; the person who can only do evil unintentionally has less power and knowledge in his soul than one capable of intentional evildoing; therefore, the person who does evil intentionally is better than the one who does evil only unintentionally. Stated more dramatically and pithily: "It belongs to the good man *(agathou . . . andros)* to do wrong intentionally and to the bad *(kakou)* to do it unintentionally." This conclusion, together with the pattern of thought that led to it and supports it, strongly suggests that by "good" Socrates means both "good at" (possessed of a relevant skill), and "morally good" (because to be possessed of a skill is better than not to be). Much more could be said about such a meaning of *agathos,* but all that's needed here is the conclusion that on some such meaning of "good" (and its antonym, "bad"), only good people can do wrong intentionally and only bad ones unintentionally. This is the most important part of what it means to be good (and bad) for Socrates. Hippias rejects the conclusion, of course, but can see nothing wrong with the argument; Socrates says that he also rejects the conclusion, but that he can't see how to avoid it because it's where the *logos,* the argument, leads. He says, perhaps with irony, that he does think the conclusion wrong, which is to say that there is some flaw in the argument by which he has led Hippias and himself to this conclusion. The dialogue rests, however, without identifying the flaw—though there is a hint in the suggestion that even if it does belong to the good man to do wrong intentionally, it may be that no good man ever does or would act in this way: "The one who voluntarily goes wrong by doing disgraceful things and unjust things would be none other than the good man, Hippias—if there is such a man." Socrates means to suggest, almost certainly, that no good man, no one with plenty of *dikaiosunē* and *epistēmē,* would ever intentionally choose to do wrong. This is a fundamentally important theme in the Platonic corpus, but not one that need be pursued further here.

There is a negative thesis that Socrates certainly wishes to establish in this discussion with Hippias. It is the denial of the claim that the man who does something wrong or inelegant (lying, limping) deliberately, with full intention and understanding, is thereby worse than the man who does these same things inevitably, without the possibility of doing anything else. And there is a corresponding positive thesis that he also wishes to establish. It is that the deliberate, intentional false-speaker is better than the one who speaks falsely without any intention to do so, precisely because the former deliberates and understands while the latter does not. There is also a third claim, intimately entwined with these first two, that is affirmed by Socrates (and agreed by Hippias): it is that the deliberate false-speaker and the deliberate truth-speaker are equally good. And finally, there is a fourth claim mentioned at the end of the dialogue, but only to be placed under erasure: I mean the claim that the intentional false-speaker is simply better than the false-speaker who can't help herself. This claim is placed under erasure because Socrates himself says that he doesn't think it right. This erasure is ironic, I think: Socrates in fact means what he says.

Suppose we take Socrates' own arithmetical example to focus the discussion: 3 x 70 = 210. Suppose, too, that we follow him in taking "false-speaking" about this to mean denying the claim, and "truth-speaking" about it to mean affirming the claim. A first Augustinian comment is that false-speaking and truth-speaking so understood need have nothing to do with the lie because they need have nothing to do with duplicity. They may have something to do with it (that is, one may speak both falsely and duplicitously); but definitionally, they do not.

This example yields the following picture: for Socrates, those who deny 3 x 70 = 210 speak falsely with respect to it, and those who affirm it speak truly with respect to it. This is so no matter what is taken to be true: if you're arithmetically challenged and you sincerely think that the product of 3 and 70 is 240, you'll deny that 3 x 70 = 210 without duplicity, but you'll still be a false-speaker in Socrates' understanding, though an unintentional (and nonduplicitous) one. If you have performed the calculation and have gotten it right, so that you take 3 x 70 = 210 to be true, but you deny the claim because you wish not to appear arithmetically competent, or for some other inscrutable reason, you'll also be a Socratic false-speaker (this time an intentional and also a duplicitous one). A similar division can be made among truth-speakers: the arithmetically incompetent person who thinks that the answer to 3 x 70 is 240 may intentionally affirm, contrary to what she thinks, that 3 x 70 = 210—perhaps because she is tired of arguing about the question, and would rather speak duplicitously than otherwise. She is still a Socratic truth-speaker. And, finally, you may be arithmetically skilled and nonduplicitous: in that case you'll be a Socratic truth-speaker who intentionally affirms that 3 x 70 = 210.

Applying the Socratic negative thesis to this example is straightforward: it is not the case that of two false-speakers (the first two instances above) the intentionally duplicitous one is worse than the arithmetically challenged nonduplicitous one. Why not? Because the intentional false-speaker (who is also the duplicitous one) has some good qualities, some powers of the soul, lacking in the false-speaker who doesn't know what she does and has no intention of speaking falsely. The most significant among these good qualities in Socrates' mind is that of being able to discriminate truth from error in arithmetic. There need be no Augustinian objection to this: it is better to be able to discriminate truth from error, in arithmetic as in any other matter. So in that respect the duplicitous false-speaker is better than the nonduplicitous one. However, it doesn't follow from this that when someone does what Socrates thinks of as "deliberate false-speaking," she is thereby better than someone who commits involuntary error. To show that the former has at least one good quality lacking in the latter is to show neither that what the former does is better than what the latter does, nor that the former is better when she does it than is the latter when she involuntarily errs. The two actions differ not only in what their agents know but also in at least one other important way: deliberate false-speaking involves duplicity while involuntary error does not. And if, as Augustine would, you think that this difference has moral weight, you'll agree with Hippias that Socrates has missed the point. He has generalized inappropriately from one difference between the agents of these two actions to a conclusion about the difference between the two agents. Involuntary error involves ignorance, which is an imperfection but not usually a sin; intentional false-speaking involves duplicity, which is always a sin. From which it follows immediately that the deliberate false-speaker is a sinner, while the one who makes involuntary error isn't. This can of course be put without the vocabulary of sin: voluntary false-speakers and involuntary false-speakers differ not only in their capacity for understanding and judgment; they differ also in their desire to misrepresent their thought in words. And while the former difference is in favor of the voluntary false-speaker, the latter difference favors the involuntary. This point is quite lacking in the Socratic argument.

And so the Socratic negative thesis is mistaken in its own terms because its conclusion does not follow from its premises. It is mistaken in Augustinian terms, too, because it neither notes or gives weight to the fundamental fact that the intentional false-speaker is a liar while the one who makes an involuntary error is not. The corresponding negative thesis can be refuted in the same way. To say that intentional false speech is better in one respect than involuntary error does not entail that it is better in all respects. And, as with the negative thesis, the essential respect (intentional duplicity) is occluded in Socrates' discussion.

What then about the claim that the intentional (duplicitous) false-speaker and the intentional (nonduplicitous) truth-speaker are equally good—that Achilles and Odysseus are interchangeable with respect to the goodness required for intentional truth-telling and intentional false-speaking? Socrates certainly shows that those who know what's the case and choose to conform their speech to their knowledge are identical in one important respect to those who know what's the case and make the opposite choice: they both know what's the case and can make a choice as to what to say about it. But, once again, it does not follow from this that Achilles and Odysseus are indistinguishable with respect to duplicity. That is precisely what distinguishes them—at least it does if we may read the *Iliad* to say that Odysseus really is the man who thinks one thing and says another, while Achilles is the man who says what he thinks. And if Socrates' third claim fails, his fourth—that the intentional false-speaker is simply better than the false-speaker who can't help herself, better not just with respect to the capacity to discern what's the case, but better *simpliciter*—must also fail, and for the same reason.

Socrates' argument is, then, profoundly confused. The very question of whether the deliberate limper is better than the involuntary limper already limps. Healthy feet are better than deformed ones, certainly; but the decision to feign a limp may be morally objectionable in ways impossible for the ordinarily involuntary limp.

To clarify differences further: Augustine and Socrates are at one in thinking that knowing the truth is a good. They also agree, therefore, in thinking that someone who does not know the truth lacks a good that someone who knows it has. But Socrates shows no interest in the question of the goodness or badness of the act of will by which the intentional liar decides to say what he thinks to be false. It is this act of will that makes the Socratic intentional liar also a liar in Augustinian terms: it is because he chooses to say what he does not think that he becomes duplicitous. And Socrates neither asks nor answers the question of the moral value of that choice. The implication of what he says is that he takes the choice to be morally neutral, for it does not seem, for him, to be relevant to the question of whether the intentional false-speaker is better or worse than the nonintentional false-speaker. This is the same as to say that Socrates does not consider the question that most interests Augustine in this connection: the question of what account to give of duplicity.

It is remarkable that this question scarcely enters Socrates' discussion, and is never clearly differentiated from the question of falsehood. This dialogue is the most extended discussion of the lie (*pseudos,* which almost always becomes *mendacium* in Latin) in Plato's work, and yet the distinction appears to have been either unavailable or uninteresting to him. It lurks in the subtext of Hippias's remarks, but no attempt is made to excavate or clarify it. It does not occur to Socrates in the *Hippias Minor* that there might be anything wrong with duplicity simply as such. Augustine's argument that there is cannot, therefore, be much illuminated by the Socratic argument that knowing false-speakers are to be preferred to those who don't know what they're talking about. For Socrates in the *Hippias Minor*, speech is an instrument of service to us, to be used by us for our own purposes; he has no thought that it might be an instrument of praise. This is the deepest difference between Augustine and the Socrates of the *Hippias Minor*, and once it is clarified it becomes clear that the only way forward in an argument between the two would be to address the question of what speech is and what it is for. Socrates would not be sympathetic to an Augustinian view on this. As the *Hippias Minor* already suggests, duplicity, even when clearly distinguished from falsehood, poses no special difficulties for Socrates. Criticisms of it, when they are made, will for him have to do with situation and result, with questions of social good and interpersonal trust rather than with questions of God and God's gift of speech.

8

Aristotle

Aristotle was aware of the Socratic argument about the voluntary lie. He comments upon it in the fifth book of the *Metaphysics,* as part of a passage analyzing the various senses of *pseudos* and its derivatives—the same Greek word played with by Socrates in the *Hippias Minor.* I'll translate it once again as "false"—though, as we shall see, this will not always work well because Aristotle distinguishes several different senses of the term. The *Metaphysics* is, notoriously, a work cobbled together by various hands from Aristotelian and quasi-Aristotelian materials. Neither its present form nor its title come from Aristotle, even though most of the material is likely to be from his hand. It therefore won't be terribly illuminating to place it in the context of the work as a whole. The passage I'm about to discuss can instead be taken by itself to represent one aspect of Aristotle's thought on the question of *pseudos;* in it, he is concerned mostly to distinguish different senses of the word and to distance his understanding of it from that of Plato in the *Hippias Minor.*

Aristotle discusses first the "false state of affairs," the *pragma pseudos.*

Some states of affairs, he says, are false in the sense that they can never occur—they cannot "be put together" in the sense that the elements of which they are supposed to consist can never be combined. Consider, for example, the state of affairs described by the claim that the diagonal of a square is identical in length to that same square's sides. This state of affairs is impossible: it is part of the definition of a square that its diagonal is not the same length as its sides, and so the claim "the square's diagonal is the same length as its sides" is necessarily false, which is the same as to say that the claim is incoherent. The state of affairs that such a claim purports to describe is one that not only doesn't occur but can't occur. Other states of affairs are false in the sense that they might occur, but as a matter of fact don't at the moment. For instance (Aristotle's example), the claim "you're sitting down" is not always true of you: sometimes you're sitting down and sometimes you're not (assuming that you're not unfortunate enough to be constrained always to sit). When you're not sitting down, the claim that you are describes a state of affairs that does not (at the moment) obtain. The state of affairs is therefore *pseudos,* false. Aristotle says that these two states of affairs, these two *pragmata,* are false in the sense that they are not *(ouk onta tauta [pragmata]):* they just don't exist.

States of affairs may be false in another sense as well: they may really occur or exist, but produce in us an impression or an appearance *(phantasia)* of something that does not occur or exist. Aristotle mentions dreams *(enupnia)* and impressionistic sketches *(skiagraphia)* as instances. These are real: the sketch exists as shades of grey on white paper, and the dream as a series of more or less vivid impressions (or, if you prefer, as a series of neurons firing in the brain). But these real things, these actually occurring states of affairs, give rise for those confronted with them to images and understandings that do not themselves exist—"the impression they produce," says Aristotle, "is of something that is not."

What Aristotle says here is ambiguous. He might mean that the visual image produced in you by looking (for example) at Georges Seurat's assemblage of tiny color-dots on the canvas called *Bathing at Asnières* is of a state of affairs that doesn't (and didn't) occur—that there aren't and weren't bathers at Asnières doing the things you're given to imagine them doing as a result of looking at Seurat's canvas. But this, of course, may or may not be so: it may be that what you imagine the bathers doing is exactly or approximately what they did (and may still be doing), and that the scene you're given to imagine by gazing at Seurat's canvas is therefore in that sense real. This is one possible interpretation of what Aristotle means. But there is another, and preferable, way to read him: it is that he means that what you imagine when you look at Seurat's canvas isn't what's on the canvas but something else. The *phantasia* conjured in you by the canvas isn't of the complex pattern of small dots on it, but rather of some people bathing, and it's in this sense that your impression is of something that doesn't exist. What conjures your impression is deeply and irreconcilably different from your impression's content. The same account can be given for what you see in dreams. But a different account is needed for what you see when you look at a real collection of bathers rather than a painting of bathers, or so Aristotle thinks. Were you yourself at Asnières, looking at the bathers, the state of affairs at which you were looking and your *phantasia* of it would be the same, or at least fundamentally similar, and so it would not be proper to say that the state of affairs you're looking at and the image produced in you by looking at it are not the same—which is what Aristotle says of the *skiagraphia* and the *phantasia*. There are difficulties here, of course; but they don't need to be pursued in order to understand what Aristotle means by saying that states of affairs are false.

States of affairs are *pseudos*, false, then, in at least three senses: first, that they can't occur (that a circle is square); second, that they don't occur (that you're sitting when you're standing); third, that they produce in those who perceive in them something significantly different from themselves (that you look at some colored dots on canvas and see the bathers at Asnières). Only the third of these false states of affairs could have anything to do with the lie. The first two don't and can't involve anyone's duplicity because they don't involve an act of representation. The third, however, does involve representation and might involve duplicity: Seurat might conceivably have been duplicitous in painting the bathers. If he was, he would have had to intend to misrepresent his thought in paint, to be duplicitous on canvas. This possibility could be analyzed in the same way as storytelling earlier was (in ch. 6): if Seurat was lying in paint, he would have had to intend his painting to express a state of affairs he did not take to obtain, and to intend that it should express nothing else—that it should not, for example, signify some truth figuratively, as Augustine thought Jesus' parables did and as I suggested Sophocles' *Philoctetes* might. We do not (or at least I do not) know what Seurat's intentions were, though it seems unlikely that the best account to give of his painting is that he was duplicitous in doing it. Aristotle's third sense of falsehood in states of affairs does not deepen or effectively challenge the account of storytelling's (or image-making's) lies in play in this book. Aristotle opens the way for a consideration of the duplicity of the artist, but he does not pursue the question. His interest in the falsity of painting (at least here in the *Metaphysics*) is only in the mismatch between what's on the canvas and what's conjured in the mind of the viewer.

But it is not only states of affairs that may be false. Aristotle also comments on the falsity of claims or statements *(logoi)*. The most fundamental characteristic of false statements is that they are misapplied—applied, that is, to "things that are not *(tōn mē ontōn)*." When, for example, you apply the definition of a circle (the object whose area is expressible by the formula πr^2) to a triangle, you're trying to describe a circular triangle, which is an object that doesn't (and can't) exist—it is a "thing that is not." The underlying idea is that each thing has a definition that captures what it essentially is. There may be different ways of verbally expressing that definition, and certainly many true things that may be said of something that do not capture what it essentially is. But the important feature of false claims is that they attempt to pick out something that doesn't or can't exist. Aristotle's account of the falsity of claims reflects his account of the falsity of states of affairs: both have to do most fundamentally with absence, with what does not or cannot exist.

Aristotle's idea that false-speakers are those who speak about what is not, and that their speech participates in the absence about which they talk, becomes a standard trope in English. Most memorably (and perhaps first), Jonathan Swift, in *Gulliver's Travels*, first published in 1726, depicted the Houyhnhnm who is teaching Gulliver to speak the Houyhnhnm language as doubting something Gulliver tells him, and saying to Gulliver (as Gulliver reports), "That I must needs be mistaken, or that I *said the thing which was not*. (For they have no Word in their language to express Lying or Falsehood.)" The Houyhnhnms are intelligent and virtuous horses who do not lie and are puzzled by the fact that Gulliver does, and that he tells them it is common among humans to do so. Gulliver is impressed by them more than by any of the other nonhuman races he finds on his travels—so much so, in fact, that when he gets back to England he prefers his horses' company to that of humans. It is possible that Swift had Aristotle in mind, consciously or half-so, when he used the phrase "the thing which was not"; it occurs often thereafter in the book, and from there it passed into the common stock of the English language. It raises echoes, as we shall see, in Newman, writing more than two hundred years after Swift. Aristotle provides its conceptual roots; he may also have suggested its very words.

The deep connection between nonexistence and falsehood in the grammar of Aristotle's thought about *pseudos* is an important point of similarity and connection between Aristotelian and Augustinian thought. Augustine's understanding of sin as what removes the sinner from being resonates with Aristotle's interweaving of falsehood with what is not. Truth as accurate representation has to do with what is; falsehood is part of the ontology of absence and lack, and this is true whether the term refers to states of affairs that don't or can't obtain, or to objects that conjure absence in the imaginations of those who use them. But this is not to say that Aristotle is an Augustinian in these passages of the

Metaphysics. At best we have here an affinity, for Aristotle has not yet addressed what from an Augustinian point of view is the lie proper.

But Aristotle's discussion does not end with false states of affairs and the false claims that purport to represent them. He treats also the *anthrōpos pseudēs,* the false person, and with his discussion of this we move as close as he will take us to the Augustinian lie proper. The false person is eager and intentional *(eukherēs kai proairetikos)* about speaking false statements as these have just been defined. False people, then, want to (and do) say the thing that is not, they want to make statements that purport to be about something but are in fact about nothing. They say things like "Socrates is sitting down" (when he's walking in the *agora*), and "a circle's radius is greater than its diameter" (when it's definitional of any circle's diameter that it is twice its radius). These are not examples Aristotle provides, but they match his account of false states of affairs and false claims, and he does clearly intend such a match: the false person speaks false claims about false states of affairs and does so with a knowing eagerness. What such a person says has no purchase on reality: it is a saying of the thing that is not, lacking in substance itself and incapable of bearing any relation to what has substance. Just as false states of affairs are not, so also false statements are not. Aristotle could have gone on to say (though he does not) that false people, to the extent that they are false, are also not: that, as Augustine would have it, false people squander their being by intentionally speaking falsely. But Aristotle has here no interest in applying this part of his analysis of the lie to the liar, and this lack of interest is perfectly congruent with the fact that he is interested more in falsehood than in the lie proper.

Aristotle is, however, interested in relating his discussion of false people to his discussion of false states of affairs—and in objecting to Socrates' argument in the *Hippias Minor* while doing so. False people, thinks Aristotle, are like sketches and dreams: these are called "false" because they are able to impress false images upon the mind—images of that which is not. Such things are false because of their effects upon those who come into contact with them. In a similar way, false speakers, in addition to being false because of their eagerness to say the thing that is not, are false because they "impress such [false] statements upon others *(ho allois empoiētikos tōn toioutōn logōn)*." Those who listen to false-speakers are as a result malformed: they come to speak falsely themselves, as like as not, and they will certainly (if they are credulous) be misled in exactly the same way that they might be by a convincing dream or an impressionistic sketch. This, for Aristotle, is one of the principal things wrong with the false-speaker and the falsehoods spoken: absence gets propagated, and the thing that is not proliferates, cancerously.

Aristotle draws the following conclusion from the analysis just offered:

> Therefore, the claim made in the *Hippias,* that one and the same person is false and true, is misleading. It assumes that the false person is the one capable of false-speaking because he knows and is intelligent. It also assumes that the person who is intentionally bad is better [than the one unintentionally so]. This false assumption is improperly concluded from the idea that one who limps intentionally is better than one who does so unintentionally. But by "limping" [in this example] is meant "pretending to limp," for if someone limps intentionally, he would in this respect be worse, just as in the case of moral character.

This is a summary of the *Hippias Minor*'s argument about the preferability of intentional false-speaking to unintentional false-speaking. It's interesting to note that Aristotle makes no comment on the fact that Plato has Socrates express dissatisfaction with the conclusion he reaches in the *Hippias Minor,* even to the point of saying that he rejects it. The absence of such comment makes it seem that Aristotle straightforwardly attributes the view he criticizes to Plato. Whether Plato meant Socrates' rejection of the view to be taken as irony or not, however, Aristotle thinks the view in question confused. In criticizing the argument that leads to it, Aristotle points to an ambiguity in the idea of the intentional limper, an ambiguity that infects Socrates' analysis of the intentional false-speaker since the latter is based upon the former. The ambiguity is this: "to limp" *(khōlainein),* Aristotle thinks, should mean (something like) "to drag a malformed or injured foot along the ground, and thus to halt in one's gait." If this is what it means, Plato's distinction between the intentional and the unintentional limper makes no sense, for the action indicated by the verb "to limp" cannot be performed intentionally. You can't decide to limp if you don't have a damaged foot, any more than you can decide to walk through a six-foot archway without ducking if you are more than six feet tall. What you can do if you lack a damaged or malformed foot is to imitate a limper, which is to pretend to limp. But this is not the same action as limping. And so Plato's question about the difference between the intentional and unintentional limper turns out to be about the difference between someone who limps and someone who pretends to limp, not about two people who perform an identical action and are distinguishable only by their understanding of or attitude to that action. If this is what the question comes to, thinks Aristotle, it is far from obvious that the one who imitates the limper is better than the one who drags his malformed foot because he can't help it.

Aristotle thinks of properties like "being a false-speaker" or "being a limper" as more or less stable characteristics, more or less fixed patterns of character. Such states are not skills or potentials or powers that you might use well or badly, or refuse to use at all. They are not like the carpenter's or navigator's skills, which require wisdom and good judgment (in addition to the skill in question) in order that they be properly deployed. No, if you're a limper, this means that your body is such that you can do nothing other than limp. If, at a particular time, you're a false-speaker, an *anthrōpos pseudēs*, this is just a fact about you, a habitual and natural, or natural-seeming, character trait. You speak falsely as naturally as you limp: once you've become a false-speaker, you have a deformity in your character, a misshapenness in your soul, of the same kind as the deformity of the foot that defines the limper. Traits of these kinds, while not completely stable and certainly alterable over time and with effort (even the limper's deformed foot can sometimes be corrected surgically), are at a particular time properties of those who have them that are beyond intentional control.

What then to say about the pretend-limper, on this (non-Socratic) understanding of what it is to be a pretend-limper? Since it is not obvious that the pretend-limper is better than the limper *simpliciter*—for Aristotle has rejected, as Augustine also would, the idea that simply being able not to limp makes the pretend-limper better than the ordinary limper—some other way of answering the question of which is best will need to be found.

Suppose we abandon the example of limping at this point and return to the question of the intentional false-speaker and the involuntary false-speaker. For Aristotle (in this text), the involuntary false-speaker is someone who speaks falsely because that is the sort of person he is: he does not see the truth, and as a result says the thing that is not and conjures the thing that is not in the minds of his hearers. He is like the man who has a real limp. Socrates' intentional false-speaker as understood by Aristotle is someone who pretends to be like the involuntary false-speaker, and in so pretending performs the act of saying what seems to him not to be the case—which is, of course, a different act from that performed by the involuntary false-speaker. Such a person is, it seems best to say, the Augustinian liar, the properly duplicitous person. Aristotle thinks it not clear which of these two acts is worse; he thinks the same about which of these two agents is worse.

In pursuing the question of which is best (act, agent, or both), we might want to know how the involuntary false-speaker got to be that way. Aristotle does not ask or answer this question, but it seems right to say that, just as a limper might have become what he is as a result of something he did (perhaps he mutilated his own foot or caused it to be mutilated by some stupidity or malevolence of his own), and as a result be morally and practically responsible for his condition, so an involuntary false-speaker might have become what he is in the same way. He might have made himself into someone who can't see and doesn't speak the truth by establishing habits of a sort that become ingrained and unshakable. If you recount an experience you've had in a way that seems to you duplicitous, and go on telling the lying story again and again, whenever occasion arises, it's likely that eventually you'll become unclear about what actually happened. You may finally come to believe your own story. When this happens you'll no longer be duplicitous when you tell it, although the fact that you aren't is traceable, causally, to a habit you established intentionally in the first place. You'll then be responsible for the fact that you have become an involuntary false-speaker. But it is also possible that both the limper and the involuntary false-speaker are what they are through no fault of their own: perhaps the limper has suffered an accident over which he had no control, and perhaps the false-speaker has malfunctioning cognitive faculties through no fault of his own. Such considerations would be relevant to the question of whether an involuntary false-speaker is better than an intentional one.

Aristotle does not, however, follow this line of thought. Neither does he address (in this text—nor in a systematic way anywhere else) the question of deep interest to Augustine, which is that of what's wrong with duplicity and whether it may ever justifiably be performed. It's clear that Aristotle thinks there's something wrong with duplicity, that what's wrong with it has something to do with the fact that it produces false-speaking, and that this in turn is implicated with the ontology of lack. But he has nothing to say about the wrongness of duplicity for the duplicitous one, and he does not introduce the Augustinian distinction between duplicity that issues in falsehood and duplicity that does not issue in falsehood—a distinction that, once introduced, forces the question of whether there's anything wrong with duplicity simply as such, independently of whether it results in falsehood.

Aristotle, in these pages from the *Metaphysics*, is perhaps best thought of as a half-Augustinian. He corrects Socrates, rightly, on the question of the involuntary lie; and he makes the connection between falsehood and ontological lack. But he does not have available to him the conceptual distinctions necessary for asking about the lie proper, which is to say that he cannot ask the question of duplicity's acceptability in any systematic fashion. It is clear from what he says elsewhere that he thinks of duplicity as sometimes acceptable even though ordinarily not, which is a position of course unacceptable to an Augustinian, though predictable given the absence of a theory of speech's nature and purposes and of a clear distinction between falsehood and duplicity.

9

Chrysostom

John Chrysostom, the golden-mouthed orator of Antioch and Constantinople, was born a few years before Augustine, probably in 349, to a middle-class family in Antioch. His mother was certainly Christian and his father may have been, though Chrysostom, as was then common, was not baptized until early adulthood. His father died when he was young, and according to his own account he lived at home until his widowed mother (who did not remarry) died, probably in 372 or 373. Chrysostom got the standard education of his time, in all essentials like that received by Augustine. In Chrysostom's case, this education produced someone whose written Greek is, according to those who can judge it, elegant and powerful; and whose preaching (again in Greek) was able to draw and keep huge crowds, reduce them sometimes to tears, and inspire them often to action. Even for someone whose Greek halts and stumbles as mine does, or for someone who can read him only in translation, Chrysostom's rhetorical skills are obvious and moving. In this he is like Augustine: a warm and excitable writer, alive to what can be done with language and eager to deploy its resources to arouse the reader's passions.

Chrysostom's education, and perhaps also his own early intentions, fitted him for the law; he could also, no doubt, have done as Augustine did and entered upon the career of a professional rhetor. But as a young man his inclinations turned him away from these possibilities and toward the ascetical life, which was then drawing many of Antioch's bright young men away from the city and toward the hermits' huts and caves scattered on the hills surrounding the city. Antioch in the late fourth century was in this respect like Alexandria: a few years as a hermit was as likely to be attractive to young men with time, money, and education as a trip to Kathmandu or Bali became to young American men and women similarly situated 1,600 years later. And so, following his mother's death, Chrysostom lived for about six years as a hermit.

He returned to the city in the late 370s, and was ordained deacon in 381 and priest in 386. During the decade or so following his ordination to the priesthood he became increasingly famous as preacher, as exegete (with a special interest in and fascination for the thought of Paul), and (to a lesser extent) as writer. One result of this fame was his appointment in 398 to the see of Constantinople, the principal ecclesiastical seat of the Eastern Empire. This made him among the most prominent figures in the Christian world of the late fourth and early fifth centuries, and it unavoidably embroiled him in the heated theological and political controversies of his time. His influence extended throughout Asia Minor: he traveled extensively, became a focus for controversy himself, and after many vicissitudes was finally unseated as bishop and forced to leave Constantinople. He died in exile in 407 at the age of 58 or 59.

His literary legacy is large, and was composed entirely in Greek. There are early polemical and pastoral works, some dating from before his ordination to the priesthood; there are letters and short treatises from his time as priest in Antioch and as bishop in Constantinople; there is an especially affecting and interesting correspondence with Olympias, a female deacon and head of a women's monastic community in Constantinople—this correspondence continued almost until Chrysostom's death, and is for the modern reader both moving and revealing of the institutional order of the fifth-century Eastern church, and the nature of the relations between men and women then. But the main literary legacy is the sermons. More than nine hundred of these survive, and though their literary style takes some getting used to for twenty-first-century readers, they repay the effort.

The work I'm about to discuss, however, is not among the sermons or the correspondence, but rather belongs to the treatises. Its title is, in Greek, *Peri hierōsunēs*, which may be rendered *Priesthood;* it is often referred to by its Latin title, *De sacerdotio*. Chrysostom composed this work in the late 380s or early 390s. It was certainly finished by 392–393, when we know that Jerome read it in Palestine. It purports to describe events in Chrysostom's life before his mother's death and thus also before his hermit years, which means that it was written at least fifteen years after the events that provide its frame. It has the form of a dialogue between Chrysostom and his close friend, Basil, and it seems on the surface to be partly autobiographical and largely apologetical. That is, it describes and justifies against detractors decisions and actions taken by Chrysostom in the early 370s. Modern scholarship, being what it is, has naturally doubted that it is either autobiographical or apologetical, and has spilled much ink in arguing about whether the events described in the first book of *Priesthood* ever happened, and about what Chrysostom's motives were in depicting them as if they had. None of this will concern me here. What does concern me is that in the first book of *Priesthood* Chrysostom offers a defense of lying, or at least of action aimed at deceit or trickery. But to call it a defense is too weak: it's really a hymn of praise to the lie, and I shall treat it as though Chrysostom means it, with the purpose of offering an Augustinian response to it. (Chrysostom writes, it is almost certain, without knowledge of or intent to respond to what Augustine had written on the lie.)

Priesthood begins with a depiction of an intimate friendship between two young men, Chrysostom and Basil, of the same social class and similar aspirations. They study together and share thoughts and aspirations. Basil is serious and ascetical: he wants to "embrace the blessed life of hermits and the true philosophy." The hermit, the *monakhos*, is the true philosopher, and Christianity is the true philosophy. For Basil, then, to live as the hermit lives is to live as a philosopher and thereby to discover and conform himself to truth. Chrysostom is more worldly and frivolous, and is not yet prepared to abandon the attractions of the world—he likes to go to the law-courts and to the theater—for the life of the hermit. But gradually Basil begins to persuade Chrysostom, and the lawyers' speeches and actors' performances start to lose their beguiling power. Basil then suggests that he and Chrysostom might live together as an initial step in beginning to follow the ascetical life together. But Chrysostom's mother (who by this time has long been a widow) objects in the strongest terms: she makes Chrysostom sit on the very bed in which she'd given birth to him, and expounds in affecting detail the troubles and difficulties that beset young widows. She talks of the *sidēran tēs khēreias . . . kaminon*, the fiery furnace of widowhood, and pleads that Chrysostom will stay with her as supporter and protector until she dies. Chrysostom is convinced, and it is difficult not to be; he wrings every ounce of pathos from the situation that he can. Rarely have the duties of sons to widowed mothers been depicted more persuasively.

Then Chrysostom and Basil learn of a plot to make them priests, to ordain them and thus elevate them to the honorable dignity, the *axioma*, of the priesthood whether they like it or not. The practice of ordaining people against their will is widely mentioned in the Christian literature of this period, and Chrysostom, like many faced with such a prospect, does not like it. It frightens him, and he says that he cannot see that he is worthy of it. This narrative opening provides the occasion for an extended depiction of just what the honor and dignity of the priesthood consists in. The bulk of *Priesthood* is devoted to this, and it is for this that it has been mostly read by subsequent generations. But the story continues before that, and provides the occasion for Chrysostom's hymn of praise to the lie.

Faced with the prospect of forced ordination, Basil and Chrysostom consider their options, which appear to be acquiescence or flight. Basil thinks that he and Chrysostom should come to the same decision and act in accord. But Chrysostom thinks that Basil will make an excellent priest while he himself lacks the necessary virtues and abilities. And so he decides to seek a way to let Basil be ordained while avoiding this for himself. He cannot, he thinks, wound Christ's body by witholding from it a young man as well fitted for priestly governance as Basil; neither can he inflict someone as unworthy as himself upon it. And so he decides, without telling Basil, to act in such a way as to bring it about that Basil is ordained and he is not. Not only does he withhold information about what he intends from Basil: he also leads him to believe that he assents to Basil's view that the two of them ought to respond in the same way to the threat of forced ordination, and that he will do what Basil does. All this is clear from the narrative portion of the first book of *Priesthood*.

When the ordaining crew arrives for Chrysostom, he hides and is not taken. When it arrives for Basil, he does not hide or run, and is taken. Those who take him trick *(ēpatēsan)* him into accepting ordination by giving him to understand, falsely, that Chrysostom has already been taken and has accepted ordination. Basil thinks this likely, and, considering himself bound by what he took to be the promises he and his friend had exchanged to do the same thing in this situation, accepts ordination. When Basil discovers that Chrysostom had avoided ordination, he comes to him in great distress, only to find that his friend is laughing with delight at the outcome. Chrysostom offers praise to God that his stratagem or machination *(mēkhanēs)* has had a good outcome. Basil, naturally enough, is even more upset at this. What can his friend be laughing about? Hasn't he just admitted to deceiving his best friend and leading him thereby into an intolerable situation?

A note on terms. Chrysostom usually uses the noun *apatē* (which is most often rendered into Latin with *dolus*) and its related verbal forms to describe what he has done to Basil. He uses this term, too, to describe what the ordainers did to Basil when they persuaded him that

Chrysostom had accepted ordination. I'll translate this term by "trick" in what follows. It indicates any action (spoken or otherwise) intended to mislead or deceive someone. It is usually a success term, which means that it tends to be used only of successful attempts to mislead or deceive. Chrysostom, then, tricked Basil into thinking that he and Basil were in agreement about their response to the threatened ordination, and he was a trickster in so doing. The same is true of the ordainers' deception of Basil as to what Chrysostom had done. This word, *apatē* (verb, noun, adjective), has also an interesting connection with pleasure. In the Gospels, for example, there is the phrase *hē apatē tou ploutou* (Matt. 13:22; Mark 4:19), which means not only the deceitful tricks of wealth, but also its pleasurable lures. Very often, when trickery is in play, the trick works best by being pleasurable, by luring the one to be tricked with what's pleasurable to him. This is very much in accord with Chrysostom's usage (he laughs with delight at the success of his trick), and this connotation needs to be borne in mind in what follows.

At this point the dialogue proper begins. Basil says that people are saying that Chrysostom refused ordination because he was too arrogant to accept it, and that Basil must have known of his intention to hide from the ordainers, and is therefore implicated with his friend's perceived wrongdoing. How, asks Basil, can he meet these accusations without saying that he knew nothing of Chrysostom's intention? If he says that, won't it show that he and Chrysostom aren't really friends at all?—for friends would have known (as Basil thought he had known) one another's plans. And if he denies knowledge of Chrysostom's escape plan, he'll be thought of as a *pseudos,* a liar, because no one will believe what he says. The text provides an affecting picture of Basil in deep distress: outraged, shaken in his confidence in Chrysostom's friendship, certain that he doesn't understand him as well as he thought he did, and deeply distressed by his own forced ordination. What then? What has Chrysostom to say about his tricks and betrayals? This is the question Basil presses.

Chrysostom answers:

> In what have I wronged you? . . . Is it that I've deceived you, or that I've hidden from you what I intended? But you were tricked for your benefit, as also were those others whom I tricked and to whom I betrayed you. If it's the case that pretense is always wrong and should never be employed even with a good motive, then I'm ready to submit to whatever punishment you like. . . . But if on the other hand an act is not always detrimental but becomes good or bad according to the intention of those doing it, then you should stop reproaching me for having tricked you, and should

show me that I acted for evil. To the extent that this [hypothesis] is not
proved, you shouldn't reproach or accuse me. Instead, it would be just that
those who want to be understood to be right-thinking should approve of
tricksters. In fact, opportune and beneficial trickery done with a proper
purpose has such great advantages that many have been punished for
not using deceit.

This is a rich passage, though also a startling and troubling one. Chrysostom speaks of deceit and trickery and pretense and betrayal. He uses
all these words to describe what he did to Basil and to the ordaining
crew. What, he wants to know, is wrong with these actions, so labeled?
He answers by asserting a principle by which the rightness or wrongness, goodness or badness of an action can be assessed (he offers it as
a hypothesis, but he means it to be taken as true): an act is not intrinsically or always detrimental *(ouk aei to pragma epiblabes),* but rather
becomes good or bad *(phaulon ē kalon)* according to the *proairesis* or
dianoia, the intention or deliberated and deliberate purpose, of the agent.
If the agent acts with good intent, then the action is good. If with bad
intent, then the action is bad. To act for evil is to act with the intention
to bring about an evil result; to act for good is to act with the intention
to bring about a good result. To call a particular act of trickery good in
this sense is to say that it is done in such a way and at such a time that
it is "opportune" *(eukairos)* and "beneficial" *(kerdos)*. Such trickery,
Chrysostom says, is not only beneficial but required: you can be, and
ought to be, punished for not doing it.

He goes on to provide examples. Generals who win battles by trickery
should be praised and imitated more than those who win by open and
straightforward combat. This is partly because battles won by trickery
are less likely to result in large loss of life than those won by ordinary
combat in which the intentions of the general are evident to his opponent.
But it is also because the general who defeats his opposite number by
trickery can claim two victories: a military one and a moral one. The
military victory is given by defeat, plain and simple; the moral victory is
given by the fact that the winning general has shown superior prudent
practical judgment *(phronēsis)*. Prudence is a moral virtue for Chrysostom, as it would have been for most Christian and pagan thinkers at
the time (it is later classified as one of the four cardinal virtues), and
to fail to develop it and exercise it when it's needed is therefore a moral
fault. Trickery in war is, therefore, not merely excusable but positively
virtuous.

Trickery *(apatē)* is also often needed *(khreia)* or necessary *(anankaia)* in politics and household affairs, claims Chrysostom. Michal, David's wife, tricks the soldiers sent by Saul to kill David into thinking that David is still asleep in bed when in fact she's just helped him escape through the window (1 Sam. 19:11–18). This, says Chrysostom, is an example of trickery approved by Scripture—here he uses the verb *paralogizomai* rather than *apataō*, following the Septuagint in doing so (he clearly means the two verbs to be interchangeable). He also mentions, as another example of scripturally approved political trickery, Jonathan's lie to Saul about David's absence from a banquet at which he is expected (1 Sam. 20:4–42): Jonathan says that David has been unexpectedly called away to Bethlehem, when in fact Jonathan knows that David is hiding in his favorite cave and has asked Jonathan to lie to Saul in order to gauge the depth of Saul's murderous intentions.

Trickery is also often and properly used by doctors, says Chrysostom. Imagine a man who has a fever and who refuses all treatments that might alleviate it. All the patient wants and demands is wine, which is the very thing that will aggravate his fever. The doctor's technical skill, his *tekhnē*, is useless in such a case, so he resorts to trickery. He takes a clay vessel and immerses it in wine; then he empties it, fills it with fresh water, and gives it to the sick man, pretending that it's full of wine. The vessel smells of wine because of its immersion, and the sick man drinks its contents thinking that it is wine. He's cured by the water he needs but would not have drunk unless he'd been convinced that it was wine. "Do you see the benefit *(kerdos)* of trickery? If one were to enumerate the ruses *(tous dolous)* of doctors, the list would be infinitely long"—and Chrysostom approves of them all so long as they're well-intentioned and have good results.

"Great," he says, "is the power of trickery, so long as it is not used only with an intention to create a ruse. In such a case [when this is not the sole intention] it should not be called trickery, but rather a kind of good management or wisdom, a technique capable of finding solutions in insoluble cases." Chrysostom here identifies trickery with *oikonomia*, good or skilled management, a term we'll see to be of importance to Jerome and Cassian as well. Doing what needs to be done in order to bring about the result that ought to be brought about—this is *oikonomia*, economical management of action. It is also *sophia*, wisdom, and an admirable technique for solving otherwise insoluble problems. In Chrysostom's time, as in ours, among the most important techniques taught and learned in medical schools appears to have been judicious trickery of patients in what the doctor takes to be their best interests.

This marks the end of Chrysostom's hymn of praise to *apatē*, to trickery and the trickster. The talk in *Priesthood* then turns to whether in fact Basil has reaped any advantage from being tricked, which provides the occasion for Chrysostom's analysis of the duties and gifts of the priesthood, which in turn constitutes the bulk of the work.

Most of Chrysostom's examples and arguments are not directly relevant to deliberately duplicitous speech. Augustinian argument against such speech therefore has no direct purchase on them. However, the principle informing Chrysostom's hymn of praise to trickery is worth comment. Interpreted broadly, it justifies particular actions by appeal to some combination of intention and result. Chrysostom's own tricking of Basil is justified by the former's good intentions (he wanted the best outcome for the church) and by the good result (Basil's ordination and his own avoidance of it is in fact the best outcome for the church). But such a principle is not easily defensible if it is taken to apply to every kind of action. It would justify (and perhaps even require) the torture of children or the incineration of civilian populations with incendiary weapons were it to be extended to all forms of action, for such things might arguably be done with appropriate *proairesis* and might also bring about good results—if "good" means something like "preventive of more suffering than is caused by them." But this is just a form of act-utilitarianism, which is the doctrine that the rightness or wrongness of any particular action is to be assessed exclusively by appeal to its quantifiable results with respect to some univocal and quantifiable understanding of the human good. The criticisms of this family of views are familiar and much rehearsed. Since it's unlikely that Chrysostom intends this view in any case (though his formulations are sufficiently injudicious that he often sounds as if he does), I won't pursue that line of argument further here.

Suppose, then, that what Chrysostom means is only that any trick, any act of *apatē*, ought to be assessed in terms of the agent's intention and the goodness of the outcome. It is likely that he does mean this. Suppose, too, that we restrict discussion to what Augustine would be happy to call lies (deliberately duplicitous speech). These are certainly included in Chrysostom's defense of the trick: he is prepared to defend his own lies to Basil and the doctor's lies to the feverish wine-bibber. As he writes the story, it is perfectly reasonable to suppose his saying to Basil, "I'll accept ordination if you will," while at the same time thinking, "I won't accept ordination under any circumstances." And as he constructs the story of the doctor and the wine-bibber, the doctor might say, "Here's your wine," while thinking, "Here's your water." These utterances would be lies according to Augustine's definition, and tricks (or contributions to tricks) according to Chrysostom's understanding. They fall under an Augustinian ban and are embraced by Chrysostom's permission.

For Chrysostom, there is nothing about speech that makes duplicitous use of it problematic as a matter of principle. He does not hesitate (not, anyway, in the first book of *Priesthood*) to praise the lie. Speech is presented by him as a morally neutral device to be deployed for good ends according to the demands of prudence. The doctor may (or should) say, "Here's your wine," if well-intentioned prudence suggests that he should; Chrysostom may (or should) say that he'll do what Basil does for just the same reasons. What's missing is any attention to the question of speech's nature and proper use. Chrysostom's assumption is that it has no nature and therefore no proper use. This is an assumption made without argument or justification, and one that does not sit well with much in Scripture and tradition.

On Chrysostom's view it would follow, for example, that one might prudentially and with good result blaspheme—insult or curse God's name, call him out of that name—and in so doing offend at least against the second commandment. Any argument against blasphemy's defensibility (which Chrysostom of course does not think defensible) would have to advert to the nature and proper uses of speech, to what God gave and intended it for. The lack of any such attention in Chrysostom's blanket justification of the lie on prudentially consequentialist grounds has implications that would be likely to disturb Chrysostom himself. It is this lack that makes his hymn of praise to trickery unacceptable as it stands.

Augustine, it's worth recalling, does permit some tricks. Jacob's deceit of Isaac would be called *apatē* by Chrysostom, and Augustine not only permits but praises it. He also, with only a few hesitations, permits jokes by excluding them from the category of the lie—though it doesn't follow from this exclusion that he's happy always to judge them proper or just. But he permits and defends particular tricks always on the same ground: that for those who perform them, what they signify or mean is a truth, which entails that they are not genuinely duplicitous. Jacob's claim to be Esau signifies (at least) two truths: that he is the one worthy of the inheritance, which is a literal truth; and, figuratively, that the inheritance has passed from the Jews (the older brother) to the Christians (the younger). Jesus' claim that there was a man who had two sons signifies among other things the truth that repentance is always possible. The justification given for these apparently lying tricks is also that given for figurative discourse in general: that the figurative claim

(Jesus is a rock) expresses a truth in the mind of its utterer (Jesus is always reliable).

Tricks can be of the right sort, then, even for Augustine. They need not entail duplicity. But can the doctor's tricking of the wine-bibber or Chrysostom's of Basil be of the right sort? No. Augustine discusses a case of this kind: imagine a doctor treating a very sick man whose equally sick son has just died. The sick man does not know of his son's death. He's desperate to know how his son does, but the doctor judges that telling him that his son is dead will bring the sick man rapidly to death himself. Should the doctor then say that the son still lives? Augustine says no: although such a lie is comfortable and easy, one to which many (including Augustine himself) will be strongly attracted, it remains duplicitous and therefore subject to all the usual strictures. It is not figurative, not a trick of the right sort, because there is no truth that it seems to the speaker figuratively to signify. It is therefore not like storytelling or prophecy, and as a result is beyond the reach of justification. It is, simply, sin. The same must be said about Chrysostom's tricks: his lies to Basil do not seem to him to figure some truth. He does not, of course, claim that they do. He claims only that his duplicitous speech was preceded by a good intention and followed by a good result, which is certainly the case. But this does nothing to remove its lying character.

Chrysostom's praise of the trick is also, in part, praise of the lie. This means that he praises sin, and in praising it praises action indistinguishable in its essentials from adultery or blasphemy. This is not coherent: commendation and encouragement of sin is commendation and encouragement of actions whose coherent performance is not possible. Commending such action is like commending the weight lifter's diet to the jockey. To resist this conclusion it would be necessary to resist also the view that human speech has a nature and a purpose, a nature given to it by the fact that we, the speakers, are formed in God's triune image, and a purpose given by the fact that breaching the invocation of thought in speech breaches, analogically, the relation between divine and incarnate word. It is striking that Chrysostom shows no awareness that the question of speech's nature and purpose needs even to be raised and answered in the light of specifically Christian conviction. In this he is not different from Plato or Aristotle, and the fact that he does not think of speech in terms of trinitarian conviction vitiates his defense of well-intentioned economizing with speech. In so thinking he is simply not thinking with sufficient seriousness as a Christian about the topic. To economize with the gift is to refuse to return it fully to its giver; to apply the category of economy to the gift is possible only if what is given is not fully understood as gift. An Augustinian reading of Chrysostom's hymn of praise to the lie sharpens and deepens the conviction that refusal of an Augustinian theology of the lie makes permission and advocacy of duplicity seductively attractive.

10

Jerome

In 394 or 395, when Augustine was about forty and shortly before he became bishop in Hippo, he began a correspondence with Jerome. They were separated by more than a thousand miles: Jerome was in Palestine, and Augustine in North Africa, and while the correspondence continued at intervals until Jerome's death in 419 or 420, it was often bedeviled by lost letters, misunderstandings, and the difficult intellectual temperament of both men. Jerome, nine years older and (at the beginning of the correspondence) considerably better known than Augustine, took offense easily and at first did not take Augustine very seriously. He responded to Augustine's queries and suggestions with condescension and insult. And Augustine, for his part, showed an aggressive confidence in the rightness of his own views, and was not (as he probably should have been) much impressed by Jerome's seniority, fame, and accomplishments, eagerly criticizing him even on his strongest ground, which was the establishment of a good scriptural text and the interpretation of its particularities. Jerome was at home with Hebrew and Greek, while Augustine had no Hebrew and relatively little Greek. But this did not stop him from calling Jerome's translations and methods into question. The letters thawed in tone a little as the correspondence progressed (especially when the two men came to agree on the necessity of combating Pelagius and his followers), but they never became entirely cordial.

Augustine's first letter to Jerome was probably prompted by his reading of Jerome's commentary on Paul's letter to the Galatians. In the second chapter of that letter, Paul had some harsh things to say about Peter and Barnabas:

And when Kephas [Peter] came to Antioch, I opposed him to his face, because he clearly was wrong. For, until some people came from James, he used to eat with the Gentiles; but when they came, he began to draw back and separated himself, because he was afraid of the circumcised. And the rest of the Jews [also] acted hypocritically along with him, with the result that even Barnabas was carried away by their hypocrisy. But when I saw that they were not on the right road in line with the truth of the gospel, I said to Kephas in front of all, "If you, though a Jew, are living like a Gentile and not like a Jew, how can you compel the Gentiles to live like Jews?" (Gal. 2:11–14)

Paul's accusation is on the face of it strong and direct. Peter, he says, is acting hypocritically (the Greek word *hupokrisei* was rendered by *simulatio* in the Latin version known to Augustine) out of fear. He pretends to think it necessary to withdraw from table-fellowship with Gentiles because he is frightened of what some Jewish Christians ("the circumcised") might do or say if they saw him eating unclean food in an unclean setting—which he would necessarily do if he lived and ate with Gentiles, Christian or not. The faction whose opinion Peter fears advocated observance of Jewish dietary law at least for Jewish Christians, and perhaps also for all Christians. Peter's conduct is a hypocritical pretense in Paul's judgment because it signals agreement to a position Peter does not in fact hold. Paul thought that Peter did not need to observe Jewish dietary law because he had been freed from such demands by his faith in Christ. The offense of taking up such observance again after having dropped it was made worse in Paul's eyes because it seemed to imply that gentile Christians need to obey Jewish law. Paul's understanding of the gospel made the rejection of any such view of the law of quite central importance, and this was why he said that Peter and Barnabas were not acting consistently with the truth of the gospel.

Jerome, in what he'd written about this passage in his commentary on Galatians, had claimed that Paul did not really think that Peter and Barnabas were offending against gospel truth or exhibiting hypocrisy by withdrawing from table-fellowship with Gentiles. Paul, says Jerome, knew perfectly well that Peter was acting according to the principles of good and compassionate management *(dispensatio)* of time and re-sources: Peter was not and did not think he was genuinely subject to the dietary requirements of the Jewish law, but he pretended (used *simulatio*) that he was in order to prevent possible offense to Jewish Christians. Paul understood this, and pretended (*simulatio* again) to rebuke Peter in order to prevent possible offense to gentile Christians. On Jerome's reading, the narrative in Galatians 2 presents two instances of compassionately managed pretense: it does not depict, as the surface of the text might seem to suggest, a church divided against itself, with one of its two most important representatives (Paul) accusing the other (Peter) of hypocrisy. Paul's words, according to Jerome, were soothing medicine: he did not think Peter a hypocrite, even though he called him one; and he called him a hypocrite only as a tactical rhetorical device.

Jerome's concern is with the unity of the church. When he claims that Paul used a tactical rhetorical device in Galatians 2 (and he is explicit in comparing what Paul wrote about Peter there with the rhetorical exercises of the schools and the law-courts), he does not think that this amounts to saying that Paul was a *mendax*, a liar. He does not, anyway, use that word in the relevant section of his Galatians commentary. Paul, in Jerome's eyes, had good ends in mind and used ordinary rhetorical means to pursue them, and in saying this he is entirely in accord with the norms of the rhetorical schools. Augustine recalls being asked to compose a speech supposed to have been spoken by Juno in her anger over the fact that she was not able to keep the king of Troy out of Italy. He knew, he says, and his hearers also knew, that Juno had never spoken these words: the words he composed would be *figmentorum poeticorum vestigia*, the traces of poetic imaginings. It is just such traces that Jerome thinks Paul has left in Galatians.

Augustine reacted to this line of interpretation with high-toned horror and indignation. Jerome's view introduced, he thought, the lie into Scripture itself. It permitted Paul to have written what seemed to him false at the time he wrote, and to have done so with the intention of deceiving his readers. Augustine thought this a disastrous move:

> Once any useful lie is admitted into such a high authority, no part of these [scriptural] books that seems to anyone difficult with respect to conduct or incredible with respect to faith will escape being referred by this same most pernicious rule to the stratagems or compassionate politeness of a lying author.

Augustine thought that Jerome's interpretation of Galatians meant that he attributed the "useful lie," the *mendacium officiosum*, to Paul, and that he therefore thought that Scripture might contain other lies of this sort. The useful lie is one told with good intentions, one that the liar thinks will have good effects and that he may take himself to be required by duty to tell. Telling the useful lie may be a matter of diplomacy, of *politesse*, of etiquette, or of compassion, and may at times hover on the edge of being (or being thought of as) a duty ("duty" is the most common meaning of the Latin word *officium*). When Augustine accused Jerome of attributing this kind of lie to Paul, he meant that Jerome thought Paul was telling diplomatically compassionate lies, lies told principally in order to comfort gentile Christians who might have been scandalized by the thought that they should observe the law, and lies that might be thought not only permissible because useful, but also required because necessary. Augustine often uses the term *officiosum* in this sense of useful/necessary himself, for example when he discusses the propriety of the patriarchs' polygamous habits.

Augustine did not question Jerome's view that lies can be well-intentioned and may have good effects. He was arguing as much himself in his first treatise on lying, which he was writing at about the same time as this first letter to Jerome. His claim was rather that permitting such lies to scriptural authors makes the job of interpreting Scripture impossible. It becomes too easy for the interpreter faced with a difficult passage to say that its author didn't mean it but was telling a useful lie. Anything unpalatable—Jesus' teaching on marriage and divorce, for example—can easily be set aside in this way, and the interpreter's authority will then be elevated above that of Scripture. The interpreter who thinks that Scripture contains useful lies can treat it like a wax nose by deciding which parts are noble truths and which useful lies. Augustine himself is often accused of treating Scripture in just this way by appealing to typology and allegory in order to interpret it. The difference, in Augustine's mind, was that principles of interpretation can be given that, when properly applied, will yield a decision as to when (and when not) to bring typological or allegorical methods to bear on the scriptural text. He did not think this possible for those who say that there are lies in Scripture. Augustine thought that heretics have often treated Scripture in this way, and that the only safeguard is to adopt the rule of interpretation that the scriptural authors do not lie. Augustine therefore asked Jerome to write a *palinode*, which is a pointed way of asking for a recantation, of his interpretation of Galatians 2 as containing a useful lie.

Jerome was pleased by none of this. He did not like having his authority as interpreter of Scripture challenged by a whippersnapper like Augustine, especially when the challenger appeared innocent of the Greek commentarial tradition that Jerome was following in claiming that Galatians 2 is a tissue of *simulatio*. Where, he wants to know, are Augustine's authorities? Where his textual support? These are the traditional responses of the senior scholar who has paid his dues and quarried his learning from the hard rock of Hebrew and Greek to the

junior who has put in no such effort and who shows insufficient respect. But the argument did not proceed only by appeal to authoritative
commentarial tradition. It moved also to the question of what Peter's
refusal to share food with Gentiles really meant; to analysis of the relation between the accounts preserved in the Acts of the Apostles about
the necessity of observing the law and this disputed text in Galatians;
and to what to say about whether it has at any time been proper for
Jewish or gentile Christians to observe the law. On this last question,
Augustine thought that at the time of Paul and Peter, Jewish Christians
ought neither to have been dissuaded from observance nor persuaded
to it, while Jerome thought that observance had never been defensible
for Jewish Christians, and was not at the time he was writing. This disagreement goes deep and has many ramifications. Its details are not of
interest here, however; we need only note that among Jerome's reasons
for rejecting the Augustinian interpretive rule that bans the lie from the
pen of scriptural authors is that it implies an unacceptable view on the
disputed question of observing the law. Augustine denied that the view
it implies is unacceptable.

Jerome does take up the terminological question that Augustine
had forced upon him. He repeats his interpretation of Paul's words in
Galatians 2:11–14, but in response to Augustine's criticisms he emphasizes that he wants to call those words *honesta dispensatio* rather than
officiosum mendacium. *Dispensatio* is not an easy word to translate in
this context. It's the usual Latin word used to render the Greek *oikonomia*, which occurs often (and usually with positive connotations) in
the New Testament. These words mean, roughly, to pay out or appor-
tion something according to the needs and merits of the recipients; the
dispensator is an administrator or manager or steward who skillfully
and appropriately orders the affairs committed to his charge; and to
act *dispensative* is to act with the pragmatic skills of the good manager
in response to the necessities of the situation, or to act under the direction of such a manager. These terms are most often used of financial
administrators who must distribute money or material goods, but for
Jerome here they are used of speakers who must distribute words.
Paul's rebuke of Peter is, for Jerome, an honest and compassionate act
of pragmatic verbal skill, a coining and distribution of words entirely
appropriate to the situation to which and in which he speaks. Paul,
on this view, says the best that could be said. Jerome's substitution of
honesta dispensatio for *mendacium officiosum* is motivated principally
by the need to avoid the word *mendacium*, "lie"; but what is meant by
the two phrases is approximately the same in his view. Certainly, both

phrases label a duplicitous act of speech, and therefore also one that Augustine would call *mendacium*.

Augustine, predictably, seized upon this term *dispensatio* like an angry terrier with a rat: "I'd like to know," he writes, "just what you meant when you said, '[Those under the law] not by pragmatic necessity *(dispensative)*, as our ancestors intended, [but really *(vere)*].' " Augustine here refers to a phrase used by Jerome in an earlier letter when explaining some passages from the fifth chapter of Galatians. Jerome had claimed that in those passages Paul was talking about those "really" *(vere)* under the law, and not about those, like himself and Peter, who sometimes pretended (by *simulatio*) to be under the law, and hence were under it only *dispensatively*, by pragmatic and compassionately motivated necessity.

Augustine continued: "Either this is what I'd label a useful lie *(officiosum mendacium)*, in which case this good management *(dispensatio)* would be a useful or honest act of lying—or I can't at all see what it is, unless perhaps the use of the words 'good management' *(dispensatio)* makes a lie not a lie?" Augustine here presents Jerome as trying to avoid use (and endorsement) of the term "lie" *(mendacium)* by now calling it *dispensatio*, the good management of words motivated by pragmatic necessity. The attempt fails, he thinks. Jerome's acts of verbal good management are no different from lies: they are all, Augustinianly speaking, just duplicitous speech, and should plainly be called so.

Augustine is not objecting to the very idea of *dispensatio*. He uses the word often, and usually in a positive sense. He applies it even to the incarnation, frequently calling it *carnis dispensatio*, an "economy of the flesh," a use of human flesh by God for good purposes. So to use flesh is God's good management, God's appropriate stewardship, and so there is a perfectly proper use of the term and the idea it refers to. What Augustine does object to is the idea that the lie can be justified by classifying it as a kind of *dispensatio*, a kind of economically appropriate use of words. This, he thinks, is sleight of hand.

Augustine goes on:

Is it the case that those who lie usefully are to be blamed, while those who do so by pragmatic necessity are to be approved? Do those who think this judge that one may lie when one chooses? It is a great question whether a good man may sometimes lie, or whether a Christian may.... But this, as I've said, is a different and important question; those who think that one may lie should choose [the justification] they want, so long as it is unshakably believed and defended that those who wrote sacred Scripture—and most especially the canonical books—were completely free from the lie.

This passage effectively ends the debate between Augustine and Jerome about lying. More letters are exchanged, but they are on other topics, and Jerome never responds to the demand made here. Augustine establishes, he thinks, that Jerome's distinction between *honesta dispensatio* and *officiosum mendacium* is not one that marks a real conceptual difference: whatever is called good verbal management may also be called a useful lie, and because both phrases indicate what Augustine calls, simply, the lie, duplicitous speech intended to deceive, they must both be rejected. But this is a point about terminology only. It says nothing about the *magna quaestio*, the great question of whether this act may properly be undertaken by anyone. This great question, Augustine says, is different from that discussed by Jerome and himself. That debate had been about whether those who wrote sacred Scripture can be said or thought to have lied, and on this he reiterates his position that they cannot.

The greater question is about whether lying can be justified at all, and on this Augustine does not engage Jerome in any way. He has a position on it, of course, as we have seen, and it is one that covers all cases of lying, not just that of lying on the part of scriptural authors. It might seem surprising that Augustine does not explain or defend his position on the broader question when discussing the narrower one with Jerome. After all, if his position on this broader question is the right one, it suggests a conclusion on the narrower one. If no one may justifiably lie, then it follows at once that no scriptural author may justifiably lie. But this is not the conclusion Augustine wants. Scriptural authors, he and Jerome both agree, are not free from sin (the account of David's adultery and murder in 2 Sam. 11–12 is the story most often mentioned by both of them to illustrate sin on the part of a scriptural author—David is a scriptural author for them because they assume that he wrote the Psalms), and so it would not follow from the claim that no one ought ever to lie that no scriptural author has ever done so. Augustine therefore argues, in his debate with Jerome, for a thesis on lying additional to the claim that it ought never to be done. This additional thesis (that no scriptural authors lie in the canonical books) is grounded independently of Augustine's larger claim, and that is why he does not appeal to that larger claim when he argues for it. In the passage translated immediately above, in fact, he explicitly rejects the need for discussing the greater question when the topic at hand is the lesser one.

Some further distinctions may be useful, although they take us beyond the scope of the present inquiry. First, to say that scriptural authors do not lie (do not represent what they take not to be the case in words preserved for us in Scripture) is not the same as claiming scriptural inerrancy. This is so because a scriptural author may err even while writing what seems to him to be the case. Augustine's definition of the lie makes this clear in distinguishing error from the lie. Augustine did also hold a subtle and interesting version of the view that Scripture does not err (one that could usefully instruct many contemporary defenders of scriptural inerrancy), but since this has nothing to do with the question of the lie, it will have to remain unexplored here. Second, the thesis that no scriptural author lies is not quite the same as the claim that no lie is endorsed in Scripture. It is at least conceptually possible that a scriptural author might endorse someone else's lie without ever writing one of his own. Perhaps the account of the Egyptian midwives' lies to Pharaoh (Exod. 1:15–22) suggests that the author of Exodus endorses that lie; and perhaps the account of Rahab's lie to the king of Jericho's men (Joshua 2) suggests the same about the author of Joshua. Augustine does not think so, and says much in support of his view; but this too is a topic not to be pursued further here.

It is unfortunate that Jerome did not respond to Augustine's fundamental position on lying. He probably never had occasion fully to understand it: there is no evidence that he read Augustine's first treatise on lying (it would be surprising if he had since Augustine did not wish it to have wide circulation, and there is, so far as I know, no evidence of its being read or responded to by anyone during Augustine's life), and the second was not written until after Jerome's death. This denies us an engagement on the matter between the two most influential fourth-century thinkers writing in Latin. Both were, in their way, ethical rigorists, and both typically attempted to derive their positions on ethical questions from fundamental Christian doctrine and from scriptural exegesis. Such an engagement would have been of great interest. But the advantage of the fact that Jerome and Augustine's discussion of the lie is limited to that of the scriptural lie is that it shows with great clarity that Augustine's view on the latter is distinct from his view on the general question. It suggests also that the Augustinian rule of interpretation which denies the lie to any scriptural author is held with vigor. Augustine would not, I think, have abandoned it even if the difficulties of reading Galatians and Acts on the question of Jewish-Christian observance of the law had been more severe than they are (or than he thinks they are). The interpretive rule that Scripture should be read as though scriptural authors wrote what they took to be the case had something close to unrestricted primacy for him: almost any contradictory rule of interpretation would have been rejected by him simply because it was contradictory. It is hard to imagine the conditions under which he would have abandoned it.

The debate also shows us that when a Christian thinker defends the propriety of acts of speech that fall under the Augustinian definition of the lie (as Jerome did with *honesta dispensatio*), such a defense is likely to involve a different view of speech and thought than that argued by Augustine in his systematic work on *mendacium*, and, concomitantly, different judgment about the relevance of attempts to justify particular lies on the ground of their good intentions or good results. Augustine's position makes such consequentialist arguments utterly irrelevant, and since he takes this irrelevance to follow from a proper understanding of thought, speech, and sin, a full engagement by a Christian thinker with his ban on the lie would have to confront what he says about these things. The debate with Jerome offers no such confrontation. Jerome's justification of Paul's supposed economies of speech simply assumes that good intentions and good results may justify or even require the lie.

Jerome's defense of the scriptural lie presupposes, then, a more general understanding of the lie's permissibility: if lies in Scripture are sometimes defensible, then lies in general must sometimes be defensible. Jerome was versed in the Greek traditions of scriptural commentary and ascetical theology, and he assumes the more general understanding of the lie scattered broadside in that tradition—as for example in Chrysostom's *Priesthood*, discussed above, and it is possible that the general defense of the lie found in its first chapter was in his mind as he debated Augustine by letter in later years on the more particular question of scriptural lies. The theoretical underpinnings of Jerome's position on the scriptural lie are found in the Greek tradition generally, and more particularly in Clement of Alexandria, Origen, and Chrysostom. I turn now to a consideration of John Cassian, a bridge-figure between the Greek and Latin Christian worlds.

11

Cassian

In the late 420s in Southern France, a monk from what is now Romania put the finishing touches to a large work on the goals, methods, and final purposes of the Christian life. This work, written in Latin, is called *Conlationes,* or *Conferences* in English. Its author was John Cassian, an almost exact contemporary of Augustine. Cassian had traveled and lived in most of the centers of the Christian world in the late fourth and early fifth centuries: for a time in a Palestinian monastery; then in and around Alexandria as the hermits and quasi-monks were following Antony's footsteps ever deeper into the silence and solitude of the desert; next in Constantinople, when John Chrysostom was bishop there, and at whose hands he was ordained deacon; next briefly in Rome, where he was ordained priest; and finally in Marseilles, where he founded at least two monasteries and wrote (or compiled) the works for which he is now remembered—including the *Conferences.*

Cassian's travels marked him as one of the last Christians to be equally at home in both the Greek-using Christian world and a Latin-using West that was already beginning to forget its Greek. Unlike Augustine, Cassian was (almost certainly) as capable of writing in Greek as Latin; and although he is considerably less subtle and interesting a thinker than Augustine, what he wrote shows much more familiarity with Greek theology than is evident in Augustine's work. Cassian's travels were in part driven by his abiding concern to understand how the still-new ascetical and monastic movements could contribute to and form an understanding of what Christian life is and is for. The *Conferences* is devoted entirely to this theme.

It purports to record conversational advice given to Cassian (and Germanus, his friend and travelling companion) by the Abbas whom they consulted during their years on the edges of the desert around Alexandria. "Abba" is the Aramaic word for father, but it is also the word used by Jesus to address God as his father (as for example in Mark 14: 36), and is thus a title of high but intimate dignity. The Abbas were reputed to be athletes of the life of ascetical prayer, as well as people from whom teaching on moral questions could usefully be sought. They were the charismatic figures of the early monastic movements in Egypt, and Cassian's *Conferences* appears to preserve for us twenty-four conversations with several among them. Each conference takes the form of a question or questions raised by Cassian or Germanus (usually Germanus) and a disquisition in response by the Abba of the day. There is occasional local color: the location is described, the sleeping or eating or praying arrangements are mentioned, and so on. But for the most part, each conference is a dialogue in which Cassian and Germanus are the passive partners, the straight men, and the Abba the teacher who does most of the talking.

What Cassian gives us is clearly not a verbatim record of what he heard the Abbas say, and I shall treat their words as his opinions. I do not mean by doing this to suggest that none of what he wrote is derived from what the Abbas taught him. I have no opinion on this, other than that there are some clear signs in some of the conferences that Cassian is responding to theological controversies that arose only after the time he spent in Egypt, and that he is happy to use the voice of the Abbas to do so. For example, in the thirteenth conference he has Abba Chaeremon speak in good set terms to what look very much like Augustine's complex views on grace and freedom as these developed in the anti-Pelagian works composed after 405. But whatever the truth about the balance between Cassian's voice and those of the Abbas in the *Conferences,* it is clear that Cassian intended not only to transmit but to endorse what he transmitted. It is quite reasonable, then, to take the *Conferences* principally as evidence of his own judgments about the matters discussed.

There is no doubt that Cassian knew about Augustine. Almost no one in the Christian world with intellectual or literary interests could have failed to do so by the end of the first decade of the fifth century, and Cassian names Augustine in what may have been his last work, an anti-Nestorian christological text. It's also likely that Augustine's thought is in play in a number of the conferences, especially when the topic is one to which Augustine gave a lot of attention. One of the conferences, the seventeenth, deals in part and at some length with the question of the lie. It's natural enough, then, to wonder whether Cassian knew Augustine's work on the topic, and whether he was responding directly to it in this conference. Unfortunately, no clear answer can be given. Cassian certainly could have known either or both of Augustine's treatises on the lie, and could also have known those parts of the Augustine-Jerome correspondence that had, against the wishes of both, become public. Both the chronology and the geography of Cassian's life and work permit this: the *Conferences* was not completed until the late 420s, some years after the second of Augustine's treatises on the lie, and three decades or so after his first. But it is unlikely that Cassian is responding directly to Augustine in the seventeenth conference. While what Cassian writes there is at variance with the line taken by Augustine, he shows no awareness of some of the most characteristically Augustinian moves, including the Augustinian definition of the lie itself. It is better to proceed on the assumption that Cassian writes on the lie independently of particular knowledge of Augustine's arguments about it. If he did know those arguments, he failed signally to represent or respond to them.

The *mise-en-scène* of the seventeenth conference is a problem of promise-breaking that presses itself upon Cassian and Germanus. They had come to Egypt from a monastery in Palestine, and before they left that monastery had bound themselves by solemn promise to a speedy return. Their intention was to learn what they could from the Abbas, and then to return to Palestine to put it into practice there. But now they have come to think that they need to stay in Egypt for a considerable time in order to learn how to practice what they have been taught. If they leave soon, as they promised they would, they will, they think, suffer a *summum detrimentum*, a great harm to their progress in the spiritual life. But if they stay, more fully to chew on and digest Egyptian wisdom, they will run the risk of lying *(mendacium)* and perjury *(periuria)* that is associated with the breaking of promises *(sponsiones, promissiones, definitiones)*. What then should they do? They ask Abba Joseph for a resolution of what seems to them a dilemma.

The connection Cassian makes between promise-breaking and lying is the first problem. Germanus's formulation of the difficulty he and Cassian are in suggests that Cassian is thinking of the two as close to identical. This is odd. If a promise is sincerely made at one time and then later broken (which is roughly what Cassian means by *periuria*), there has been, in Augustinian terms, no lie, no duplicitous speech. When the promise was made, if it was made sincerely, the one who made it fully intended to keep it: there was no gap between speech and thought. The promise's later breaking may well be morally problematic, but it is not an example of the lie. Reasons to criticize promise-breaking will therefore not be the same as reasons to criticize the lie. Why then does Cassian bring the two so closely together? It is difficult to be sure because one of the striking lacks in Cassian's discussion of lying and promise-breaking in the seventeenth conference (not remedied elsewhere) is any attempt at defining what it is to lie or what it is to break a promise. The reader is forced to look at the examples he offers, and to reason back from those to what he might mean by lying. I'll return to this difficulty, but before doing so it's important to restate Cassian's defense of at least occasional lying and promise-breaking, however exactly these are understood.

The central concern of the *Conferences,* and of Cassian's work as a whole, is to describe the central point, the *scopos,* and the final goal, the *finis,* of the monastic life, which is in turn depicted as the ideal type of the Christian life in general. The central point is the attainment of *cordis puritas,* purity of heart; and the final goal, for which purity of heart is utterly necessary, is entry into the kingdom of heaven, which will only be achieved finally and irrevocably after death. The heart is purified by prayer, principally, and by removal of obstacles to prayer, among the most important of which are the unrestrained and disordered passions. The Christian life, on this view, is understood as progress toward a particular end, and this suggests (though does not immediately entail or require) that when a Christian is faced with a particular ethical or practical question—"should I do this or should I not?"—she should answer by considering only whether doing or not doing what is at issue best serves purity of heart. And this is often just what Cassian recommends, frequently under the description of "salutary discretion" *(discretio salutaris)* or "advantageous counsel" *(salubre consilium).* What he wants is flexibility, not legalistic rigor; and he wants it because he thinks it better serves the central point and final goal of the Christian life.

Consider the following passage, spoken by Abba Joseph in response to the initial question about whether promise-breaking is ever defensible:

> When a thoughtless promise has brought you to a situation in which you will suffer grievous harm whichever alternative you take, your choice should turn to the option in which the costs are more tolerable or may more easily be given satisfaction for. . . . In every situation, therefore, consider the final goal of the course of your life, and be guided by it. If we judge on the basis of later and more salutary advice that we have made an inferior choice, it is preferable to change to the better by abandoning

the worse than to subject ourselves to worse sins by obstinately sticking to what we'd already promised.

Cassian here accepts the possibility of a genuine ethical dilemma, one in which sin will result whatever you do—one, that is to say, in which any action you perform will be a sin. If you're bound by an unsuitable promise (Cassian calls it *inconsulta*, "thoughtless," suggesting that more thought and better advice would have permitted you to avoid it at the outset), you'll sin if you break it by going back on your sincerely given word, and you'll sin if you keep it by making yourself subject *peccatis gravioribus*, to heavier or worse sins. In such a dilemma, the only proper course is to start weighing the costs of each sin, and to decide to do the one that will cost you least, the one in which *tolerabiliora dispendia*, "the costs are more tolerable." You must, in short, submit yourself to consequentialist reasoning, and not only that: your reasoning about costs and benefits must be guided by a single overarching principle, which is that of the *scopos*, the central point of the Christian life—which, recall, is purity of heart. The result in the case of Germanus and Cassian's problem is clear: they should break their promise because doing so will better serve their final goal than will keeping it.

The passage just translated suggests that Cassian assimilates sin to harm. Anything that detracts from progress toward the attainment of purity of heart is certainly a harm in his view, because progress toward that goal is the greatest good, and anything that hinders it must therefore be a harm. But Cassian is usually equally happy to call such harms sins. The slippage from harm to sin is clear enough in the passage translated, and is found scattered broadside through his work. Particular sins, for Augustine, are always a matter of the will, of decision and intention on the part of the sinner. But harms, clearly, can be done to you without or against your will: you can be killed, tortured, imprisoned, quite without consent. It is this tendency to assimilate the idea of harm to that of sin that makes it possible for Cassian to recognize the possibility of genuine dilemmas, of situations in which (what he calls) sin is unavoidable, in which whatever you do will be a sin. This is not a possibility for Augustine. For him, there is no situation in which we must sin, for we can always refuse to act. This may entail great harm, to ourselves or to others, but it does not (or need not) involve us in sin. There are therefore no dilemmas in the strict sense, none that involve sin's inevitability.

For Cassian, however, there are dilemmas, or at least situations in which harm-assimilated-to-sin cannot be avoided. His own and Germanus's situation in Egypt is one. They would sin by deciding to keep their promise and return to the Palestinian community, for this would be to postpone and perhaps altogether prevent further progress toward *cordis puritas*, and any decision to do that is a decision to undergo great harm. But they would also sin by deciding to stay in Egypt and thus breaking their promise, for promises do in fact bind, and it is therefore sinful to break them. And yet they must either stay or go, which is to say that they must sin. It is in situations like this that Cassian advocates the consequentialist calculation mentioned in the extract given above: figure out, if you can, which course of action involves the least weighty sin/harm/damage, and do that. This is why he represents Abba Joseph as advising promise-breaking in this situation.

To this point the discussion has been about promise-breaking rather than the lie. But now Germanus quotes Matthew 5:37, on letting your yes be yes and your no be no, and asks whether this doesn't mean that Christians are bound by their words. Abba Joseph's response shows that he takes this text to apply indifferently to promise-breaking and lying, since both are examples of refusing to be bound by one's speech. From this point onward, the conversation in the seventeenth conference moves back and forth without apparent tension or difficulty between examples of promise-breaking and of lying. Both are treated with the same conceptual frame and are given the same potential justification. The first element in this we've already seen: recognition that dilemmas are possible and resolution of them by application of a consequentialist calculus.

The second element in Cassian's justification of occasional lying or promise-breaking is the assertion of the primacy of intention over result. "God," he says, "does not search into the outcome of what you do, but rather into the mind's goal." The question of *processus*, of outcome, is here contrasted with that of *mentis destinatio*, the goal at which the mind aims when it undertakes a particular action. The latter is what counts and is what ought to be paid principal attention to when you consider whether to do something. Your lie or your promise-breaking may turn out well or badly, which is to say that it may or may not be instrumental in your advance toward purity of heart. Whether it will cannot be fully known to you when you make the decision to lie or to break your promise; neither can the extent of collateral harms brought about by it. This, however, doesn't matter. What counts in God's eyes is the aim or intention with which you undertake the action. If this is appropriate, then your decision to undertake the action will also be appropriate, even if the outcome is bad.

At first blush it seems that this emphasis on intention over result stands in tension with the first element in Cassian's justification of the lie, which was that you should apply a consequentialist calculus when faced with a dilemma. If what makes your action right in the face of a dilemma is that your intention is right—that your action has the right goal—then why should you need to pay attention to what the consequences of your action are likely to be? Why must you consider which of your two courses of action subjects you to the graver sins? But this difficulty can be resolved. What Cassian means is that the mind's goal ought always to be purity of heart, and that when this is its goal, its primary and ultimate intention, it will at once follow in the case of an apparent dilemma that choice will be made of the action that seems best suited to serve that goal. Such choice will inevitably involve some assessment of outcome: Cassian and Germanus will, if they have the *scopos* of monastic life as their mind's goal, inevitably assess the merit of promise-breaking over promise-keeping in terms of which is likely best to serve that goal. But Cassian's view is that they don't have to be correct in the assessment they make. They have only to be sincere in their making of it in the light of an aspiration toward purity of heart. If they are, it will follow that they have done the right thing: "There is no harm in setting aside a rash promise so long as the *scopos,* the pious goal undertaken, is held to."

But Germanus is still uneasy. Isn't it the case, he asks, that there are direct and unambiguous scriptural injunctions that forbid the lie? Can these be properly circumvented by appeal to aspiration for purity of heart? Abba Joseph's response to this makes use of an idea already familiar from the debate between Jerome and Augustine: that of the divine *oikonomias* or *dispensationes* (Cassian, writing in Latin, helpfully provides the word in both languages). God is a good manager, the best possible manager of everything. When necessary, then, he permits exceptions to or exemptions from an otherwise binding rule. This is his *oikonomia* or *dispensatio.* God, according to Cassian, dispenses or exempts many scriptural figures from the demand not to lie. He includes Rahab, who lied to the king of Jericho's men (Josh. 2) at the request of Joshua's spies and later (Josh. 6) seems to be rewarded for having done so; he also includes Jacob, who lied to Isaac about his identity (Gen. 27), and is rewarded by getting the inheritance to which he was not, as younger son, entitled. Both Rahab and Jacob, on Cassian's interpretation of these texts, are not only exempted from the punishment that would normally come from breaking God's law, but are instead blessed and rewarded for having broken it. Abba Joseph puts this by saying that some people reached the very summit of righteousness *(ad summam iustitiam)* by lying.

Cassian does not mean by this, however, that the lie's proscription be taken lightly. To underline this he has Abba Joseph say that lies should be used like hellebore, a plant that can cure you when you have some particular deadly diseases, but that will kill you if you take it when you're healthy. When you lie, then, you should be in desperate straits, faced with a situation in which sin is unavoidable. Even then, you should lie only with the *scopos* of the Christian life in view. If all these conditions are met—and God will know, for God pays close attention to the *intima pietas,* the interior disposition, of the speaker, not just to whether what's said is a lie—then you may (and perhaps should) lie.

By saying that God dispenses people from the ban on the lie in special circumstances Cassian means to reject the view that the lie is like concubinage: that there was a time when it was freely permitted or even required, but that this is no longer so. Both Augustine and Cassian held this view about the polygamous habits of the Old Testament patriarchs (as did most of the fathers of the church), and Germanus is represented as suggesting that the same pattern of thought might be applied to the lie. But Abba Joseph quickly rejects such a view. The lie was forbidden to Jacob and Rahab as much as to Christians, and when God dispensed or excused them from the ban on the lie, he did so for just the same reasons that he might now dispense Germanus and Cassian from the rule against promise-breaking.

To this point, Cassian's argument that the lie may sometimes be permitted comes to this: ordinarily, the lie is banned; but when you are faced with a dilemma in which sin is unavoidable, you may sometimes be dispensed by God from the ban; this requires, however, that the principal motive with which you lie (purity of heart) is the right one, which is the same as to say that when you lie it must seem to you that among the courses of action open to you, the lie is the one most likely to serve your heart's purity.

But Cassian does not stop there. He adds a further claim, which is that sometimes the *caritatis viscera,* the very guts of love, will require that you lie. Even the apostle Paul, says Abba Joseph, "condescended to relax a little from the rigor of his perfection," when, by pretense *(simulatio)* he behaved as a Jew to Jews and a Greek to Greeks (commenting on 1 Cor. 9:20–22). Should we do less? If we "look for what's ours and obstinately work to hold on to what is useful for us, we shall have to speak the truth even in cases where doing so results in another's death." Cassian means this to be a *reductio:* if holding on to the ban on the lie means that another person will die, love requires that we break the ban.

This bullet, as we have seen, Augustine was quite prepared to bite. If your refusal to lie meant that someone else would die, so be it: harms like the death of the body or its suffering cannot properly be thought to outweigh decisions to sin. But even for Cassian, this claim—the claim that love sometimes requires the lie in order to prevent physical harm—is at first sight odd. Is it meant as a case of the justifiable lie in addition to those already canvassed? If it is, it needs additional justification, for it implies that the need to protect others from physical harms outweighs the need to obey God's commands, and this, as a principle, would have such broad and damaging results that it seems unlikely that Cassian would want to defend it. Many sins, offenses against God's commands, could protect the alien from physical harm. I could, presumably, protect the life of another by idolatrously worshiping some god other than the Lord of Hosts, the God of Abraham and Isaac and Jacob. Does Cassian mean that I should? It seems unlikely.

A slightly more promising route for defense of the claim that the guts of love may require the lie is to say that intending the protection of the other from physical harm in a situation where one can only effect such protection by lying may in such a situation be identical with having purity of heart as the mind's goal. If this line is taken (Cassian does not explicitly take it), the argument from love's guts would reduce to the argument from heart's purity. This is perhaps a more charitable interpretation of what Cassian intends by the appeal to love's guts, but it too has the disadvantage of making the situations in which one may safely ingest the otherwise-fatal hellebore vastly more common than one would expect, and vastly more common than seems capable of reconciliation with Cassian's claim that the ban on the lie should be taken with great seriousness.

The inner logic of Cassian's thought on the permissible lie is clearest, perhaps, in the examples he offers from the everyday life of monks. Suppose, for instance, that you're fasting and as a result have decided to postpone or abandon your evening meal. A fellow monk arrives as it's getting dark and asks whether you've eaten. Should you hide the fact that you're fasting in order to comply with Jesus' command not to let your fasting be publicly evident (Matt. 6:18)? Or should you tell your visitor that you're fasting, and as a result have no plans to eat tonight? Cassian's view is that you should keep hidden from your guest the fact of your fast, and that to do so is clearly an instance of the lie *(profecto mentimur)*. The rationale, predictably, is that it is more sublimely virtuous to observe humility by lying than proudly to tell the truth. Here again Cassian relies upon the idea that aiming for purity of heart, which the humility of hiding your fast would instance, trumps the ban on the lie. Making public the fact that you're fasting would be opposed to purity of heart.

In this case it isn't at all clear whether an Augustinian lie need be involved at all. It certainly would be if you said something like "Let's eat: I'm not fasting just now," for that would clearly be a duplicitous statement. But, of course, you could perfectly well obscure the fact of your fast without saying any such thing. You could offer your guest dinner; you could join him in eating it; and you could talk of other things. To refuse comment or statement on a topic is not to lie, and from this it at once follows that Cassian's concern to avoid prideful display of discipline can be accommodated without the lie. There may be other reasons to worry about misleading your interlocutor with silence, but they won't be connected directly with the question of the lie. Cassian's view, put into Germanus's mouth, that responding rightly to this situation makes the lie inevitable *("nos quoque fatemur inevitabile esse mendacium"),* is therefore incorrect. Or if it is to be defended, this can only be done by giving and defending an understanding of the lie according to which it might be true.

A second example makes a little clearer Cassian's views about silence and the lie. Suppose you have miraculous powers (many of the Egyptian Abbas were thought to have). You know that discussing and explaining the nature, significance, and danger of such powers when instructing young monks in conference is of great value for their advancement in purity of the heart. But you want to avoid boasting by claiming that your teaching about such powers is based on knowledge derived from your own possession of them. What should you do? It seems, says Cassian, that you have three options. The first is to claim the powers you're talking about as your own. The second is to refuse to speak about such powers at all. The third is to speak about them, but to attribute their possession to others. Cassian's view is that the third option is the right one:

> It is better to lie in this way than, out of an irrational respect for the truth, either to hide by inappropriate silence things that might edify your hearers, or to speak truthfully about yourselves and thereby to run headlong into the noxious vanity of boasting.

The first option—explicitly and truthfully claiming the powers you're teaching about as your own—is ruled out because it involves *iactantia,* boasting or bragging, and this is an unacceptable offense against the *scopos* of the Christian life. The second option—to refuse to teach about such things at all—is judged unacceptable because it would withhold from your students something that might be of great benefit to them in their own quest for purity of heart. This would be *incongrua taciturnitas*, inappropriate silence. Both these rejected opinions, says Cassian, are likely to be attractive *"pro observantia inrationabilis istius veritatis,"* because of an irrational respect for the truth.

This last phrase shows the depth of Cassian's disagreement with Augustine more clearly than anything discussed to this point. If *veritas* here means nonduplicitous utterance—and it is difficult to be sure because of Cassian's usual lack of interest in saying just what he does mean by his own terms of art, though the example in play does strongly suggest that something like this must be meant—then to say that one could have an irrational concern for it is from an Augustinian viewpoint oxymoronic. Could one have an irrational interest in praising God? In doing with speech the only thing coherently possible to do with it? No: to say such things would make no sense for Augustine, and that Cassian can say them shows that his understanding of what it is to speak is naïvely instrumental. For him, speech is ours, an instrument properly used in the service of a greater good (purity of heart), appropriately used as seems good to us in the service of that good. This difference between Augustine and Cassian goes deep; its resolution would require a full justification of Augustine's understanding of speech as gift, and his rooting of that understanding in the triune image that constitutes us. All I can say here is that Cassian's treatment of the examples under discussion shows no awareness of a fully Augustinian position on the lie, and is equally lacking in awareness that it might be good to have a fully Christian understanding of speech rather than a technical-instrumentalist one.

But more can be said about this example. Cassian's three alternatives do not appear to exhaust the possibilities. One could, presumably, offer explicit teaching about such powers in monastic conference without claiming them as one's own (truthfully) or attributing them to someone else (mendaciously). If that line was taken, it would be possible to avoid both boasting and silence: you could edify your students without lying to them. It is not clear why Cassian does not consider this option. Following it might meet both his needs and Augustine's. This lack of imagination on Cassian's part (if that is what it is) illustrates an important truth about the Augustinian position. From that position, it will often (surpisingly often, perhaps) be possible to avoid the lie with a combination of silence and indirection while still meeting other needs (teaching your students, protecting the innocent from physical harm, and so on). The Augustinian is never forced into a dilemma as is the follower of Cassian.

A final example, this time a scriptural one. In Genesis 27, notoriously, Jacob, Isaac's second son, appears to lie to his father as a way of getting the inheritance that should have belonged to Esau, Isaac's first son. The blind Isaac calls Jacob to him and asks, "Which of my sons are you?" Jacob's reply—"I am Esau your first-born" (Gen. 27:19)—seems the clearest case possible of the Augustinian lie, for Jacob knows perfectly well as the words leave his lips that he is not Esau, and is therefore speaking duplicitously. Cassian takes Jacob's words as a clear case of the lie, of *mendacium*, and says that Jacob ought to have lied and was rewarded by God for lying: the act, being a lie, was bad, but the intention, being good, trumped and overcame the act's badness. What was the intention? It was not, says Cassian, a desire on Jacob's part covetously to get what was not coming to him. No. It was done *"ex fide sanctificationis perpetuae,"* out of faith in eternal sanctification—sanctification, that is, of himself and of God's chosen people through him. In Cassian's view, the whole act—the lie told with precisely the intention just identified—was rewarded by God, rewarded with a blessed and everlasting inheritance. There is a telltale phrase in Cassian's explanation of why God rewarded Jacob's act: God judged Jacob as liar—the one who presumed to offend against the lie's ban—"excusable, or rather praiseworthy" *(excusabilem immo laudabilem)*. The move from excusing the act to praising it is what's striking here: if Jacob's presumption is excusable, then the lie is wrong and regrettable, but understandable and forgivable because of the great benefit attainable only by its means. But if the lie (or Jacob's presumption in telling it) is praiseworthy, then we have the view that there is nothing to be excused, understood, or forgiven. Jacob's lie was the right thing to do *simpliciter.*

It isn't easily possible to determine which of these positions Cassian would have adopted if he'd made the distinction. I doubt that the question would have been of much interest to him. What does clearly concern him is to find a way to moderate an unacceptable rigorism, and this he has found so long as he has a way to permit Jacob's lie, whether thought of as excusable or praiseworthy. If avoiding the lie offends against purity of heart, then the lie should be told; and this was, in Cassian's mind, exactly Jacob's position.

Augustine's understanding of Jacob's lie is of course different. He prefers to read Jacob's claim to be Esau parabolically or figurally, claiming that Jacob's intention in claiming to be Esau was to signify "one thing by way of another, so that a truth might be understood," and that an intention like this can well serve purity of heart. What Jacob signified by his lie was a *mysterium*, which is only inadequately rendered "mystery" in English. The *mysterium* in question is the church's reception of the inheritance once promised to the Jews. Along with this goes Jacob's mysteriously symbolic act of putting on a goatskin in order to feel to his blind father's touch like the hairy Esau and unlike his smooth self. This action signifies—indicates, points to, proleptically teaches about—the one who will take upon himself sins not his own. Just as the goatskin is not Jacob's own skin and is put on with a result that is unambiguously and importantly good (Jacob becomes Israel), so the sins that Jesus takes on are not his own, and his donning of them becomes the crux of the world's salvation. Through his acceptance of the sins of others, Jesus becomes the scapegoat beyond compare, a scapegoat after which no other is needed. At this point all the depths and difficulties of Augustine's thought about the atoning significance of Jesus' death open before us. Fortunately, we don't need to follow Augustine in exploring them. We need to note (in passing) that the line Augustine takes in his interpretation of Jacob's lie commits him to a problematically supersessionist interpretation of the relations between Christians and Jews, one shared by almost all his contemporaries. It also moves rather rapidly from the literal sense of Genesis 27 to its figural sense in order to preserve Jacob from the burden of having told a lie.

Of this last difficulty Augustine was very much aware. It concerned him because he resisted, as a matter of general principle, a too-rapid move from literal to figural reading, and his method of dealing with the difficulty in this case was to claim that Jacob had already become the elder son, the rightful recipient of his father's blessing and inheritance, before the apparent lie of Genesis 27:19. This was described, says Augustine, in Genesis 25:31–33, where it is recounted that Esau sold his birthright to Jacob for a mess of pottage. Jacob was thus already the rightful owner of the inheritance by the time he claimed to be Esau in Genesis 27, and so if "Esau" is taken according to the element of that word's sense presumably uppermost in Isaac's mind when he asks Jacob who he is—that element being "rightful recipient of the gift of my estate"—then Jacob was quite right to say, "I am Esau," because by then he was the rightful recipient of Isaac's inheritance. And so he was not lying when he spoke those words. This piece of interpretation, if successful, permits Augustine to say that Jacob's words were not a lie even at the literal level, and certainly not in their mysteriously proleptic figural sense.

Cassian has the better of the exegetical argument here. Augustine's reading is possible, certainly, on both the figural and literal levels, and is certainly richly suggestive as to the figural sense of what Jacob said to Isaac. But Augustine is forced to attribute to Jacob a subtle and precise distinction between one element of the sense of "Esau" (rightful inheritance-recipient) and its reference (to the boy who came out of Rebekah's womb first) in order to preserve his view that Jacob did not lie to Isaac. And this is perhaps hyperingenious. It is also not really necessary. Augustine's own assumptions about how to read Scripture on the question of the lie require not that no lies are depicted in Scripture, but only that no lie is told or approved by a scriptural author. And it would certainly be possible to argue that the author of Genesis (whom Augustine took to be Moses) depicted Jacob as lying to Isaac without thereby signaling approval of the lie. The good things that come from Jacob's lie would then have to be shown not to require the lie nor to be a reward for it, but this is an easier exegetical task than the one Augustine chose to undertake.

The differences between Cassian and Augustine on the question of the lie should now be clear. They differ as to whether the lie is ever acceptable; they probably differ as to what it is to lie; they differ as to how sin should be understood; and they differ, as a result, over whether there are any sin-requiring dilemmas. It's now time to see whether and to what extent their views can be drawn closer together, and how the differences that remain might be adjudicated.

Cassian claims that the *scopos* or central point of the Christian life is purity of heart. He thinks (roughly) that the extent to which you have purity of heart is the extent to which your desires and passions are in harmony with God's intentions and hopes for you—that, to put it negatively, the extent to which you defect from divine intention in what you want, think, or feel is the extent to which you lack purity of heart. This view understands the heart's purity as a matter of more or less, a condition in which there can be progress and its opposite. In Cassian's mind, too, the heart is never finally or irreversibly purified before death, which is to say that the kingdom of heaven cannot be entered in this life.

But suppose there are some actions that necessarily oppose advance in purity and instead cause retreat from it. Suppose some actions, by their very nature, require the will of those who perform them to be out of harmony with God's will. Suppose, to put matters as bluntly as possible, that some actions just are defections from purity of heart, that they just are defilements rather than purifications of those who perform them. Would it follow that such actions ought never to be performed, that Christians are bound, nonnegotiably, not to do them?

Cassian thinks so. He thinks that there are actions intrinsically opposed to the heart's purity, and that such actions should never be performed. In response to a question from Germanus as to whether there aren't some commitments to which we should unmovingly hold (immobiliter custodire), commitments to which we are bound come what may, Cassian has Abba Joseph say that there are some "principal mandates" (mandata) whose observance is necessary for our salus, our salvation, and that nothing, not even the certainty of death, can justify abandonment of them. Among these principal mandates are, he says, the "custody of love" (custodia caritatis), the "purity of chastity" (castimoniae puritas), faith, sobriety, and righteousness. Each of these is "to be held to with unchanging perseverance," for to fall back from them even slightly is, strictly, damnable ("paululum recessisse damnabile est"). By contrast, there are some patterns of action that we can take or leave, perform or not perform, depending upon our judgment as to their utility (and Cassian does use, frequently, the noun utilitas and the adjective utilis, for this point) for the goal of heart's purity. The lie belongs, for Cassian, to this second category.

Augustine and Cassian do not, therefore, disagree on whether some actions should be placed under a rigorously exceptionless ban. Neither do they disagree about why this is so: some actions are simply noncompossible with the Christian life, which means that they and the Christian life cannot coherently be undertaken at the same time. It is these actions that are to be exceptionlessly banned, and precisely because they bear this property. Cassian's advocacy of discretion in living the Christian life—which seems on its face to call such rigorism into question—in fact does not: all it does is limit the kinds of actions to be treated with rigor. Augustine and Cassian are in perfect agreement, for instance, that chastity (limiting sexual activity to marriage) is a demand to be treated with rigor, to be banned without exception. But they disagree with equal depth about whether the lie is to be treated rigorously.

What then can an Augustinian learn about the lie from Cassian? Not much. Is there anything in Cassian's discussion in the seventeenth conference to give an Augustinian pause? Again, not much. Cassian's permission of the lie on consequentialist grounds shows that he thinks of it as an action preferably not to be undertaken but defensibly performed when its refusal seems to the liar likely to lead to more damaging results than its acceptance. But he nowhere explains why: he does not offer an account of the lie (nor even a definition of it) that supports his view that it is more like wine-drinking, which Cassian takes to be generally not a good idea but sometimes permissible, than like unchastity, which the two agree is never permissible. Augustine does offer, as we've seen, an account of the lie that shows that and why it is never to be performed, why the lie is more like unchastity than wine-drinking. In order for an Augustinian to learn from or be persuaded by Cassian's defense of the lie, a rival account of what it is to lie would be needed. Otherwise, Cassian's position remains a mere assertion without argument.

12

Aquinas

Thomas Aquinas was born in 1224 or 1225 in Roccasecca in southern Italy and died in 1274. He became a Dominican against the wishes of his family; studied under the greatest teacher of his time, Albertus Magnus, in Paris and Cologne; taught at Paris and in Italy; reached the heights of academic life when such life was new; composed works in almost every literary genre; and is said to have come by the end of his life to judge all of them worthless when compared with the vision of God he was given a few months before his death. His subsequent reputation fluctuated: he was thought by some in the decades following his death to have been flirting with heresy (too much use of Aristotle, "the Philosopher," as Aquinas always called him); was largely ignored even by other Dominicans until the sixteenth century; and then gradually came into his own during the Counter-Reformation, becoming a dominant force in the Catholic intellectual world by the mid–nineteenth century, and remaining so until very recently. Now, as he has lost his central place in Catholic thought, he is being increasingly discussed and appealed to by philosophers without Catholic sympathies.

Aquinas began to compose one of his most-read works, the *Summa Theologiae*, at Rome in 1265. The *Summa* is a large work, a conspectus of all the major topics of theology, intended, as Aquinas writes in the prologue, *ad eruditionem incipientum*, for the intellectual training of beginners. The erudition it would provide for them was to have to do with the *res christiana*, the things that have to do with the Christian religion, and Aquinas says in the prologue that he intends to be brief and clear to the extent that the material to be covered permits. The *Summa* contains perhaps 1.5 million words, and Aquinas had not finished it when he stopped writing in 1273, a few months before his death, early in 1274. If this is brevity, libraries could not contain prolixity. But the range of matter covered is vast, and Aquinas's style is telegraphically compressed; so perhaps the aspiration to be brief was realized.

The fundamental unit of the *Summa* is the question. There are 512 of these: each treats a particular topic in a few thousand words. These questions are collected and ordered into parts, of which there are three (*prima pars,* I; *secunda pars,* II; *tertia pars,* III), with the second part being further subdivided into two (*prima secundae,* IaIIae; *secunda secundae,* IIaIIae). Each question within these parts is further subdivided: first into articles, which treat subtopics under the main topic; and then into objections and responses, a citation of authority, and Aquinas's developed argument for his own preferred position.

For example, Question 110 of the second part of the second part of the *Summa* has as its topic-heading "the vices opposed to truth." These vices are said in the question's prologue to be four: the lie *(mendacium),* pretense *(simulatio),* boasting *(iactantia),* and self-depreciation *(ironia).* The first of these four, the lie, is the only one treated in Question 110, and the question is divided into four articles in order fully to analyze it. The first article asks whether the lie is always opposed to truth; the second, whether it is adequate to classify the lie into three kinds (useful, jocular, harmful); the third, whether every lie is a sin; and the fourth, whether every lie is a mortal sin. This question is my chosen text for this chapter; I'll refer to it simply as "Question 110."

The first part of the *Summa* (I) treats God and creation—or, as Aquinas puts it in the prologue to the second part, "God and those things that proceed from the divine power according to the divine will." The second part (II) treats human beings as God's image, which is to say according to our capacity to judge and to act freely in accord with our judgments. Aquinas here provides an analysis of the nature of human acts and their proper ends or goals (IaIIae), and of the virtues and their corresponding vices (IIaIIae). In the third part (III) he treats Jesus Christ, as he explains in the prologue to that part: "In order to complete our entire theological enterprise, consideration of the Savior of all, in himself and with respect to the benefits he has given to the human race, follows upon consideration of the final end of humanity together with the virtues and vices." The *Summa* as a whole thus reflects in its structure the order of the creeds: God-creation-incarnation-redemption-consummation.

The whole of the *Summa's* second part (IaIIae and IIaIIae together) treats human life: what it is, what it's for, how human action is and ought to be ordered. Within this overarching concern, Aquinas uses the schema of the seven virtues, together with their annexed or associated virtues and corresponding vices, to order his exposition of particular actions, both those good for us and those bad for us. These seven virtues are: faith, hope, and love, categorized together as the three theological virtues; and prudence, justice, temperance, and fortitude, categorized together as the four cardinal virtues. All particular vices and virtues are annexed to, and therefore treated under the heading of, one of these seven principal virtues. The particular vice that concerns me here is of course the lie, *mendacium,* which Aquinas treats in Question 110. It's to what he says in this question that I shall offer an Augustinian response. But before turning to the particulars of this question, Aquinas's discussion of the lie needs to be located within the broader structure of the part of the *Summa* within which it is found. This can be done by moving outward in concentric circles, as it were, until the lie is placed in relation to one of the seven principal virtues.

First, the lie is called one of the vices opposed to truthfulness *(veritas)*. These include pretense *(simulatio),* hypocrisy *(hypocrisi),* boasting *(iactantia),* and self-depreciation *(ironia).* Truthfulness, in turn, is classified as one of the parts of justice (the fifth of the seven principal virtues), which is to say as one of the many virtues annexed to justice and treated under its head. To say that truthfulness is annexed or connected to justice means that in part it coincides with justice's definition, but does not do so fully. Truthfulness, says Aquinas, coincides with justice's definition in two respects: first, that it is an act directed toward another, which is so in the case of truthfulness because it is a communicative act; and second, that it is an act that "establishes a certain equality among things." Justice establishes such an equality by giving exactly what is owed. Truthfulness does so analogically by establishing a proper relation between signs and things. A truthful communication "adequates" the word to the thing (or at least intends to do so), which is to say that it creates a properly reflective expressive relation between the one and the other. Truthfulness is, therefore, one of the many virtues annexed to justice (there are more virtues belonging to justice than to any other of the seven principal virtues); and the lie is one of the several vices or lacks opposed to it.

In locating his discussion of the lie in this way Aquinas is already non-Augustinian. If truthfulness is understood to be annexed to justice, and if the lie is seen as an offense against truthfulness so understood, then the starting point is already fundamentally mistaken. To offend against justice is a complex matter (there are kinds and modes of justice for Aquinas), but it is essential to all such offenses that they fail in one way or another in the sphere of external interpersonal actions, and that they do so most basically by not giving what is due, what is owed, to some other or others. What is wrong with offenses against justice is precisely that they so fail. This starting point ensures that Aquinas's discussion of the particularities of the lie will consider its wrongness principally in terms of its relation to and effects upon someone other than the liar—and will therefore move in the sphere of (what we might call) interpersonal and social ethics. But from an Augustinian point of view this is a mistake to begin with: what matters most fundamentally about the lie is not what it does to the liar's relations with others but what it does to the liar's relations with God. This difference ramifies and goes deep.

The detailed architectonic of the *Summa* is clearly not Augustinian in inspiration (its governing genius is Aristotle). Even less so is its style. Augustine's prose is poetic, hot, elegant, excitable, full of the tricks and techniques of the professional rhetor and the accomplished preacher. Aquinas's prose is, by contrast, dry, precise, compressed. Precision has its elegance, no doubt, but even such crystalline beauty as it can possess is hard to find in Aquinas. His sentences are usually short and simple, easy to construe grammatically even when they are conceptually subtle. He seems not to be interested in arousing the passions of his readers, and the result is that the principal pleasure to be had from reading him is conceptual and analytical. But this he provides in spades: the distinctions he creates and deploys in order to further understanding of some topic are often dazzling, as is the complexity and range of the systematic frame within which he places his particular distinctions. Aquinas is a systematic thinker and a precise one. Augustine is neither.

These differences do not necessarily mean that Aquinas was not an Augustinian thinker. Aquinas quotes Augustine more frequently than most Christian thinkers—perhaps more than any. (Still, Aristotle is probably quoted by Aquinas more often, and Aquinas certainly devoted more intellectual energy to the Aristotelian corpus than to the Augustinian.) He quotes, too, from a wide range of Augustine's works, and always with the professed intent of endorsing the positions in those works. Among Augustine's Christian interlocutors with whom I deal in this book, Aquinas is certainly the closest to Augustine on the lie. There are, nonetheless, important differences between the two, some of lack and some of supplement, and they do not show Aquinas's thought to advantage.

In the first article of Question 110, Aquinas asks whether the lie is always opposed to truthfulness, and if so, why. The answer is clearly yes: for Aquinas, *veritas* (truthfulness) and *falsitas* (falsehood) are opposites, contradictories, which means that where one is present the other must be absent. If, then, the lie is intimately and always connected with falsehood, it will follow immediately that the lie and truthfulness are always and necessarily opposed. As always, Aquinas approaches the task of showing this to be so by clarifying his terms. Truthfulness, the act of truth, is a signifying act, an *enuntiatio* or act of communication that uses signs with the intention of accurately referring them to an idea, a *conceptum*, of a thing. Such an act requires reason: animals can't do it precisely because they lack reason. It is also an act of moral significance: to do it is to do something good, to use verbal signs as they were meant to be used, which is to say in accord with their proper end.

Mendacium, the lie, is opposed to all this. Its moral significance is found in two intentions: the first is to say something false, and the second thereby to deceive someone. But, says Aquinas, only the first intention is proper to or definitive of the lie. Only it belongs to the lie's species, as he likes to put it, which is to contradict the mind with speech or some other sign (he mentions nodding the head). Aquinas emphasizes the centrality of the first intention by explaining the word *mendacium* to be derived from the expression *contra mentem dicitur,* to say something opposed to the mind, against the content of the speaker's mind. Aquinas does not mean this as a historical claim about *mendacium*'s etymology, but rather as a grammatical gloss upon the word, a linguistic emblem of its definition.

The second intention with which the lie's moral significance is connected, the intention to install a falsehood in someone else's mind *("falsitatem in opinione alterius constituere")* is not intrinsic to the lie. In Aquinas's terms it belongs not to the lie's species but to its perfection. This means that the deceptive lie is successful, but the lie that fails to deceive is nonetheless a lie. Unlike Augustine, Aquinas is not interested in (or at least doesn't in Question 110 address) the question of whether all liars do intend or hope that their lies will deceive. No doubt this is the ordinary case; but Augustine's interest in the lie told just for the pleasure of telling it shows more psychological acuteness than Aquinas's assumption that the *perfectio* of every lie is the deception of an interlocutor. Aquinas and Augustine are, however, entirely at one on the question of the lie's definition. It is for both of them an act of intentional duplicity (though this is not a term that Aquinas uses in Question 110), a communicative act intended to misrepresent what the speaker takes to be the case.

Aquinas agrees with Augustine, too, that the lie has nothing necessarily to do with falsehood. To speak what's false while believing it true is no lie; and to speak what's true while believing it false is a lie. Aquinas's conclusion on the definitional question is straightforward: the lie is clearly, directly, and formally *(directe et formaliter)* opposed to truthfulness's virtue. So far, then, Aquinas and Augustine have no substantive disagreements.

Aquinas then turns to the question of the lie's kinds. He inherited a threefold division of the lie, into the useful *(officiosum)*, the jocular *(iocosum)*, and the harmful *(perniciosum)*. This division has some roots in Augustine's work, and in the vocabulary and interests of Latin thinkers of the fourth and fifth century, as we have already seen. But the firm threefold division of the lie as Aquinas inherited and treated it is a much later creation whose history and vicissitudes need not detain us. Aquinas interrogates this division. Is it adequate? Are there lies that fall outside its scope, and are there other divisions and classifications equally or more defensible?

One such alternative division, suggests Aquinas, is based on what the lie essentially is. The lie's definition, recall, is speech (or other signification) *contra mentem*. A division based upon this definition would consider how—in what ways—speech might oppose the mind. In providing such an analysis, Aquinas follows not Augustine but Aristotle: a division of the lie *"secundum ipsam mendacii rationem"*—according to the lie's very definition—yields lies that go beyond the truth by excess and lies that fall short of the truth by lack. The former are lies of boasting *(iactantia)* and the latter lies of depreciation *(ironia)*. The idea behind this division is that the lie's essence is found in its opposition to truthfulness, and this opposition may go in two directions: excess, which claims more than what's true; and depreciation, which claims less. Truth-telling, then, is the mean between these two. The truth-teller claims just what seems to him to be the case, no more and no less. All this is entirely Aristotelian (see ch. 8 and notes thereto).

Aquinas's examples of boasting, of the lies of excess, include the king of Tyre, who is reported by the prophet Ezekiel (28:2) to have said, "I am a god," which clearly exceeds what's the case. He also mentions the Pharisee's claim, "O God, I thank you that I am not like other men" (Luke 18:11), which is also clearly an excessive claim, since with respect to the relevant property—that of being a sinner—the Pharisee is just like other men. These examples fit Aquinas's (Aristotelian) definition of the excessive lie: you boast, he says, when you extol yourself, which means when you say of yourself more than you are *("de se supra se aliquid dicit")*. But, interestingly, these examples do not clearly fit—or perhaps clearly do not fit—Aquinas's own definition of the lie. This is because while they are good examples of claims false by excess, they are not necessarily good examples of claims *contra mentem* by excess. The king of Tyre may very well have believed that he was a god; the Pharisee may very well have believed that he was unlike other men in not being a sinner. Indeed, the whole point of the parable of the Pharisee and the tax-collector is that he did believe this and was sinfully confused precisely in believing it. To speak what you take to be true when it is in fact false is no lie, as Aquinas himself has already said. Better examples of the boasting lie would be exaggerations of qualities the liar knows herself to have but not to have to the degree she claims. I might say, for example, "my Latin is good enough to read Augustine with ease," while at the same time knowing that it isn't, that although I can usually make sense of Augustine in Latin, it is sometimes a struggle to do so, and that it is even more difficult for me to appreciate the aesthetic qualities of Augustine's prose. This would be a boasting lie because it would seem an exaggeration to me as I uttered it.

There are similar difficulties with Aquinas's examples of the lie of depreciation, the ironic lie. Here too what's needed are instances of claiming less than one should claim, and doing so knowingly. Should I say, "I can barely read Latin at all," this would be such a claim. It will not do, though, to offer examples of claiming less than one should while thinking that what one claims is just what one should claim. This, again, is falsehood, but not the lie. Aquinas's attempted classification of the lie by excess and lack fails to the extent that he forgets his own definition of the lie, which he often does. He forgets it, I suspect, because of Aristotle's influence: Aristotle's understanding of the lie does not focus upon duplicity (he is more concerned with falsehood and lack, with saying the thing that is not), and when Aquinas moves from Augustine to Aristotle, as he does in this classification of the lie by excess and lack, he is liable to forget the Augustinian definition with which he is supposed to be working.

The lie may also be classified into kinds according to end or result, says Aquinas, and this is how the threefold classification (useful, jocose, harmful) is arrived at. Jokers aim at getting laughs, those who lie to protect the innocent aim to be useful, and those who lie to defame or destroy aim to hurt. And so, "It's clear that the greater the good intended the more the fault of the lie *(culpa mendacii)* is decreased." This is ambiguous. Aquinas might mean *culpa* with respect to ancillary intent, not *culpa* with respect to the act of the lie itself. The lie itself, after all, is always the same: it is to speak against the mind, to speak, as Augustine would have it, duplicitously. Accompanying intentions (to deceive, to help, to amuse, to hurt, and so on) have their various merits and demerits, but none of these belongs properly to the lie. What Aquinas ought to mean, therefore (and were he to mean this he would be in complete agreement with Augustine), is that the lie's fault is not altered by the goodness or badness of particular accompanying intentions. Saying so is perfectly compatible with saying that some such intentions are good and some bad. The sense in which it is better to lie usefully than harmfully, then, would be just the sense in which it is better to want to be useful than to want to harm. And this has nothing at all to do with the lie. But I suspect that this is not what Aquinas means, as will become apparent in his application of the distinction between mortal and venial sin.

Aquinas next asks whether every lie is a sin, and answers that, yes, the lie is evil by definition *(malum ex genere)*, which is to say that it is an act that inevitably arrives at a place where no one should go. This is because words are by their nature signs of thought, and it is therefore improper intentionally to voice, to invoke, something other than your thought, to speak something other than your mind. Therefore, the lie should never be performed. This sounds terribly Augustinian, as stark and uncompromising as is the master himself. This impression is reinforced by what Aquinas says against objections to this view. One objection is that lies are said to be rewarded in Scripture, as in the case of the Egyptian midwives, who are said to have had houses built for them by God as a result of having lied (Exod. 1:21); Aquinas replies, ventriloquizing Augustine, that they were not rewarded for their lie, but rather *pro timore Dei*, for the fact that they showed proper fear of God. Another is that Jacob lied to Isaac, to which Aquinas offers an essentially Augustinian interpretation of that prima facie lie as speech that should be interpreted *figuraliter* and *prophetice*.

Most strikingly, Aquinas responds to the lesser-evil argument—that, for instance, one may or should lie in order to prevent someone from committing or suffering a murder—by saying that since the lie is intrinsically disordered *(ex sua inordinatione)* it may never be permitted in order to block harm to another: "It is not permitted to lie in order to save another from any danger whatsoever." But then Aquinas goes on to say: "It is permitted prudently to hide *(occultare)* the truth under a certain dissimulation *(sub aliqua dissimulatione)*, as Augustine has said in *Against Lying*." A difficulty here is that Augustine said no such thing in the work in question. Aquinas most likely has in mind Augustine's discussion of the Abraham/Abimelech/Sara story from Genesis 20 (discussed in ch. 1). But what Augustine concludes there is that hiding the truth *(occultare veritatem)* isn't the same as lying. Augustine's approval of hiding the truth in certain circumstances is in accord with his view that silence is not a lie, and that if it is sometimes wrong to hide the truth by silence *(tacendo, silentione)*, this is not because doing so is a lie. But Augustine does not mention dissimulation approvingly, in *Against Lying* or elsewhere. When he does use the word in his discussions of lying, it is disapprovingly: dissimulation for him is just another word for the lie. Is there then a disagreement between Aquinas and Augustine here? And why does Aquinas misrepresent Augustine at this place?

The second question is difficult to answer. Perhaps Aquinas read a version of Augustine's *Against Lying* different from the one that has come down to us. A more likely explanation, though, is that the approving mention of dissimulation here serves those among Aquinas's intellectual purposes that clearly separate his position on the lie from Augustine's. For Aquinas, it seems, to dissimulate is not the same as to simulate: *dissimulatio* differs from *simulatio*. The latter is active pretense: it occurs when "someone signifies by [nonverbal] signs of things or actions something about himself that is contrary to what he [actually] is." This is just a nonverbal lie, and in this it is the same as hypocrisy and other associated ideas. Like the verbal lie, this is, for Aquinas, intrinsically disordered and (thus) evil: it can never permissibly be done. Dissimulation, by contrast, is concealment: you dissimulate when you act in such a way as to hide qualities you have. On this understanding, dissimulation is a species of silence, and this is why Aquinas permits it—as Augustine also would. There is certainly a difference between the two men as to the proper use of the word *dissimulatio*. Perhaps, too, there is a conceptual difference. To see whether this is so, Aquinas's discussion of whether the lie is a mortal sin needs to be explored.

For Aquinas, a mortal sin *(peccatum mortale)* is one that opposes love, and by so doing separates the soul from God—for it is principally by love *(caritas)* that the soul maintains its connection to God. The result of mortal sin is the soul's *perditio* and *mors*, its ruin and death. To ask whether the lie is a mortal sin, then, is to ask whether it is opposed to love in the appropriate sense. How might the lie be opposed to love? The first possibility is that the lie might be opposed to love *secundum se*, according to what it is, which Aquinas here takes to mean according to its *significatio*, according to what the lie is told about. If the lie is about things having to do with God, or about things that serve the human good, then it is opposed to love, and as a result is a mortal sin. But if the lie is about something insignificant and contingent—last year's Chicago White Sox win-loss record, say—then the lie does not oppose love in the relevant sense, and is as a result not a mortal sin.

I pause here to observe that it is odd, even in Aquinas's own terms, to equate the lie considered as such, considered *secundum se,* with what it is told about—with, that is to say, its topic. Considering the lie *secundum se* should be to consider it according to its definition. And this definition (as Aquinas has already given it) is speech *contra mentem,* speech taken by the speaker to contradict what she thinks, what she takes to be the case. This definition applies to all lies, no matter what their topic. How then does it make sense to say that a particular lie's sinfulness can depend upon its topic? If the lie-as-such is sinful, the sense in which and the extent to which it is sinful will remain the same for all lies. To say that a particular lie's mortality or veniality depends upon its topic is to say that no lie is intrinsically mortal—for if it were, no change of topic could make it cease to be so. If the lie considered *secundum se* were mortal, all lies would be mortal. This suggests that Aquinas thinks that the lie-as-such (intentional speech *contra mentem*) is venially sinful only.

The second way in which a lie can be mortal, says Aquinas, is that it can be opposed to love by having a particular end or purpose. If, for instance, you blaspheme, or lie with the goal of damaging your neighbor, your sin is mortal. But if you lie with the goal of getting a laugh (the jocose lie) or giving help (the useful lie), then your sin is not mortal.

The third way in which a lie can be mortal is that it can have as a side effect, an epiphenomenon, scandal or other damage—even if that scandal or damage was not the aim or purpose of the lie; this means that any lie can become a mortal sin if circumstances change.

It follows from all this that only the harmful lie, the *perniciosum mendacium,* is clearly a mortal sin. The lie of the Egyptian midwives, for example, is not such because it does not have as its aim or goal anything contrary to love. It may even, says Aquinas, merit or deserve a temporal reward (he has in mind the houses built for the midwives mentioned in Exod. 1:21).

All this is a bit puzzling from an Augustinian point of view. Perhaps it can be clarified by considering more closely what Aquinas means by distinguishing mortal from venial sins. The distinction between the two is easy to state formally: mortal sin is *contra caritatem,* which is to say directly opposed to and noncompossible with the realization of our proper end, which is eternal happiness with God. The result of such unrepented sin is eternal and infinite punishment. Venial sin is any sin not so characterizable, which is to say any disordered act whose remedy lies within human power, and that does not separate those who do it from God's love. Sin in general is, for Aquinas, any disordered act, which is to say any evil human act, or, following Augustine with some qualifications, anything said, done, or desired against the eternal law. Venial sin is thus less disordered, less evil, less contrary to the eternal law than is mortal sin. The distinction between the two kinds of sin requires that the variables be quantifiable and arranged hierarchically, and sometimes Aquinas writes as if venial sin is not really sin at all, or at least that it belongs to sin's definition only analogically. Recall that the reason given by Aquinas for the lie being sinful is that it misuses words by misrepresenting thought: words are by their nature signs of thought, and it is therefore sinful intentionally to voice, to invoke, something other than your thought, to speak something other than your mind. All lying partakes of sin in this sense.

But, as Aquinas's application of the distinction between mortal and venial sin to the question of the lie shows, it is not a mortal sin to misuse words in this way. If it were, all lies would be mortal sins, and they are not. Misusing words, then, is by itself only a venial sin (if even that). What makes a venial sin of this kind mortal has nothing to do with words and their relation to thought—nothing to do, in Augustinian terms, with duplicity (and this may be among the reasons why Aquinas does not use the Augustinian vocabulary of the *duplex cor,* the rupture between thought and speech, to discuss the lie). What it does have to do with is external harm and damage, with matters extrinsic to the lie considered simply as such. This is a completely non-Augustinian position, for it rejects the Augustinian position that the lie is essentially and constitutively an internal matter, which is to say that what is wrong with the lie as such can have nothing to do with external and collateral harms. That Aquinas takes the line he does is a direct result of his classification of the lie as a sin against justice.

Matters are, however, more complex. While the distinction between mortal and venial sin is one of kind (the defining characteristics of the one differ from the defining characteristics of the other, and it follows directly that no particular act can at one and the same time be both mortally and venially sinful), it is not always easy to tell to which category a particular act belongs. Consider, for example, ordinary cocktail-party chatter, most of which is vain, idle, inattentive, self-glorifying, flattering, casually facetious, gossipy, and so on. This is what Aquinas calls *verba otiosa,* idle chat (Aquinas has in mind here, probably, Matt. 12:36–37). Such chat is (or may be) intrinsically sinful, but the sin involved will be venial since it will not usually be an offense against love and there-fore not something that separates its speakers from God to the extent that they become worthy of infinite and eternal punishment. However, circumstance can alter the act. It does this not by making a particular act more weighty or grave or significant: circumstance cannot "increase gravity infinitely," as it would have do if a venial sin were to become mortal. A change in circumstance cannot alter the kind to which an act belongs. What it can do, however, is change the description under which the act is identified, and therefore also its kind.

Suppose, to return to the cocktail party, you make a casual joke of an off-color sort to the person you're talking to. So far, this is an example of idle chat, which is at worst venially sinful. But suppose this particular instance of idle chat is undertaken with the principal intention of en-couraging the person you're talking to to have adulterous sex with you. Now the act must be described differently. It ceases to be idle chatter, and becomes idle-chatter-motivated-by-adulterous-desire. And that (so Aquinas would say) is a mortal sin. A venial sin cannot straightforwardly become mortal, then; but a component or element of an act that would by itself be venial can, by being combined with a particular end that doesn't intrinsically belong to it, constitute a new act, which may be mortal. Idle chatter (venial) may become idle-chatter-with-the-purpose-of-inciting-lust (mortal).

But an act that is intrinsically (according to its definition and so also according to its kind) mortally sinful cannot with equal ease be altered by addition or subtraction into a venially sinful act. If one component of an act is mortally sinful, then the entire act is mortally sinful. There is (to oversimplify only slightly, and not so as to misrepresent Aquinas) only one way in which a mortally sinful act can cease to be so, and that is by losing or failing to have some element essential to its definition. Aquinas tends to put this by saying that a mortal sin may become venial *propter imperfectionem actus,* "because of the imperfection of the act," which is to say when it isn't really the act it might seem to be because it lacks some essential element. Suppose, for example, it is suggested that adultery or murder (mortal sins, both) is committed by a sudden involuntary motion of the body: imagine that you fall from a high place onto the body of another and as a result kill or sexually penetrate him or her—perhaps both at once. This act lacks deliberative decision: in the imagined case you didn't decide to do anything, or if you did, it certainly wasn't to commit adultery or rape or murder. Without deliberative decision, no act can be a mortal sin. But this is not to say that a mortal sin can cease to be so. It is only to say that when an act otherwise identical in form and result to a mortal sin is performed without intention or deliberation, it is not in fact a mortal sin.

The application of these technicalities to what Aquinas says about the lie's sinfulness in Question 110 is straightforward enough, and it issues in a deeply non-Augustinian position. Aquinas thinks that the lie—deliberate speech *contra mentem*—is intrinsically sinful but only venially so. It is not an offense against love. It becomes so only when joined with additional factors of various sorts. This is why the useful or jocose lie is venially sinful, and the harmful lie mortally so. The lie in Aquinas's view, then, is *malum ex genere* (properly evil), but is not an offense against love. This means that the intentional use of words to misrepresent the speaker's thought is also not an offense against love.

The contrast with Augustine's position is dramatic. For Augustine, duplicitous speech is a rupture of the divine image, a recursively incoherent act best characterized as a refusal of the divine gift by attempted expropriation. It is sin's very paradigm. In Aquinas's terms, this would be an offense against love, and thus a mortal sin. That Aquinas does not so understand it shows that he has a different evaluation of the seriousness of the act in question. And this is scarcely surprising since an Augustinian trinitarian analysis of the act of speech is altogether lacking in Aquinas's discussion of the lie. Augustine's analysis of what is wrong with the lie is simply absent in Aquinas, and it is absent because of a refusal to think of speech in terms of the triune image. As with Cassian and Chrysostom (though for different reasons), Aquinas here shows himself insufficiently serious as a Christian thinker: the act of speech, while not for him morally neutral, has begun to move in the direction of being so considered. Aquinas does not yet think of speech as something we own and can do with as we will. But the fact that he considers the lie as such *(per definiens, ex suo genere)* to be only venially sinful is evidence of a significant move in that direction. Aquinas's position on the question of the lie is thus closer to that of Jerome and the majority of the Greek tradition than it is to that of Augustine—and this despite the frequency with which Augustine is quoted in Question 110. Aquinas differs from Jerome, Cassian, and Chrysostom in categorizing the lie as always sinful; but he is like them (and unlike Augustine) in not considering with sufficient depth just what it is about speech that makes its deformation by lying a sin. A Thomist is thus much more likely than an Augustinian to offer justifications for particular acts of intentional duplicity in terms of motive or result, and the extent to which this happens is precisely the extent to which a fully Christian mode of thought about speech has been abandoned.

The essential mistake is to think of the lie as if it were principally or exclusively an offense against the requirements of justice, of what is properly owed to the other. If this is the starting point, then it will be very difficult to avoid the seductive conclusion that some lies, some instances of speech *contra mentem*, are justifiable. If, for example, speaking *contra mentem* is not meant to deceive; if those to whom a lie is spoken (the Nazis at the door) have placed themselves outside the circle of those deserving of justice; and if the results of some lie are good for those to whom or for whom it is told, it will be inevitable, or almost so, that lies will begin to be sorted and organized into more or less harmful kinds (Augustine does this too), and then likely that some lies will come to be thought of as not really sinful, or not sinful in the same way as others. This is the deep grammar of Aquinas's classification of speech *contra mentem* as venial sin, and it stands in an opposition to the grammar of Augustine's thought about the topic that could only be resolved by deciding whether the lie is principally a willed rupture of the divine image or principally a sin against justice. Aquinas is of course not alone in locating the problem of the lie within the sphere of justice; this was implicit already in Cassian and Chrysostom, as we've seen in chapters 9 and 11, and it becomes even clearer in Kant, to whom I now turn.

13

Kant

In early 1797, an essay by Benjamin Constant, a French politician and littérateur, appeared in German translation. The original French version of the essay was titled "Des réactions politiques"; in German it became "Von den politischen Gegenwirkungen"; and it can be Englished as "On Political Reactions." Most of Constant's essay has nothing to do with lying, but one passage from it does address the topic, and this passage caught Kant's attention when the German version of the essay came his way within a few months of its publication. It prompted him to write a reply, which he called "Über ein vermeintes Recht aus Menschenliebe zu lügen"—"On a Supposed Philanthropic Right to Lie." I'll call this the lying essay. Kant begins it by quoting the offending passage from Constant:

> The moral principle that it is a duty to speak the truth would, were it taken by itself and without conditions, make any society impossible. We have proof of this in the very immediate consequences a German philosopher has drawn from the principle. He goes so far as to maintain that it would be a crime to lie to a murderer who asked you whether your friend whom he was pursuing had hidden in your house.

Constant had not named the "German philosopher," but Kant took it to be himself, and was provoked by Constant's words.

When he read Constant's essay Kant was already an old man (he would die a few years later, in 1804, at the age of 80). The development of the critical philosophy of the 1770s and 1780s, according to which the claims of theoretical reason must be chastened and limited "so as to make it possible for practical knowledge to reveal how pure rational faith has an absolute claim on us," was well behind him. He had shown, he thought, what were the limits upon what human beings can know about the way things really are, and in so doing had provided (among many other things) a new grounding for our ethical duties.

These duties, these *Pflichten,* he understood in terms of what we can coherently think it right to do: if you have a formal duty to do something this means, roughly, that you can coherently intend that the goals, methods, and circumstances of your action—its "maxim," as Kant likes to call it—be universalized, which is to say applied as a universal law, understood as something everyone should always do in a like situation. If you can coherently so intend, then your action has the character of a formal duty, which means that when occasion arises you must do it (and, correspondingly, refrain from doing what opposes it). Further, formal duties are the only actions that meet this criterion, which means that the criterion is both necessary and sufficient for an action to be a formal duty. Formal duties are, then, to use a non-Kantian language for a moment, exceptionless moral norms: there are no circumstances in which they can properly be set aside or acted against, and no results that might follow from acting upon them that could require their abandonment. This is not the only way in which Kant states his understanding of an exceptionless moral norm. Another formulation—which he takes to be equivalent—is "Act in such a way that you treat humanity *(Menschheit),* whether in your own person or in someone else's, always as an end *(Zweck)* and never just as a means *(Mittel)."*

There are difficulties in deciding whether Kant is right to think of these two formulations (and there are others) as equivalent. There are difficulties, too, in deciding just what they come to, and how particular, substantive moral duties about such things as killing, lying, committing adultery can be derived from them. But this is no place for the exploration of such difficulties. What I've said, too abstractly and too briefly, about formal duties will suffice to serve as backdrop to Kant's particular argument in the lying essay, and so to a reading of that I now return.

Having quoted Constant on the unacceptable results of the unnamed German philosopher's views of the *sittliche Grundsatz,* the moral principle, that one has a duty *"die Wahrheit zu sagen,"* to speak the truth—these results include the claim that you'd be wrong to lie to a murderer even if you could save innocent life by doing so—Kant goes on to quote Constant further on what's wrong with this understanding of the duty to tell the truth:

It is á duty to speak the truth. The concept of duty cannot be separated from that of right: one man's duty corresponds to another's right, and where there are no duties there are also no rights. To speak the truth is therefore a duty, but only with regard to someone who has a right to the truth. But no one who harms others has a right to the truth.

This is Constant's argument. Its understanding of the meaning of duty (*Pflicht*) means that no duty can be understood *unbedingt und vereinzelt*, "by itself and without conditions," for every duty must be understood in terms of its corresponding right. If I have a duty to do something, part of what this means is that someone else has a right to have it done: if I have a duty not to kill or rape or torture you, part of what this means is that you have a right not to be killed or raped or tortured by me. Likewise for truth-telling: if I have a duty to do this to you, it must be because you have a right to have it done. It follows immediately from this understanding of the syntax of duty and right that if someone places himself outside the circle of those who have a right to have the truth told to them, then no one can meaningfully be said to have a duty to tell it to them. Constant applies the principle by saying that the murderer, the "one who harms others," has removed himself from that circle, and so there can be no duty to speak the truth to the murderer at the door.

So far Constant's position. He rejects the idea that any duty can be considered apart from its corresponding right; he thinks that murderers have no right to have the truth told them; and he therefore rejects the idea that there is a duty to tell the truth to murderers, from which it follows that there is no formal duty to tell the truth. What he says is clearly coherent, which is to say that the conclusion of his argument must be accepted if the understanding of the reciprocity of rights and duties from which it begins is accepted. It is to this understanding that Kant's response is directed. But before turning to that, it's interesting to note that no definition of truth-telling is offered in the lying essay. It seems reasonable to assume that both Kant and Constant mean by *die Wahrheit zu sagen* the opposite of what Augustine means by *mendacium*. If to lie is to seem to oneself to speak against one's thought and thus to be duplicitous, then to speak the truth means to speak with sincerity, to say what seems to one to be the case. So, in any case, I'll assume.

Kant's argumentative response begins with what may be a little philosophical joke. The *prōton pseudos* in Constant's argument, he says, is the claim that truth-telling is a duty only to those who have a right to the truth. The Greek phrase *prōton pseudos* is rightly glossed by the editors of the German text as *der erste Trugschluß*—the first fallacy, or logical error. But, of course, *pseudos* can also properly be translated as "lie" (in English) or *Lüge* (in German) or *mendacium* (in Latin). Kant is joking, then, by accusing Constant not only of error but also of lying—it is the deep-going ambiguity in the European conceptual vocabulary of the lie that makes possible this bit of philosophical humor at Constant's expense. If it's not humor, then Kant is exhibiting his own subjection to the confusion between error and lie, and this seems unlikely. The error, in any case, is that Constant's formulation of the idea that it is possible to have a right to the truth might be taken to mean that it is possible to have rights over whether any particular claim—such as that the grass is green, that Augustine was an African, or that God necessarily exists—is true or false. And this idea, as Kant rightly says, is *ohne Sinn*, senseless. Claims just are true or false: rights are neither here nor there. But this is just a debating point on Kant's part. Constant clearly means not that we can have rights over a claim's truth, but that we can have rights over whether what someone says to us seems to the person saying it to be true. We can, to put this in Latin, have rights over *veracitas* but not over *verum*—over truthfulness but not over truth.

Leaving this debating point aside, Kant turns to the real questions raised by Constant's remarks. The first of these, he says, is whether in cases where one cannot avoid saying yes or no, one can have a right (*Recht* again) to be untruthful *(unwahrhaft zu sein)*. And the second is whether, in similar cases, one is ever bound *(verbunden)* to be untruthful. The first question asks whether it is ever proper to be untruthful, and the second whether it is ever required. On Kant's understanding, the answer to the second question follows directly from the answer to the first: if you can never have the right to speak untruthfully, then you can certainly never be bound by duty to do so. In what follows, therefore, I'll restrict my remarks (as Kant mostly does) to the question of whether it's possible to have the right to lie—which is the question enshrined in the title of Kant's essay.

I note, too, that it seems reasonable to assume that Kant means by speaking untruthfully just what Augustine means by the lie: knowing duplicity. Kant's question—can one ever have the right to do this?—would of course be answered by Augustine with a resounding and unambiguous negative. Kant answers it in the same way, but for different (and incompatible) reasons, as we shall see. Before turning to the reasons, however, it's worth noting that neither Kant nor Constant pays sufficient attention to the possibility of silence. Are there actually cases in which an answer to a question is compelled? In one sense there clearly are. Speech is in part a physical act, requiring movement of the tongue and vocal chords, and it seems clear enough that all physical acts may be compelled. One can be forced to walk where one would not; one may also be forced to speak what one would not, whether by crude manipulation of the organs of speech, more subtle manipulation of patterns of neuronal firing in the brain, or complex conditioning over time, such as that used in preparing victims to give self-damning testimony in the Stalinist show-trials of the mid–twentieth century. There is no reason to doubt the efficacy of such techniques, especially when complemented by a twenty-first-century pharmacopeia and understanding of brain physiology. But though these techniques may compel speech, they do not support the Kantian assumption that there are situations in which, although one is not constrained in these ways, one must nevertheless speak. A situation of this sort would be one in which one can speak duplicitously or nonduplicitously, but needs must (and knowingly) speak in one way or the other. But there are no such situations. Speaking duplicitously is an intentional, uncompelled action: those who do it (liars) must know what they do and intend to do it. If their vocalization is forced, what they do is not lying because it does not meet these criteria. If duplicitous speech is possible, silence is also possible, as is nonduplicitous speech. And so Kant's easy assumption that there are cases in which one must say yes or no is altogether too facile. This, however, is only a prelude to the main Kantian argument.

To return, then, to that argument, Kant has asked whether one may or must lie. He understands this to be a question that—as Constant raised it and as he will respond to it—belongs only to the sphere of the doctrine of right *(Rechtslehre)*, which is to say to the laws or principles that govern duty to others. He does not consider it as a question that belongs to ethics in the strict sense, which is to say that he doesn't discuss in this essay what might or might not be wrong with the lie if considered only in terms of the liar's duty to himself. To discuss it in this second way would be to enter the "doctrine of virtue" *(Tugendlehre)*, and Kant is explicit about his intention to avoid doing so. In connection with duty to others, then, Kant says that truthfulness is a "formal duty of man to everyone," which he explains by saying that every lie (now, for the first time since the essay's title, he uses the standard German word, *Lüge*) is an offense against duty *überhaupt*, duty considered most generally, no matter what the particular circumstances. To say that truthfulness is a *formale Pflicht*, a formal duty, is then for Kant the same as to say that it is always an offense against duty, which in turn means that no one may ever justifiably do it. Formal duties bind without respect to result or ancillary intention. So, Constant's murderers and the death of their victim notwithstanding, Kant thinks that you may never lie to another, and that if you speak at all it must always be nonduplicitously.

Kant's conclusion is the right one from an Augustinian point of view, but when he comes to say more about just what the offense of the lie consists in, the depth of his disagreement with Augustine becomes dramatically evident. For Kant, what's wrong with speaking duplicitously to someone else is that the liar brings it about (or contributes to bringing it about) that "speech—declarations—in general can't be trusted, with the result that all contract-based rights fall away and lose their power, which is a wrong done to humanity in general." The lie, to put the same point differently, always does harm, if not to some particular other then to humanity in general, for it vitiates—brings to nothing—the very source of right *(Rechtsquelle)*, which is the trustworthiness of speech.

Kant here makes much play with the word *Recht,* not all of which is easy to reproduce in English. His use of the word gives it a range of meanings: legal right, right in general, what's right as opposed to what's wrong. The lie breaks, empties, or vitiates right in all these senses. Most significantly, the fundamental assumptions of the law of contract, which include the idea that the speech of parties to contract is nonduplicitous, are broken by it. This is an *Unrecht,* a wrong, that goes beyond what's taught under the head of contracts and civil wrongs in contemporary law schools: it's a wrong that dissolves the glue of trust that binds together the fabric of society. And this, most fundamentally, is what's wrong with the lie, what makes it wrong. The inevitable conclusion of this line of thought is: "Truthfulness in all statements is, therefore, a holy and unconditionally commanding demand of reason, without limit by expediency."

An example of limit by expediency—limit, that is, to the formal, unconditioned duty to speak truthfully—is lying to murderers. The expediency in question is the saving of innocent life, and Kant certainly does not deny that it is possible to save innocent life by lying in such situations. Like Augustine, he is perfectly alive to the fact that particular lies may have particular effects, good and bad; but, also like Augustine, he thinks this fact irrelevant to the lie's wrongness. To lie in order to prevent harm, as Constant advocates, is quite compatible with thereby doing a wrong (Kant at this point retreats into Latin, using a juridical distinction between *nocere,* harm, and *laedere,* wrong). Harming someone is not the same as wronging them, and where your only alternatives are to harm by doing right or to prevent harm by doing wrong, you should choose to harm by doing right. Were you to choose to prevent harm by doing wrong, you would choose an action always and essentially wrong (such as lying), which only accidentally, in this particular case, has the effect of preventing a harm. If you abandon the right (truth-telling) in order to avoid a local and contingent harm that might result from it, you'll do something that Kant thinks literally senseless: you'll do something not coherently defensible. In fact, says Kant, it is not even correct to say that telling the murderers where their victim is has the effect that the victim is killed. Instead, it is the "accident" (and here Kant again uses Latin, *casus*, for technical effect) of the particular circumstance in which the truth is told, not the telling of the truth itself, that gives rise to the unpleasant effects.

For Kant to characterize the claim that one should speak truthfully whenever one speaks as a "principle of right" *(Rechtsprinzip* or *Rechtsgrundsatz)* is precisely to say that it is a rule without exceptions. And he makes this very clear toward the end of the lying essay by considering the case not of the liar, but of someone who (like Constant) is prepared to consider whether particular lies might properly be told:

> The one who is asked whether what he's about to say will be truthful or not, and who does not react with indignation at the suspicion thereby expressed that he might be a liar, but instead asks first whether he might consider possible exceptions—he is already potentially a liar. This is because he has shown that he does not recognize truthfulness in itself as a duty, but reserves to himself exceptions to a rule whose nature permits no exceptions because to do so would contradict itself.

The rule is exceptionless: it is contradicted by admitting a single exception, and so anyone who considers whether there might be exceptions is in fact considering whether to jettison the rule altogether. This is why such a person is a potential liar. In the same way, a potential prostitute is someone whose reaction to the suggestion that he might accept money to have sex with a stranger is to ask about the price. The only way to avoid being a potential liar is to consider the ban on the lie to be exceptionless, and as a result not to consider whether the situation might justify an exception.

The formal duty to speak nonduplicitously when you speak is for Kant (to return to the brief sketch of his ethical theory given at the beginning of this chapter) a duty informed and expressible by a maxim that can coherently be applied as a universal law—that is, coherently be thought of as incumbent upon everyone in all circumstances. The maxim in question is not stated clearly by Kant in the lying essay (like the absence of a clear definition of the lie itself, this is an important and surprising lack), but the most charitable interpretation of what he does explicitly say suggests that it is probably something like: *when you speak declaratively, do so nonduplicitously.* Kant most often uses the general term *Aussagen* (acts of speech, speakings) for that which you must not do duplicitously, but at least twice in the lying essay he glosses this term with others: *Deklarationen* (declarations), and *Erklärungen* (statements). This suggests that he does not mean to have the maxim cover all types of speech, but only those in which the speaker is likely to be taken to be speaking his mind, saying what he thinks. Kant's placing of the discussion within an analysis of the law of contract also suggests this, for when you enter into a binding contract (financial, matrimonial, adoptive, and so on) you are performing an act that implies the concordance of what you say with what you think.

If this is the right reading of the lying essay—that it is a formal duty to speak truthfully when you speak in such a way that you will likely be taken by others to be speaking your mind—then it follows at once that not all acts of speech, not all utterances, are covered by the formal duty. Kant does not, in the lying essay, provide examples of utterances that are not such as to make it likely that those who speak them will be taken to be speaking their minds. All (or most) of the stereotyped formulae of courtesy are free from this expectation: when I ask a casual acquaintance how he is, he's unlikely to think I want to know; when I sign a letter "Your obedient servant," its recipient won't think that I take myself to be his obedient servant—if he does, he is not at home with the ordinary etiquette of a society that uses such signatures. These utterances, and others like them, are, presumably (Kant does not say), exempt from the formal duty to truthfulness, which is to say that it is coherently possible to apply the maxim that you may untruthfully (duplicitously) say such things. Kant's ban on the lie is exceptionless with respect to the class of utterances it covers; but it has no purchase on some (perhaps many) utterances, and so does not ban duplicity with respect to those.

Kantians and interpreters of Kant's thought have not, in general, been very happy with the line of thought offered in the lying essay. This is mostly because they have wondered why speech to homicidal maniacs falls under the class of utterances in which you're expected to be speaking your mind. If it does not belong to this class then there's no immediate reason to think that there's a formal duty not to do it, any more than is the case for insincere use of the formulae of courtesy. It might, for example, be possible to understand the lie spoken to a homicidal maniac who knows that you think him to be a homicidal maniac—or at least knows that you know him to have murderous intentions; perhaps he's brandishing a revolver and muttering bloodcurdling threats as he asks you his questions—as an instance of actions whose maxim is (something like): *speak duplicitously in a situation where nothing else is expected by your interlocutor.* A maxim of this sort does not raise any difficulties for the trustworthiness of speech in general, and would therefore not obviously fall victim to the argument Kant offers in the lying essay. It would generate some paradoxes, of course: if it were a generally known maxim, then the would-be murderer would expect you to lie to him, and your lie might thus be made less effective. But these paradoxes, and the inner-Kantian discussions to which they lead, are not my concern here. In order to fulfill my purpose of using Kant as stimulus for Augustinian thoughts, I must now turn to the clarification of differences between the two, and to suggestions about how these might be resolved.

The similarities between Kant and Augustine on the lie are significant. Both want an exceptionless ban on duplicitous utterance of a certain sort, and both want to separate this ban from consideration of the circumstances surrounding individual instances of the speech-act in question, and most especially from consideration of intended or actual results. This means, among other things, that for both Augustine and Kant no instance of duplicitous speech can be justified by appeal to the good intentions that accompany it or the good results that flow from it—though each is clear that particular lies may be well-intentioned and may have good results. What is wrong with the lie, for both of them, is something unavoidably present in every instance of it, not something that may be present in only some instances. They agree, as well, that the ban on the lie is more than presumptive: it is not that what's wrong with duplicitous speech means that you should not so speak unless by not so speaking you'd be forced to do something worse. Lying is not like obeying traffic laws: those it is good to obey and bad to disobey, both Augustine and Kant would agree. But if obeying them means killing an innocent person, you'd better not obey them. The ban on obeying traffic laws is presumptive in the sense that it should be abandoned as soon as it becomes evident that something worse than disobeying traffic laws will result from obeying them. The ban on lying cannot be treated in this way: there is no conceivable circumstance in which it would make moral sense to abandon it.

But at this point the similarities cease. The first and deepest difference is in the analysis of what's wrong with the lie, or, better put, of what it is about the lie that makes it wrong. Kant's view is that the lie is to be placed under an exceptionless ban because of public, social facts—facts about the relations among human beings. If a juridical right to the lie in particular cases is established (and recall that in the lying essay Kant's discussion moves only in the sphere of *Recht* and *Pflicht*, of public rights and duties), thinks Kant, this will contradict at least one among the conditions of the possibility of a rightly ordered human society. Permitting the lie in order to save innocent life (or for any other particular consequence) stands in direct opposition to one of the necessities of social existence, which is that declarative speech be understood as trustworthy. Legislatively to understand declarative speech so that it is only sometimes to be sincere contradicts the very nature of such speech: it makes public declarative speech not-speech by placing under erasure something that must, if coherence is to be maintained, be protected from just such erasure. Kant's view of what it is about the lie that makes it subject to an exceptionless ban, then, depends on a particular view of the nature of public declarative speech, and sees the lie's occasional permission as contradicting precisely that nature.

Augustine's view of what's wrong with the lie, by contrast, has nothing to do with public space, social facts, or the relations among human beings. It has, in the end, only to do with facts about God, and about human nature as created in the image of God. These facts—that speech is gift, that its proper use is a return of gift to giver, and that the lie is a paradigm case of the attempt to expropriate the gift—make the lie performatively incoherent quite without respect to the public features of speech.

This difference between Augustine and Kant leads to a difference in defining and delimiting the speech-acts to be banned. Both agree that duplicity is the essential property of such acts—or, as the discussion earlier in this chapter should have made clear, this is probably what Kant means in the lying essay, though he is not quite explicit about it; but what it means for an utterance to be thought duplicitous cannot be quite the same for both. If lying is essentially a public or social fact, then duplicity will also have to be understood in the public sphere: it will have to belong to duplicitous utterances not only that they seem to their speakers not to make public what they take to be the case, but also that they are offered as public tokens of what they do not take themselves to think—tokens intended as counterfeit communicative currency whose endorsement (Kant thinks) would debase all genuine (nonduplicitous) communications. For Kant, then, the lie must not only be duplicitous but also intended to deceive. Indeed, it's the latter property that must be more important, for it is principally this that produces the contradiction that Kant appeals to in order to ground his ban upon the lie.

Augustine, by contrast, is more interested in duplicity than in the intention to deceive. Duplicity is a fact about the speaker best known to himself. In fact, as Augustine understands it, it must be known to the speaker. You can't be duplicitous without knowing that you are. This difference means that what counts as a lie for Kant will not always do so for Augustine, and vice versa. It is possible to intend to deceive without duplicity, as Augustine's discussion of the case of the skeptical friend (analyzed in ch. 1) shows.

But if what Kant bans under the label *Lüge* and what Augustine bans under the label *mendacium* are really different in this way, then it is clear that what seemed at first to issue in a conclusion very like Augustine's exceptionless ban is in fact deeply and irreconcilably different. Kant, like Aquinas, is led by his location of the analysis of the lie within the sphere of justice simply to exclude from his ban much of what Augustine embraces with his. Kant of course does not consider Aquinas an authority, so what in Aquinas was a mixed and half-Augustinian position has become in Kant a full-blown displacement of the question of the lie (and of speech more generally) from the sphere of human participation in the divinely given order of things to the sphere of relations among human beings, and (even more restrictively) to what goes on in the juridical and political arenas.

So much for the clarification of differences. In spite of some surface and some structural similarities, the differences go very deep and issue in two quite irreconcilable positions. How might resolution of these differences be attempted? It will do no good to criticize Kant for thinking with insufficient seriousness as a Christian thinker, for in his work on the lie, as elsewhere and always, he makes no attempt whatever to think as a Christian thinker. To think as a Christian about the lie is to begin from substantive assertions about human nature, divine nature, and the nature of human speech, assumptions given by an authoritative tradition constituted largely by Scripture as read and interpreted by the church. In the first half of this book I've shown how this works in Augustine's case. Kant does not, in this sense, think as a Christian about the lie. He does think of himself as a Christian thinker, but the sense in which he understands this bears little or no similarity to the way in which Augustine understands it. Kant wants a formal exercise of pure thought, free of assumptions about God or human nature, by means of which he can show the lie's occasional permission to be incoherent and the duty to abjure it exceptionless. There is no easy way to resolve by argument the differences between these two modes of approach to the question. An Augustinian reading of Kant on the lie shows, certainly, how deep the differences go and how sharply pointed they are; it does not show that Kant is wrong (though of course if Augustine is right he must be wrong). Exactly the same is true of a Kantian reading of Augustine on the lie.

However, the Kantian method raises some difficulties for itself from which an Augustinian account is free. Augustine may begin his analysis of the lie from a substantive metaphysic—from, that is, richly complex claims about God and speech and us. He then derives from that metaphysic, as we've seen, the conclusion that the lie is a recursively self-contradictory act, a self-canceling act. Kant cannot do this: he must show, or try to show, that permitting the public lie is a formally or logically contradictory act, and he must show this without making use of substantive claims about human nature or God, or speech. But this is not so easy to do. It is far from clear that every instance of the lie is also an instance of actions whose maxims cannot coherently be universally willed, and this is largely because Kant's implicit understanding of what it is to lie—publicly to misrepresent what you take to be the case with the hope of deceiving your inter-locutors—locates the lie firmly within the public sphere, the sphere of justice. And in that sphere, as was evident already to Aquinas (ch. 12) and as will be clear again in Newman (ch. 14), some instances of the lie just don't meet the Kantian criterion of actions that must be banned on pain of formal contradiction. You can, it seems, perfectly well coherently intend that lying to those with murderous intent be universally practiced. So doing would not (or would not obviously) bring the trustworthiness of speech into general disrepute, any more than would lies of etiquette or jocose lies. It is therefore difficult for Kant to defend his advocacy of an exeptionless ban on the lie given his own assumptions—and this is the consensus of his interpreters. If you want an exceptionless ban on the lie, whether as understood by Augustine or as understood by Kant, you're better off as an Augustin-ian than as a Kantian.

This Augustinian commentary upon Kant's lying essay deepens the sense that the adequacy of the Augustinian position on the lie depends upon the adequacy of an Augustinian metaphysic of participation and the application of that metaphysic to speech. Kant's lying essay in no way challenges this, and while Kant's thought as a whole no doubt does provide a competitor for Augustine, it is not one that there appears any pressing necessity to engage. Or, to put the same point more modestly, the need that Augustinians have to engage Kant is of the same kind as the need that Kantians have to engage Augustine. It is not a deep need on either side. For Augustinians, Kantian thought can only appear as an instance of pagan thought whose starting point and fundamental assumptions are wrong to begin with. Argument is unlikely to be efficacious here. If Kantians are to become Christian—which would in the end mean abandoning Kantian ways of thinking and accepting broadly Augustinian ones—they will have to be among those "taught to listen to the divine Scriptures." Argument is unlikely to bring that about.

14

Newman

In January 1864, a review by Charles Kingsley of J. A. Froude's *History of England* appeared in *Macmillan's Magazine*. Froude's book was Whig history written from a hyper-Protestant position: it identified all that was or could be good in Europe with a pan-German Protestantism of a rationalist and muscular sort. This was a set of prejudices largely shared by Kingsley, then Regius Professor of Modern History at Cambridge and a man with a high public profile as novelist, historian, and controversialist. Kingsley took the opportunity given by reviewing a deeply anti-Catholic book like Froude's to air some of his own fixed ideas about the Catholic church and its clergy, including the following gem:

> Truth, for its own sake, had never been a virtue with the Roman clergy. Father Newman informs us that it need not, and on the whole ought not to be; that cunning is the weapon which Heaven has given to the saints wherewith to withstand the brute male force of the wicked world which marries and is given in marriage. Whether this notion be doctrinally correct or not, it is at least historically so.

The references to "brute male force" and "the wicked world which marries and is given in marriage" are quintessential Kingsley. The depiction of cunning as what opposes the laudable masculinity that marries (so runs the deep grammar of Kingsley's thought) was meant to identify those who advocate and use cunning with the feminized celibates also known as the "Roman clergy." A central element in Kingsley's anti-Catholic polemic is the unnaturalness of a church that (in his view) denigrates

heterosexual sex and the muscular masculinity that goes with it. It is
striking that he manages to smuggle this in even to the topic of truth
and the lie, which is what the quotation above is putatively about.

The "Father Newman" in question was John Henry Newman,
England's most famous nineteenth-century convert from Anglicanism
to Roman Catholicism. The conversion had occurred in 1845, when
Newman was forty-four. Kingsley's accusation came almost twenty years
later: memories were long, and Newman's duplicitous treachery, as it
had seemed to many in England, in abandoning the Church of England
for Rome remained fresh in many minds and was often the occasion for
barbed remarks like Kingsley's. Newman's habit was to let these pass
unremarked and uncontested, but this jibe, he decided, could not be
left alone. It called into question, he thought, not only his own probity
and veracity, but also that of the Roman clergy in general; and that, he
thought, could not be left unanswered.

This was the beginning of one of the more colorful episodes of intellectual controversy in mid-Victorian England. The rhetoric of insult
was then highly refined, and was deployed to striking effect by both
men. Kingsley, for example, says that Newman has been led by an
oversubtle intellect and an oversensitive temperament to become "the
slave and puppet seemingly of his own logic, really of his own fancy,
ready to believe anything, however preposterous, into which he could,
for the moment, argue himself." He says that Newman has been led
by his Romish interest in miracles and saints to become imaginatively
"more materialist than the dreams of any bone-worshipping Buddhist";
and he likens Newman to "a treacherous ape, [who] lifts to you meek
and suppliant eyes, till he thinks he has you within his reach, and then
springs, gibbering and biting, at your face." Newman was not much
more restrained. One example will suffice:

> [T]here are people of matter-of-fact, prosaic minds, who cannot take in
> the fancies of poets; and others of shallow, inaccurate minds, who cannot
> take in the ideas of philosophical inquirers. In a Lecture of mine I have
> illustrated this phenomenon by the supposed instance of a foreigner, who,
> after reading a commentary on the principles of English Law, does not get
> nearer to a real apprehension of them than to be led to accuse Englishmen
> of considering that the Queen is impeccable and infallible, and that the
> Parliament is omnipotent. Mr. Kingsley has read me from beginning to
> end in the fashion in which the hypothetical Russian read Blackstone; not
> I repeat, from malice, but because of his intellectual build. He appears to
> be so constituted as to have no notion of what goes on in minds very dif-
> ferent from his own, and moreover to be stone-blind to his ignorance.

The loss of these rhetorical habits is regrettable. Not only is our own argumentative discourse less colorful and less interesting than that of almost any other age (Augustine and Jerome could rival Newman and Kingsley in the imaginative use of the rhetoric of insult); but also our elevation of the virtue of politeness and courtesy over that of passionate and pointed argument suggests that we don't think our disagreements very important. For Newman and Kingsley a great deal was at stake, and their rhetoric reflects this. Would that ours did.

The chief interest of the Kingsley-Newman debate for my purposes is that it prompted Newman to devote some intellectual energy and some prose to the question of the lie. This was a topic that had interested him in a passing way since his days as an Anglican: he was widely read in the Greek patristic tradition (rather less so in the Latin), and as a result he knew the positions on the question represented by Origen, Clement, and Chrysostom. But it is unlikely that he would have written more about the topic if he had not been prompted to do so by Kingsley's accusation that he, like the "Romish clergy" in general, depreciated the virtue of truthfulness.

Newman's response to Kingsley's charges was to write the *Apologia pro Vita Sua*, an intellectual history of the process by which he became convinced that the Anglican Church was not in fact part of the one, holy, catholic, and apostolic church in which Anglicans then and now confess belief Sunday by Sunday. He wrote this book-length document in a frenzy of effort between March and May of 1864; most of it deals with the changes in his ecclesiological and historical views from the 1830s to his conversion in 1845, and although he told this story in order to rebut the charge that he had been duplicitous in pretending still to have Anglican convictions long after he had in fact abandoned them, he says little in the body of the book about the particular question of the lie. But in the *Apologia*'s concluding part, published as an appendix both in the work's initial serial publication and in its first edition as a book (both in 1864), he gave a detailed response to most of Kingsley's particular charges. Among these were that he advocated "the economy" with respect to speech—meaning, roughly, that he supported the ideas about *oikonomia* and *dispensatio* discussed above in connection with Jerome, Chrysostom, and Cassian; and that, more generally, his attitude to and understanding of the lie's moral character made it too often permissible. Beginning in 1865, this appendix was recast into a series of lengthy notes in which reference to Kingsley's particular charges was dropped, but the substantive discussion largely retained. I shall draw upon this later version in what follows: the relevant material is in note F

("The Economy") and note G ("Lying and Equivocation"), and in the last ten pages or so of the main text of the *Apologia* in its 1865 version.

First, then, "the Economy" (usually capitalized by Newman). In writing about his early studies in the Greek Fathers, Newman rhapsodizes about a "sacramental principle" he found in Clement, Origen, and Athanasius, according to which "various Economies or Dispensations of the Eternal" were depicted. It is worth quoting him at length on this:

> I understood these passages [that is, those on economy/dispensation in the fathers] to mean that the exterior world, physical and historical, was but the manifestation to our senses of realities greater than itself. Nature was a parable; Scripture was an allegory: pagan literature, philosophy, and mythology, properly understood, were but a preparation for the Gospel. The Greek poets and sages were in a certain sense prophets, for "thoughts beyond their thought to those high bards were given." There had been a directly divine dispensation given to the Jews; but there had been in some sense a dispensation carried on in favour of the Gentiles. He who had taken the seed of Jacob for His elect people had not therefore cast the rest of mankind out of his sight. In the fulness of time both Judaism and Paganism had come to nought; the outward framework, which concealed yet suggested the Living Truth, had never been intended to last.

Newman here summarizes (he must have had the book open before him) a part of what he'd said about the economy in his book about the Arians of the fourth century, on which he'd worked as a young man in 1831–1832. In that book, the principle of the economy had been identified as a contribution made to Christian thought by the Alexandrians (Clement and Origen in particular). Newman's understanding of the principle did not change much from the 1830s to the 1860s. According to it, the visible and transient world is ordered by God in such a way as both to conceal and suggest what is finally real, which is eternal. The events of the created order cannot fully reveal what they suggest because the temporal is in principle incapable of fully communicating or showing the eternal. God must, therefore, dispense or economize eternal truth by using temporal devices—covenant with the Jews, inspiration (half-understood, naturally) of the pagans, and so on. Newman's favorite examples of divine economy are the incarnation (the flesh of Christ both conceals and suggests the godhead) and the eucharistic elements. These ideas and terms are present in Augustine, too: I've noted his use of the phrase *carnis dispensatio* to describe the incarnation, and as Newman's patristic work showed him, such an idea of the divine economy is scattered broadside through the works of the fathers, Greek and Latin.

Application of such an understanding of the economy to human speech is, however, more controversial. Augustine resisted it, as we have seen; Newman embraces it. He takes it to be obvious that we need some principle by which to assess when and to what extent we may properly intend that our speech not fully reflect our thought, and he thinks (along with Jerome, Chrysostom, Cassian, and many others) he has found it in the economy. But the "Rule of the Economy," as he likes to call it, does not justify any and every intentional separation between thought and speech. What it does denote, he says, is a "cautious dispensation of the truth, after the manner of a discreet and vigilant steward." The principle governing this cautious dispensation is that you ought to choose from among permissible or licit utterances whichever is "most expedient and most suitable at the time for the object in hand." Newman provides scriptural examples of the application of this principle, among which are: Jesus' pretense of going farther on the road past Emmaus when in fact he intended to stop and break bread with those he'd been accompanying (Luke 24:28); Jesus' harsh words to the Syrophoenician woman whose daughter he was about to heal (Mark 7:24–30); and Paul's circumcision of Timothy when Paul thought circumcision useless (Acts 16:3; Gal. 5:6; 6:15).

The illustrative scriptural examples Newman gives are not all of the same sort. Each seems meant to illustrate some division or dissonance between what is thought and what is done or said; but in the case of the Syrophoenician woman, at least, it isn't obvious that there is any such dissonance. The most natural reading of that story is that Jesus changes his mind about being willing to help the woman and her daughter, not that what he thinks is at odds with what he does and says. It seems, however, that Newman did cite the story to illustrate a disharmony between Jesus' thought and action, like that between Paul's circumcision of Timothy and his view (or at least his claim) that circumcision is never necessary or efficacious, and like that between Jesus' gesture of continuing to walk and his intention not to do so. Other interpretations of these scriptural texts are possible, too; but since Newman takes them to be illustrative of the economy as applied to speech and action, I assume that he understands them all to depict instances of intentional dissonance between thought and speech or action.

Newman emphasizes that these scriptural instances show the principle of the economy applied to speech (and action) because none of them involves intrinsically illicit or sinful speech. If they did, he acknowledges, then economizing speech would be an example of doing evil in order that good might come, and this is neither what the economy advocates nor what Newman accepts. The economy advocates only finding and using the most appropriate and effective words for the situation in which you find yourself, and this is a "rule which nature suggests to everyone." There is no Augustinian objection to the rule as framed: if you have a choice among licit or permissible utterances, then of course your choice should be guided by considerations of expedience and effectiveness. But the principle as it stands gives no guidance as to what makes an utterance licit, and so the principle of the economy as Newman states it stands neutral to the Augustinian ban on the lie. Determining whether, from an Augustinian point of view, Newman's doctrine of the economy is acceptable depends entirely upon whether the criteria he uses to determine an utterance's permissibility are defensible.

So much, in a preliminary way, for the principle of the economy. An Augustinian application of it to the question of whether one may ever lie (intentionally speak duplicitously) would yield the conclusion that one may not. How, then, does Newman apply it?

He is slippery on the question of the lie's definition. He notes, forcefully and repeatedly, that the definitional question is difficult, no less so for Protestants than for Catholics; and that even forceful proponents of muscular Christian virtue like Milton (and, he clearly thinks though doesn't say, Kingsley) have been troubled by it and have often ended by defining it in such a way as to make particular lies defensible or required. But in the end, Newman forces himself to the sticking point, and makes some necessary distinctions.

The fundamental question, he thinks, is whether "some kind or other of verbal misleading" is licit for just cause. Newman's answer to this question is yes, and he thinks that everyone will agree that it should be yes. What, then, are the kinds of verbal misleading, and what the just causes that do (or might) permit them? This way of posing the question shows clearly that Newman's thought on the lie is framed by the question of justice, as Aquinas's also was. This predisposes him toward the use of a consequentialist calculus to decide particular disputed cases: if what's wrong with the lie is that it offends against duty to others, then it will not be difficult to justify particular lies when they seem likely to prevent more damaging transgressions of duty to others, such as murder or rape. The phrase "verbal misleading," too, as a portmanteau-word for kinds of lie, suggests that Newman's interest is in the lie's effects, actual or intended, upon its hearers rather than upon its speakers.

Newman distinguishes four kinds of verbal misleading that might be justifiably performed under some circumstances (*ex iusta causa* as he likes to put it). The first is silence, which he thinks, as Augustine also does, poses no particular moral problems. Since not to say something can scarcely be categorized convincingly as a kind of verbal misleading, and since from an Augustinian point of view Newman's defense of it raises no difficulties, I'll say no more about his discussion of silence.

Second, there is evasion. To evade, on Newman's understanding, is for someone to "state some truth, from which he is quite sure his hearer will draw an illogical and untrue conclusion." "Illogical" here means a conclusion that does not strictly follow from what has explicitly been said; and "untrue" means that the conclusion drawn by the hearer will be one not taken as true by the speaker. Newman's example of evasion is the famous story about Athanasius: Julian the Apostate sends some soldiers to find and arrest Athanasius, bishop of Alexandria, as part of his attempt to proscribe Christianity and reestablish paganism in the early 360s. Athanasius has left Alexandria in disguise. Julian's soldiers come upon him on the road and, not seeing through the disguise, ask him where Athanasius might be found. Athanasius answers, "He is not far from you." What Athanasius says is true and is so taken by him. But the soldiers, as he intends, take it to imply that the man saying these words is not Athanasius. They go off to search the neighborhood and Athanasius safely escapes. Another example (not Newman's but mine): you ask me whether I have any children; I reply, "I have a son," as indeed I do. You conclude, as I mean you to, that I have just one child, the son I mentioned. But in fact I also have a daughter, and that fact had not escaped my mind when I gave you my answer. A third example, this one Newman's: you ask me whether Christians believe in a Trinity; I reply, "We Christians believe in one God." Among the conclusions you draw from this is—contrary to what I take to be the case—that Christians do not believe in a Trinity.

These examples are identical in the following respects: a speaker says something that seems to him true, and he says it in a situation in which he reasonably expects his hearers to draw from what he says a false conclusion about what he takes to be the case. Newman's formulation is not so precise (he does not consistently make the distinction between "a truth" and "what a speaker takes to be true"), but this is what he means. This is evasion, and as Newman rightly says, it is pervasive in some areas of human life: "The greatest school of evasion . . . is the House of Commons," he says, quite rightly. A thread running through the Newman-Kingsley debate is the question of Englishness. Kingsley thinks that any permission of the lie is fundamentally and essentially un-English (he also thinks Roman Catholicism incompatible with the English character). This is an accusation worrying to Newman, for he knows that many English people will agree with Kingsley about it, and he is half convinced of it himself, thinking as he does that some Catholic devotional habits and patterns of reasoning are inappropriate for the English. Newman takes, therefore, every opportunity he can to suggest that essential elements of Englishness (the House of Commons) are deeply and constitutively implicated with evasion, and perhaps, too, with what Augustine would call the lie. In doing this he is trying to suggest that the English character is not consistently opposed to the lie, and that Kingsley cannot therefore win the debate by simple jingoism.

Newman's judgment about evasion is that it may be justifiable in some circumstances (he does not provide examples). He thinks, too, that evasion is morally dangerous, especially to the clever, who will find it easy and perhaps attractive because of its ease. He wants, therefore, to avoid evasion as much as is consonant with justice and prudence, but doubts that such avoidance will always be possible. An Augustinian response to this can be brief: as Newman has defined evasion, it is never what Augustine would call a lie. Discussion of its acceptability or otherwise will then have to rest upon grounds other than those used to ban the lie.

Newman's third "kind of verbal misleading" is equivocation, which he also calls a play upon words. This he understands to occur when a speaker, knowing that a particular word has two or more acceptable senses, uses it in one of them (according to which he takes what he says to be true) while intending that it be taken in one of its other senses, according to which he takes what he will be understood to mean to be false. Again, Newman provides no examples, but the idea is clear enough. For example, the verb "to let" has still in English at least two different and almost diametrically opposed senses: it may mean "permit" or "prevent" (the latter more common in legal usage)—British passports until recently included the request from His (or Her) Britannic Majesty that the bearer be permitted to pass "without let or hindrance." If I know this, I may say, "I'll let you borrow my car," while thinking that I intend to prevent you from borrowing my car and at the same time intending you to think that I will permit you to do so. This is equivocation, and the speaker who equivocates in this way says something he takes to be true while knowing (and intending) that his words might be taken in such a way as to convince his listeners that he thinks the opposite of what he thinks.

Equivocation and evasion, on Newman's understanding of them, are identical in intention and effect. But while Newman allows the latter, with regret and reservation, he rejects the former completely, because, he says, he has "the English habit" of directness and straightforwardness. Newman does not expound his reasons for rejecting equivocation. I don't doubt that the depth of Kingsley's scorn, shared by many Anglican thinkers, for the equivocations permitted and argued about by eighteenth-century Catholic moral casuistry (adjectives such as "Jesuitical" are favored on this topic, and Alphonsus Liguori, though no Jesuit, is a frequent whipping-boy, and is Jesuitical at least to the extent that he is anti-Jansenist) made it impossible for him to do anything other than deny the propriety of this mode of verbal misleading on the simple ground of Englishness. But perhaps a more developed and more theoretically convincing reason for rejecting equivocation can be offered. Equivocation differs from evasion by requiring that the speaker have in his mind (at least) two different senses of a word important to what he's saying. Evasion does not. This is the only significant difference between the two modes of misleading. It can be made a reason to have more doubts about equivocation than about evasion, for it requires the equivocator to approach more closely to duplicity than does the evader. If you know the range of meanings possible for "let"—which you'd have to in order to equivocate with it—you'll have to make serious efforts to ensure that your utterance is sufficiently well-formed to make it express what you take to be the case at the same time as be likely to mislead others about what you take to be the case. As suggested in the discussion of figurative talk and jokes in chapter 1 above, the necessity of such effort moves equivocation closer to the Augustinian lie than is the case with evasion. An Augustinian line of thought of this sort about equivocation would suggest likely difficulties, but such difficulties would not always or inevitably make equivocation into a lie, and therefore would not ban it for that reason.

But this is not Newman's reason for rejecting equivocation. He is simply revolted by its calculating deviousness, by its incompatibility with the mid-Victorian ethic of the gentleman, and by its general inelegance. He would never do it or advocate it, he says, and would rather "lie materially" than equivocate. In saying this he mentions his fourth kind of verbal misleading and at the same time shows how very far he is in thinking about the lie from an Augustinian position. The material lie as Newman understands it is "saying the thing that is not," by which he means (though does not quite say) speaking against the mind, uttering what one takes to be false (he usually calls this just "falsehood," with some evidence of the usual confusions that this can lead to). "Saying the thing that is not," then, just is the Augustinian lie. To lie formally, as distinct from materially, is then to say the thing that is not, without just cause. The presence of just cause is what distinguishes the material lie from the formal lie. The latter is always and without exception forbidden, says Newman; but the former may be allowed just because there is just cause for it.

Newman draws upon analogies with murder and theft for this position. Materially, he says, murder is killing: killing another human being is its matter, the action in which it essentially consists. But formally, murder is killing in the absence of just cause: this is the full form of the act. And clearly, he thinks, there are material murders (killings) that are not formal murders precisely because there is just cause for them: killing in self-defense, killing done by the state of those guilty of capital crimes, and so on. Similarly with theft: its matter is taking what you don't own without permission; but just cause (imminent starvation, perhaps) can exempt some acts of this sort from the formal category of theft.

These analogies show as clearly as anything could that Newman thinks of the lie's matter—saying the thing that is not, simple Augustinian duplicity—as capable of exemption from the category of things that should never be done. This exemption can be given only by something external to the matter of the act itself: by the agent's intention, the intended result, the pressures upon the agent, or even, interestingly, the clarity with which norms about the acceptable untruth have been communicated by elites. On this last Newman writes:

> I would oblige society, that is, its great men, its lawyers, its divines, its literature, publicly to acknowledge as such, those instances of untruth which are not lies, as for instance untruths in war.

Why is it important for élites to provide clear and systematic guidance as to when an untruth (an Augustinian lie) is not a lie? Because without it, our consciences will be confused and our habits ill-formed. We know (thinks Newman) that when a soldier on the right side kills another in a just war no murder has happened. We know this because the messages we are sent about it from our élites are unambiguous and frequent. We are not generally confused about the difference between killing-for-just-cause and simple murder. But we have no such clarity about the situations in which untruths are not lies; and because Newman is sure that there are such situations, he thinks it possible and desirable that there be such clarity, or at least that we approach more closely to it.

Newman's position offers no new challenge to an Augustinian view of the lie. Like Jerome, Cassian, and Chrysostom, Newman is sure that there are defensible (perhaps even required) Augustinian lies. And he is like Aquinas in thinking about the lie largely within the frame of justice understood as duty to other human beings, and as a result exempting those deliberately duplicitous acts that don't obviously offend against justice from the category of sin *stricto sensu*—or, if a distinction between mortal and venial sin is allowed, from the category of mortal sins. This explains why Newman can say with such assurance that he'd rather lie materially than equivocate. For him, the ethic of the English gentleman (in this matter at least) trumps that of the Christian. Or, to put the same point in another way, there is no hint in Newman's thought on the lie of any attempt to think about the nature and purposes of speech as governed principally by the triune image in which we are made. This lack in turn leads to the absence of an attempt to think of the lie in terms of God rather than in terms of us. And this is the fundamental reason why an Augustinian answer to the great questions of the lie is not only not given by Newman, but not even seriously engaged or raised by him.

15

Nietzsche

Nietzsche writes extensively about truth and lies, especially in his essays and notebooks from the early 1870s, though he nowhere treats the topic in any systematic fashion. This is not unusual: he is an aphoristic writer with his own good reasons for avoiding the systematic treatise, and so it is difficult to find a systematic treatment of any topic in his work. In this chapter I'll comment upon the essay "Über Wahrheit und Lüge im aussermoralischen Sinne," which in English is "On Truth and Lie in an Extramoral Sense." I'll call it "the truth essay" in what follows. It was begun in 1872 and completed in 1873, before Nietzsche was thirty, and well before he wrote the major works of the 1880s. The later Nietzsche's interests shift to some extent to different matters, and even where they do not, he often uses a vocabulary significantly at odds with that evident in his early work. So the usual warnings apply: the remarks that follow are relevant mostly (and in some cases only) to what Nietzsche writes in this essay.

Nietzsche's style is warm, contrived, and overexcited. He strives for effect and often overreaches. But because of the idiosyncrasy and intensity of his style, I've chosen to quote him more than most of my other conversation-partners for Augustine. The flavor and texture of the prose is, in Nietzsche, itself a part of the argument, and in this he is more like Augustine than any of those other interlocutors.

Nietzsche begins by writing of the invention of knowing *(Erkennen)*. This, he says, occurred in a moment of supreme arrogance and mendacity *("Es war die hochmüthigste und verlogenste Minute")*. It is arrogant because the human intellect, that which knows (or takes itself to know), becomes self-important as soon as it begins to understand itself as a knower: the philosopher, the ideal type of the knower, begins to think that he is the center of the universe, that the eyes of the universe are "focused telescopically upon what he does and what he thinks." But this is an illusion. The universe has no interest in human acts of knowing: we are ephemeral, without significance to the universe, and so our pride in our knowings is deceptive, mendacious:

> The arrogance connected with knowing and sensing is a fog that blinds the eyes and senses of men. It deceives us about what human existence is worth, and carries with it a supremely flattering estimation of the worth of knowing itself. Its most general effect is deception, but even its particular effects carry with them something of the same character.

Deceit *(Täuschung)* is what overestimating the significance of our capacity to know does to us. We misunderstand ourselves as knowers, and the very fact that we do so has survival value because it permits us to pretend to be what we are not, which in turn helps us to survive, to flourish in an inhospitable universe and among the threats and dangers of human society. Nietzsche is eloquent about the varieties of pretense and posturing:

> Here [among the arts of dissimulation] are deception, flattery, lying, deluding, talking-behind-the-back, the false front, living with borrowed splendor, the mask, hiding behind convention, posturing in front of others and in front of oneself.

All this flows from arrogance and toward vanity; it is in equal parts deceit of others and deceit of self. Notice that Nietzsche says that we posture in front of ourselves as much as in front of others. Overestimating our capacity to know—glorying in it, elaborating and ornamenting it—is what makes all this possible; what motivates it is principally the desire to maintain ourselves in the face of competition with others.

Combined with this tissue of deceit and pretense, says Nietzsche, is a surprisingly profound and passionate drive for truth *(Trieb zur Wahrheit)*. In part this drive is a social necessity: we need to be able to speak to one another, to check the Hobbesian war of each against all, and so we need a "linguistic legislation" by means of which we can agree which words stand for which things and how language is properly to be used. These are necessities of communication and therefore also necessities of social existence; they lead, says Nietzsche, inevitably to the establishment of a contrast between truth *(Wahrheit)* and the lie *(Lüge)*. "The liar," he says, "deploys the proper designations, the words, in order to make the unreal appear as real." The liar is one who misuses linguistic conventions for his own benefit: he calls himself rich when he is poor, clever when he is stupid, truthful when he is mendacious. This is not approved by others: there is a social need for truth, and this is the first explanation of the drive for truth about which Nietzsche has raised a question. It is a drive for what makes social life possible and comfortable, and it explains the shunning of the man who comes to be known as a liar.

The act of speaking truthfully, for Nietzsche, is then most fundamentally an act of abiding by convention. Nietzsche had almost certainly read Kant's lying essay (ch. 13); and he was persuaded by part of the argument of that essay, as well as by elements in his own thought uninfluenced by Kant, that the liar who lies by offending against socially established convention is indeed committing an offense against trust. But it is important to note that Nietzsche's defense of truth-speaking in this sense of abiding by convention is always understood by him to be a eudaemonistic defense, a defense, that is to say, of a broadly consequentialist kind in terms of the benefits to be had by it. Refusing to use the names that have been agreed upon would, he says, be discourteous and confusing to all concerned. The offense is one of manners, not morals, and it is fair to assume (though Nietzsche does not say so) that in cases where failing to use the agreed words would not cause such a breach of manners, there would be no offense. The offense of the conventional liar is defined by its context and its result, which means that it is still an offense, but not a nonnegotiable demand. There may be contexts in which committing it has better results than refusing to commit it.

But there is another sense of truth and truthfulness whose very possibility is rejected by Nietzsche. Suppose language were capable of reflecting or imaging the essence of things. Suppose "speech was the adequate expression of all realities." Utterance might then be true in the sense that it adequately and accurately described, imaged, or referred to its topic. This, says Nietzsche, is not possible. All language is metaphorical: it has its origins in physiology, in what he usually calls the stimulation of the nerves; its middle point in irreducibly particular mental images; and its end in words, combined to make utterances. At each point there is a move from one sphere into another of an entirely different order: the physiological sphere is not the sphere of mental images, and neither is the sphere of words. The move from one sphere to another cannot be captured by talk of imaging or reflecting; it can at best be suggested by talk of creative acts of translation, each of which is finally metaphorical in the sense that it carries over something from one sphere to another, and none of which is literal because none can simply image, reflect, or refer to that to which it is causally related.

This lack of capacity to image, reflect, or refer is especially obvious to Nietzsche in the case of the relations between words and the mental life to which they are causally related, and which they might mistakenly be supposed to image. A word, for Nietzsche, is best understood as the sonic effect of a neural excitation. An illustration he uses for the kind of effect he has in mind is a device developed by the German physicist Ernst Friedrich Chladni to represent the vibrations of sound in a visible medium. Chladni attached a series of strings to a sand-covered flat surface, and then caused the strings to vibrate at different frequencies. The resulting patterns in the sand he called "sound figures." These sand figures don't image or reflect the music of the vibrating strings. They can't do so because they occur in a different medium. But the sand figures are caused by the vibrating strings, and (Nietzsche would prefer to say) figure them metaphorically. The representation of nerve-stimuli and mental images in words, says Nietzsche, is inevitably like this, and this is why literal representation in words of what language is supposed to be about cannot be achieved.

From this view it follows that all utterance (and all writing) is figurative. It follows further that language and reality can be related only aesthetically, through tropes, and, further yet, that the artist, the one especially skilled with tropes, will be the one able to figure the relation with the greatest intensity. It is this universalization of metaphor which underlies Nietzsche's definition of truth as

> [a] movable host of metaphors, metonymies, and anthropomorphisms . . . a sum of human relations which have been poetically and rhetorically intensified, transferred, and embellished, and which, after long usage, seem to a people to be fixed, canonical, and binding. Truths are illusions which we have forgotten are illusions; they are metaphors that have become worn out and have been drained of sensuous force, coins which have lost their embossing and are now considered as metal and no longer as coins.

The upshot is that Nietzsche recognizes (at least) three senses in which utterances may be true, and connects each with a particular kind of lie. The first sense in which utterances may be true is by agreement with convention. This is the conventional sense of truth. The second is by imaging or reflecting reality in a literal way. Let's call this the nonmetaphorical sense. The third is by attaining a high degree of metaphorical intensity. Let's call this the artistic sense. He affirms both the possibility and the desirability of utterances that bear conventional truth, but in so doing he acknowledges that these are true only by courtesy, and so he often calls them lies. He denies, as we've seen, for his own theoretical reasons, the possibility that any utterance could be nonmetaphorically true. Thinking that it could is a delusion, and also a special kind of lie. And he affirms both the possibility and the desirability of utterance that bears artistic truth: it is what he strives for himself, what he recognizes in the early Wagner and excoriates the absence of in the later Wagner. But here too Nietzsche often resorts to the language of lies: the truths of creative artists are lies because creative artists are, inevitably, liars (here Nietzsche consciously plays with Plato) in the sense that they reject both conventional and nonmetaphorical truth; but they are the best liars (here he rejects Plato), the liars who speak the most truth, because it is only in the intensity of rhetorical play found in their modes of expression that language comes close to producing the kind of figure that cannot be transfigured, the supremely figurative figure.

But these remarks are, perhaps, almost as cryptic as Nietzsche himself. They need expansion in order for it to become clear just what he thinks is wrong with lying in the various senses in which he uses that term. Consider the columbarium: this is an image Nietzsche uses to figure the lies required by conventional truth. A columbarium is a pigeonholed container for the ashes of cremated bodies (*columba* is the Latin word for "dove," and so a columbarium is a dovecote; the Romans appear to have liked to keep pigeons as much as the working-class English used to, and to have kept them in much the same way). It serves for Nietzsche as a figure for the "great edifice of concepts" produced for us by the social demand to use the customary metaphors. Concepts are the ashy residue of metaphors, just as the contents of a columbarium are the ashy residue of living bodies. Concepts are still metaphors for Nietzsche; but they are metaphors that no longer seem like metaphors to their habitual users. They have become frozen, petrified, dead, spread out in changeless spatial form with a rigidity that encloses their users in a pattern from which they cannot escape. Seeking to speak in accord with this dead residue is what Nietzsche means by seeking to speak conventional truth. It is, to put the same thing only slightly differently, seeking to lie, because the ashy metaphors in the columbarium are neither ultimate nor artistic truth: they don't reflect the way things are because they can't, and they aren't living, creative metaphors because they have been consumed and can be present only as a constricting, dead presence. Recall that for Nietzsche speaking the lying truths that are demanded by our social being is both inevitable and proper. But it is also a mendacious act that deals death when it is misunderstood as a reflection or imaging of the order of things.

The ashily inevitable lies of conventional truth are always called into question by the *Trieb zur Metapherbildung*, the drive for the development of new metaphors. This drive finds its paradigmatic expression in artistic creation—musical, literary, and visual. But here too there is inevitably lying and deception. The artist is, according to Nietzsche, best understood as a "master of representation," which is to say that all his work bears the mark of dissimulation. In this the artist's speech is no different from that of the conventional speaker, trapped in the columbarium. But it is different in that the lies told by conventional truth-tellers are indigent, needy of security and a sense of firmness and accuracy to the concepts they use. The lies of the artist, by contrast, use new metaphors to smash to pieces the edifice of concepts, and do so in conscious understanding that this is what they do. Nietzsche identifies science (and a certain kind of philosophy) as devoted to building up the columbarium, and art as devoted to breaking it down. Both lie and both deceive. But art does so freely and with poetic ecstasy; science does so grimly, without understanding what it does. The rational man, the philosopher-scientist (Nietzsche tends to use Heraclitus as the ideal type) is opposed to the artist. The former lives in the columbarium of concepts; the latter in the freedom of metaphor understood as such. The former is inartistic; the latter irrational. The former wants mastery by science; the latter mastery by heroic entry into the illusion of beauty. When the artist is dominant there is the possibility of culture, because "art's mastery over life" *("die Herrschaft der Kunst über das Leben")* is then apparent. What the artist invents, the products of his dissimulation, his lying invention, are not invented out of need but out of joy. Those of the lying philosopher-scientist are predicated precisely on a need to pretend to himself that he is not lying.

This explains why Nietzsche sometimes identifies the quest for nonmetaphorical truth as pathetic. Those who seek such truth are pathetic because they do not understand that what they are makes nonmetaphorical truth inaccessible to them. They have only the irreducible particularity of their own consciousness (this is the Kantian restriction on knowing modulated into a Nietzschean key), and the attempt to see through this into ultimate truth is doomed: it leads only to imprisonment. The better way is through art, which desires life and contributes to its richness, and as a result is happy with the lies that are all it can speak. For Nietzsche, the world cannot make any particular utterance true. This is not in its gift, even though we would desperately like it to be, and to say this clearly is as far as epistemology can go; it is a denial that any nonmetaphorical truth can be spoken. The truths of convention may and should be spoken, but always under the sign of the lie, because they have a tendency to convince those who speak them that they are nonmetaphorically true. And the truths of the artists, which are what the world most needs to hear, are the best and most glorious lies: they are to be sought and increased. As Nietzsche puts it elsewhere, "Our salvation does not lie in *knowing* but in *creating!* Our greatness lies in supreme semblance, in the noblest fervency. If the universe is no concern of ours, then at least we demand the right to despise it." The "supreme semblance" about which Nietzsche talks is, of course, the work of the poet, which is a lie from beginning to end. But Nietzsche's tropes about this lie, scattered broadside through his early work, show that he sees this lie as something rare, surprising, exciting, stimulating. By contrast the lie evident in the search for philosophico-scientific nonmetaphorical truth is common, familiar, dull, and deadening.

At the core of the grammar of Nietzsche's thought about the lie is the familiar Kantian claim that the nature of human beings and their relation to the world make the utterance of nonmetaphorical truth an impossibility. All human utterance is therefore a lie in the sense that it fails to attain this reflective status. Conventional truth-telling is a kind of lie that most people agree to tell for social benefit. Such lies may be told in the awareness that they are such, or in forgetfulness of this fact. In the former sense they are recommended and in the latter despised. Philosophico-scientific truths are lies of a more ambitious kind, lies that seek a nonmetaphorical truth that cannot be found; rationalist philosophers are therefore the most deeply self-deceived of all liars. And the lies of the artist (which are also artistic truths) are the best, the highest form of human utterance, though still lies for all that.

What, then, are the deepest differences between Augustinian thought on the lie and what Nietzsche has to say in the truth essay? The first point to make is that Nietzsche has nothing direct to say about the complex speech-act that Augustine identifies as *mendacium,* the lie. This is because Nietzsche takes the act identified as a lie by Augustine (and banned under that description) to be impossible. Recall that an Augustinian lie requires the liar to know her own mind and to misrepresent it to her audience: she has one thing locked in her heart and another ready on her tongue. Such a definition assumes the possibility that what the liar says might be begotten by and thus accurately represent (or image or reflect) what is in her heart; and such a possibility is ruled out by Nietzsche's theory of the relation between words and things. It follows that Nietzsche can neither ban nor permit such an act, since for him the conditions of its possibility do not obtain.

Another way to put this fundamental difference is to say that Nietzsche identifies actions that Augustine would call lies in a different way. Consider an example. If, being a Catholic Christian, thinking that I am, and taking being a Catholic Christian to rule out being a Buddhist, I try to get my interlocutors to think I'm a Buddhist by saying, "I'm a Buddhist," I lie, Augustinianly speaking. My thought, in such a case, does not beget my speech. But Nietzsche, though he might call this an instance of *Lüge*, the lie, would understand it as an instance of refusing to abide by socially given convention—an example of the conventional lie. Both Nietzsche and Augustine would, for the most part, agree in saying that such actions should not be performed. But an Augustinian must judge that Nietzsche's refusal of such actions is inadequate because it is based solely upon the calculation of consequences—as was also the case for Kant. I've already had occasion to note Augustine's refusal of such an attitude to lying, and his reasons for it.

An Augustinian reading of Nietzsche will not, however, stop there. Why is there this difference, and what may be done to resolve it? For Augustine, the possibility of uttering our thoughts in such a way as to reflect or image them in words is a gift of God. We have it because we are creatures made in the image of the triune God, and this means, among other things, that our words have the capacity to be begotten by our thoughts. We have been given the possibility of relating words to thoughts in the same way that the second person of the Trinity is related to the first. And it is just this possibility that permits the Augustinian lie. Here we have an ontology, a view about the nature of persons and their relations to God that is an outgrowth of a particular trinitarian theology. Intrinsic to this theology and its concomitant ontology is the idea of the gift. The possibility of telling the truth and of lying is then understood by Augustinians as an example of sheer gift—the gift of both thought and speech.

Nietzsche's thought on the lie—and, more broadly, on the nature of human speech—does not have this idea of the gift. In its absence, the nonmetaphorical correlation of word to thought and of thought to reality cannot be affirmed. Once the idea of the divine gift of such a possibility is lost or otherwise rejected, only two roads are open. One is the attempt to argue for the possibility that one can nonmetaphorically speak one's mind and that one's thought, nonmetaphorically spoken, can image the order of things, and to do so by appeal to nothing other than concepts and patterns of argument that can be understood and deployed (in principle) by all rational people. But Nietzsche assumes Kant's conclusion on this matter, which is that this can't be done. The possibility of nonmetaphorical truth, he assumes, can't be demonstrated by reason. Such attempts always fail, and, Nietzsche would say (and Augustine would agree), they always produce a columbarium of concepts, a rigid structure entry into which produces only death.

The second road from the denial or forgetfulness of the gift ends in the simple denial that nonmetaphorical truth-telling is possible, and so also the denial that Augustinian lying is possible. This is Nietzsche's position. The sin that Augustine identifies is, for him, based on a confusion. Truth-telling, for Nietzsche, is in the end a matter of manners, sanctioned as all etiquette always is by social pressure and in extreme cases by the force of law. The Nietzschean conventional lie is in its mild forms an offense against good manners and in its strong forms an offense against the legal constraints of contract.

Augustine and Nietzsche agree that the possibility of nonmetaphorical truth-telling and its concomitant form of lying cannot be demonstrated or refuted by the use of autonomous reason. For Augustine, the possibility of speaking one's mind and the possibility of the sinful lie are both given by God, as is the capacity to know that these are possibilities. For Nietzsche, the chastening of reason by the failure of attempts to offer autonomous demonstrations leaves only physiology and manners as resources for understanding what it is to lie and when to do it. Neither shows any evidence of thinking his position demonstrable in noncircular fashion to those who don't already share it. For Nietzsche, such people are either philistines or noble but self-deceived and inhuman philosophers. For Augustine, they are pagans or heretics. In neither case are they reachable by anything other than a form of catechesis, which in Augustine's case would take the form of the catechumenate, and in Nietzsche's of an artistic apprenticeship.

But this is not to say that either man takes reason to be utterly impotent in this matter. While it cannot show by arguments comprehensible and convincing to all that either position is wrong (or right), someone thinking from within one or another of the positions can indicate what can be learned from the other and what rejected. Following this line, there are four Augustinian points to make about Nietzsche's views on lying, three critical and one appreciative. They will not convince followers of Nietzsche that they are wrong, but they may indicate strategies for further thought about the matter in the future.

First, an Augustinian must say that Nietzsche's position on lying exhibits in a peculiarly sharp and elegant way the results of abandoning the idea of the divine gift. Without this idea, language becomes disconnected from a disenchanted world, and thoughts become explicable in terms of physiology. Language becomes an artifact, one that may trap its makers as it does when it is used to construct a columbarium, or one that may force them into the endlessly repeated activity of forging new metaphors—the *Trieb zur Metapherbildung* connected with the likelihood of eternal recurrence. In either case, language and its makers assume an importance whose weight they cannot, from an Augustinian perspective, bear. The strong poets whose work is advocated by the early Nietzsche, whose own work, early and late, itself bears the marks of just such a strongly poetic temperament, are always, as he acknowledges, vastly outnumbered by the philistines and the self-deceived rationalists. The upshot, then, from an Augustinian point of view, is that Nietzsche's radical attempt to take freehold possession of language by emptying it of its intimately symbiotic relation to the second person of the Trinity collapses under its own weight. Such a view cannot be borne (not even, finally, by Nietzsche), and almost all of us are relegated by it to self-deceit and the stasis of conceptual death. This is exactly what an Augustinian would expect. Language brings life, paradoxically, only if it is possible to tell nonmetaphorical lies with it, which in turn is possible only if speech (and writing) can be begotten by thought. Otherwise, the death that Nietzsche finds in the conceptual columbarium cannot be escaped, and loving language, as Nietzsche does, can only be to embrace a corpse.

Second, there is a self-referential problem with Nietzsche's views. If nonmetaphorical truths can't be spoken, and if, as seems to be the case, a theory of language is offered to show why this is so, then it seems at first blush that the theory of language in question needs to be nonmetaphorically true in order for it to do the work its constructor made it to do. But if the theory of language is nonmetaphorically true (recall that Nietzsche's theory of this sort moves, in the truth essay, from physiology to image to word), then it has refuted itself, for it ought, if true, to guarantee that there are no nonmetaphorical truths. There are, perhaps, ways around this difficulty, and I think it very likely that the later Nietzsche saw the difficulty and made some adjustments to his theory in order to meet it. But it remains a difficulty, nonetheless, and one that an Augustinian would expect to be present in all theories of the sort recommended by Nietzsche.

Third, Nietzsche's views about (what he would call) conventional lying are deeply inadequate, from an Augustinian perspective, to constrain our tendencies to tell such lies. They, and theories like them, inform the tendencies that most of us have to think about such lies chiefly in terms of manners. We don't like to be caught lying; we acknowledge the social undesirability of widespread and habitual lying; but we don't think of lying as something that, by itself, carries much moral weight. And so we lie with relative frequency and not too much discomfort.

Fourth, and finally, Augustinians should appreciate Nietzsche's emphasis on and positive assessment of the drive toward metaphor. Nietzsche, it is true, places this drive at the service of the heroic artist's self-assertion, while Augustine places it at the service of confession before God. But the two are at one in seeing the importance of the human capacity to play with language's endless possibilities for ornamenting and dramatizing the truth (as Augustine would call it), or the lie (as Nietzsche would call it). They place this capacity at the service of different ends, and they provide incompatible theoretical understandings of it. But each of them performs as virtuoso poet, and an Augustinian should appreciate and show reverence for Nietzsche's rhetorical capacities (even while judging his understanding of them to be deficient) just as much as Augustine appreciated Vergil's God-given skills as poet. For Nietzsche (at least the early Nietzsche) redemption is possible only through art; for Augustine, the possibility of art is a sign of redemption. Augustine provides a good counterexample to the Nietzschean thought that the metaphysician (and especially the Christian, but also the Platonist) is the enemy of art.

In chapter 3 I quoted Nietzsche's remarks on his reading of Augustine's *Confessions:* "O this old rhetorician! How false and eye-rolling he is! How I laughed—for example about the theft of his youth, nothing more than a student escapade." The letter in which he wrote these words continues:

> What psychological falsity! (for example when he talks about the death of his best friend with whom he shared a *single soul,* he "resolved to go on living, so that in this way his friend would not wholly die." Such things are revoltingly dishonest.) Philosophical value zero! *vulgarized* Platonism—that is to say, a way of thinking which was invented for the highest aristocracy of soul, and which he adjusted to suit slave natures. Moreover, one sees into the guts of Christianity in this book.

Nietzsche is right that in the *Confessions* one "sees into the guts of Christianity." But when he accuses Augustine of falsehood and mendacity, does he think that Augustine lies by offending against social convention (the first Nietzschean sense of the lie)? This seems unlikely. Is it, then, that Augustine lies by attempting to image or reflect reality, to depart from metaphor and to attain transparency of speech and thought—Nietzsche's second sense of the lie? This is possible; Augustine is, after all, a Platonist. But the very passage from the fourth book of the *Confessions* quoted (paraphrased, actually) by Nietzsche in this letter is saturated with metaphor, and the tools of the rhetor's trade. It should be the case, then, that the falsity Nietzsche accuses Augustine of is the artist's lie, the third sense of the lie. That it is not suggests that Nietzsche's disapproval of Augustine has nothing to do with the intensity of his metaphors, nothing to do with the extent to which his figures transfigure, but everything to do with the fact that what Augustine's figures serve—the God of Abraham and Isaac—is an object of horror to Nietzsche. Nietzsche is selective about the art he praises, and is so on the basis of convictions of a nonartistic sort (concepts drawn from the columbarium) about what is and must be the case.

Part Three

The Community of Truth

To say that we should not lie—that the lie is banned—can easily seem like an exhortation to pull up our socks, clean up our acts, and just stop lying. This is not what Augustine means. To think in such a way about the problem would be to think as a Pelagian, which would be to grant a power to the human will that it does not, since the fall, possess. The ban is not, therefore, meant as encouragement to effort. Such effort would inevitably fail. What is it then?

First, it is an element of central importance in Augustine's analysis of what it is like to be a speaker, a user of language, under the sign of sin. The lie is the ideal type of sinful speech, speech distorted by disordered desire. Arguing for a ban on the lie illuminates sin's nature. Second, the ban on the lie is a signpost toward what it would be like to speak without sin. Augustine's analysis of what's wrong with the lie is carried on always as counterpoint to his recommendation of confession and adoration as the only kind of nonsinful speech. Banning the lie serves in this way to show, seductively as much as argumentatively, what it would be like not to lie. This is far from the same thing as encouraging the liar to make an effort to stop lying. It is, instead, an attempt to depict what it would be like to turn the gaze away from the lie and toward the truth—which is to say, toward God.

This way of understanding Augustine means that his ban on the lie only makes sense in the light of God's graceful gifts. If the lie is avoidable only by reordering one's loves, and if such a reordering can take place only by turning one's gaze from self to God (from lie to truth), then it follows at once that a necessary condition for all this is that God gives himself to be gazed at, that God ceaselessly batters our hearts with the gift of himself. For Augustine, as for all Christians, that prevenient gift and remorseless offer is always to be understood as an act of the Triune God, the God who created the cosmos, who elected a people, who become incarnate, who was crucified and resurrected, who orders and inspires the church, and who makes himself available for our contemplation and consumption in the eucharistic worship of that same church. The lie is speech under the condition of sin: speech transformed by God's gift is the praise-shout of the church. The lie's ban has sense and purchase, then, only when understood and expressed as an element in the syntax of grace.

But this in turn means that the lie's ban can only be taken with full seriousness by those prepared to enter a community in which the praise-shout, the alleluia of worship, is the principal and fundamental act. This community is the church. In that community, God's remorseless offer is evident in fullest and liveliest glory. Apprenticeship to and forma-tion by the habits of that community constitute the only way in which Augustine's ban on the lie can make sense and become a real possibil-ity. The fact that we are made in the image of the Triune God explains what is wrong with the lie—why we should not do it. But it is far from sufficient as a condition for the possibility of abandoning the lie. Such a relinquishment requires the sanctifying grace of the church.

The church, however, has always its other. It is never the only com-munity in which Christians live: there is always a human city as well as a city of God, and it is always incumbent upon Christians to pay atten-tion to the norms and habits of their particular human city, for these necessarily provide particular challenges and obstacles to the life of the church. This will be true with respect to lying as much as with respect to anything else. If it is true that the ban on the lie can only become anything more than notional in a community of worship, then it will be normal that the human city will at all times find particular ways of avoiding the ban, praising the lie, and treating speech as an object to be owned. This is certainly true of our time, and while it is probably not the case that the inhabitants of the human city in the twenty-first century are more likely to be liars than those who've claimed citizenship in it at other times, it is the case that our particular human city has its own peculiar and characteristic ways of advocating and practicing the expropriation of speech.

The depth with which the norms and habits of our human city have entered into our souls is suggested by the fact that thinking as Augustine does about the lie is unlikely to be attractive to many. You, as reader of this book, are almost certain to have moral and practical intuitions that make the Augustinian ban on the lie unacceptable and the reasons for the ban dubious. This will be true whether or not you are a Christian: the distance between Augustine's metaphysic and ours is great; greater still would be the distance between a community that took the Augustinian ban seriously—a community of truth—and the forms of social, political, and economic life in which we live and move and have our being.

Autonomy and ownership are the two fundamental values of late-capitalist polities such as those of the United States, Western Europe, the former Soviet Empire (increasingly), and much of East Asia. The United States is the ideal type, the polity toward which in its own eyes all others should tend, and which in the eyes of others is either a city on a hill to be emulated or a Great Satan to be destroyed before its ambitions to Americanize the earth can be realized. In the United States, the twin ideals of autonomy and ownership are more deeply entrenched than elsewhere; there (here; it's where I live) they've taken on the most extravagantly rococo institutional forms and ordered the syntax and flavor of ordinary speech and behavior most comprehensively.

In the United States and its satellites and imitators the person is understood to be ideally autonomous in the sense that dependence upon others, while acknowledged as not quite avoidable—we all have to be born; we all need, from time to time, physical help and care—is seen as something to be minimized. We would, if we could, remove it altogether. And so we can (we do) justify killing those who will, because of physical or mental defects, lack autonomy in significant degree. We can (we do) justify letting such people kill themselves. We can (we do) justify killing those who threaten our autonomy with violence. We can (we do) permit and encourage the dissolution of binding vows (of marriage, for example) and irrevocable relationships (of parenthood, for example) if it seems to us that preserving such vows and relationships encroaches unduly upon the autonomy of those bound by them. And so on: the catechism of what commitment to autonomy requires by way of violence and blood is long.

Ownership goes almost as deep. Status is given principally by display of what is owned, and by capacity to increase what is owned and displayed. Among thoughts not thinkable is the idea that display can be excessive or that it is possible to own too much. The grammar of ownership has the syntax of consumption as a dominant element: the owner is someone who can buy; the act of buying, of purchasing, is the act by which owning is made real; and so the purchasing act is one (like orgasm) that ought to be performed as frequently as possible. To limit it, ascetically to constrain it, is understood not only to be odd and peculiar and strange, but also antisocial, a virus within the body politic. Frequent purchase, the orgasmic act of consumption, is what we are urged and exhorted to; and so ownership is front-loaded into purchase, and purchase front-loaded into consumption. We become, ideally, owners who will not be deterred by the fact that we already own something from repurchasing it. We define ourselves, and are defined by others, principally in terms of what we like to purchase. And when our autonomy is threatened by violence from without, by the decay of the body, or by betrayal, we comfort ourselves by going shopping. We can (we do) justify—even glory in—a deep divide between rich and poor in the name of maximizing shopping's possibilities. We can (we do) resist external constraints upon our freedom to shop to the point of permitting our schools to decay, our public space to wither, and our idealism to be occluded by the lust for ownership. We can (we do) collude, as good shoppers, in our own tranquillization and the evisceration of compassion, sensibility, and love. We can (we do) deprive ourselves of the joy in the material world available only to those who refuse ownership of it.

None of this is to say that there is no construal of ownership acceptable to Christians. The tradition for almost the last thousand years has taught that there are some such interpretations of what it means to own. The Catholic Church especially has in the last century or so devoted considerable attention to the notion of private property, as is evident in the body of Catholic social teaching that extends from Leo XIII's *Rerum Novarum* (1891) to John Paul II's *Centesimus Annus* (1991). But the understandings of ownership and property defended there are very far from those dominant in the contemporary Western world.

The ideal citizen of a late-capitalist polity is, then, the autonomous owner. But it is not only material goods that we consider subject to ownership. We also think of ourselves as owners of our words. Such an attitude is written into copyright law, whose history is not much more than two centuries long: I can sue you if you do not seek my permission to make use of what I have written. It is implied also in our unremitting emphasis upon the evils of plagiarism: to present another's words as one's own is, for us, a moral failure and (sometimes) a punishable crime. We urge our students not to do it, we castigate public figures if they are found to have done it, and we place a high value upon novelty, newly minted words. We reward those who produce (and, thereby, own) words not previously produced, not previously owned. What better compliment for a writer than to say of her that she has a style all her own? What higher praise for a researcher or scholar than to say that his findings are new, challenging, will push back the frontiers of knowledge, will transform a discipline or lay the groundwork for a new enterprise? To say, as medieval commentators so often did at the beginning of their commentaries, that nothing new would be said here—that would, for those who think of speech as autonomously produced and owned by its producer, be an admission of failure.

A community in which the Augustinian ban on the lie was taken seriously—a community of truth—would look very different from any we now know, and would have an uneasy relation with a polity dominated by autonomy and ownership. The community of truth would have repudiated autonomy and ownership as these pertain to speech, and would, as a result, appear sometimes callous and often puzzling to those subject to such values and to the tropes through which they are expressed. The community of truth would, had it the strength to live by its convictions, be known as a community that valued the avoidance of duplicity more than the preservation of life. It would be known as a community whose members' speech would be reliable: you would know, in talking to them, that what they were saying would seem to them at the time they said it to be what they thought. A community of truth would be a community that could be trusted.

It would also be a community that could not easily act as advocate for or supporter of a late-capitalist democracy. This is because it is likely that such democracies can only function if those who seek and assume elected office understand lying to be an essential part of what they do as politicians. If this is so—and it is indisputably so in practice; any dispute can only be about whether it is so in theory—then Augustinian Christians cannot seek and assume elected office in such a democracy, and must think at least several times before acting as advocates for such a political order. It is perhaps sufficiently obvious not to need argument that the economic practices of such democracies—their necessary reliance, for example, upon the expansion of markets by the use of mendacious advertising—require the systematic use of the lie.

The community of truth will also be one for which silence will become increasingly attractive. If the lie is as ready to the tongue as Augustine says, silence will often be the tongue's only proper use. This is the intuition behind the tradition of encouraging *linguae castitas*, the tongue's chastity.

But membership in the community of truth will not be easy for most of us. We can scarcely avoid understanding speakers as autonomous owners of their speech because of the depth with which such a view has become inscribed into our political and educational institutions. This means that it is easy for us to tell and to defend the lie. Being formed as we have been explains why you (and, much more than I would like, I) have moral intuitions that make it seem obvious to us that the Augustinian lie can be defended in a broadly consequentialist way. It is common among expositors of Augustine (and, indeed, of Kant) to say that it is obvious that someone who won't tell a lie to save an innocent life has made a moral mistake. For an even stronger example, consider the following: you're the navigator in a warplane carrying a nuclear bomb; you know that the pilot has received orders to drop the bomb on a city; you know, too, that if the bomb is dropped on the city at least a million people will be incinerated. The pilot asks you for the coordinates that will get him to the drop-site. You think that it would be profoundly wrong to drop the bomb on a city (you'd signed up for this military duty in the belief that you'd never be put into this situation), and you know that the only safe and sure way available to you of preventing this eventuality is to give the pilot the wrong coordinates—that is, to speak duplicitously to him. If you refuse to give him any coordinates he'll know there's something wrong and will figure out a way to get himself to the target without your help. And, obviously, if you give him the right coordinates, the bomb will get dropped. A million innocent lives against a lie.

The answer seems obvious: the lie should be told. Aquinas would say so: it would be a venial sin. Newman would say so: it would be a lie for just cause. Cassian and Chrysostom and Jerome would say so without a moment's thought: economizing with speech like a skilled steward of words would permit and perhaps require such a lie. There is no consistent ban on the lie in Plato or Aristotle, so they would permit this lie without much hesitation. Nietzsche would have no difficulty with it. Kant would have a difficulty, but a consistent Kantianism would permit and perhaps require such a lie. Only Augustine would accept the terms and ban the lie. The consistent Augustinian cannot lie to save innocent life, whether one or a million; he cannot lie to comfort the sad, preserve public order, prevent physical suffering, or even to prevent apostasy or blasphemy.

This means that God's gift of speech to us will seem, to those who so regard it and who think of it as Augustine thought of it, a violent gift, a disruptive offering. Should I lie to save the life of my child? No. Should I lie to prevent war, encourage peace, soothe the weary and discouraged, instruct the foolish, or liberate the innocent from torture? No. But then, violence is done to very many of my intuitions and judgments about what I ought to do, about what is proper. Acknowledging my giftedness disrupts my comfort with what seems to be the voice of my conscience: to remain comfortable with what my conscience seems to say places that voice before the gift of the God who has gifted me with demand before comfort, whose word divides bones from marrow and judges the thoughts and intentions of the heart.

This apparent violence and disruption should be no surprise. If my conscience has been systematically malformed, as it inevitably has by the culture of autonomy and ownership in which I live, then a reformation of it will be radical. The demand to relinquish ownership of speech and to acknowledge, instead, that speech is gift will require radical alteration of speech-habits: loquacity will have to give place to silence, and self-assertion to praise.

Notes

Conventions

For quotations from Scripture I use, without comment, the English given in the New American Bible unless the Latin used by Augustine is sufficiently different that there is reason to translate and comment on it. When this happens I make it clear. For citations of Scripture I use the book names and chapter and verse divisions of the New American Bible, which in turn are the same as those of most other modern English Bibles, Catholic and Protestant. This will usually cause no problems, for Augustine rarely identifies scriptural quotations or allusions by anything more than the barest mention of the author or book in play. Identifying them by chapter and verse is a courtesy of modern editors, translators, and commentators for those of us who have memorized rather less of Scripture than had Augustine. But there are special difficulties with the enumeration of the Psalms, and I make an exception to my usual practice for citation and quotation of Augustine's *Enarrationes in psalmos* by following the enumeration of the Septuagint, the Greek version of the Old Testament, which differs from that of the Hebrew text and (therefore) from that of most modern English Bibles. This enumeration was the one familiar to Augustine, and modern editions and translations of his expositions of the Psalms usually follow it. This can cause difficulties when trying to locate Augustine's comments on a particular psalm. A quick rule of thumb is that beginning at Psalm 10 and ending at Psalm 146 you need to subtract one digit from the enumeration given in modern English Bibles in order to arrive at Augustine's numbering, or to add one if you're converting in the opposite direction. So Psalm

51 in your English Bible is Augustine's Psalm 50, and Augustine's Psalm 128 is your English Bible's Psalm 129.

For citations of Augustine's works in the notes I give the Latin name of the text, the relevant sectional number, and the source in which I read the Latin text. I have not always used the best critical editions, but rather those easily at hand in my own library or those in which I happened to be doing the work. Sources are given in full on their first mention in the notes to each chapter, and thereafter in abbreviated form (usually just the author's name). The only exception to this is J.-P. Migne's *Patrologiae Cursus Completus Series Latina*, 221 vols. (Paris: Garnier, 1844–1864). I cite this always as "Migne," followed by volume and column number. All translations from Augustine are mine, though I have benefited from consulting translations made by others, and have sometimes silently adopted or adapted their felicitious phrases.

Further Reading on Lying

There's a vast literature on the lie. The few works mentioned here do no more than scratch the surface of that literature, but many of them contain rich resources for further reading.

Among nonscholarly works I've profited and derived enjoyment from: Angela Opie, *Illustrations of Lying in All Its Branches* (Hartford: Andrus, 1827), which is a popular semidevotional how-to-avoid-lying book for the uneasily upwardly mobile in early-nineteenth-century England; Philip Kerr, ed., *The Penguin Book of Lies* (London: Viking, 1990), which is an immensely entertaining anthology; Oscar Wilde, "The Decay of Lying: An Observation," in Edgar Saltus, ed., *Intentions*, Complete Works of Oscar Wilde (Garden City, N.Y.: Doubleday, 1923), 5:5–63, which is an elegant lament for the loss of boldly mendacious art and of the impoverishment thereby of life, which is in any case a pale imitation of art; Diane Komp, *Anatomy of a Lie* (Grand Rapids: Zondervan, 1998), which is a moving and direct record of one woman's lies and her attempts to avoid them; Paul Lombard, *Ma vérité sur le mensonge* (Paris: Plon, 1997), a witty set of confessions of the inevitability and occasionally transformative effects of lying; Lauren Slater, *Lying: A Metaphorical Memoir* (New York: Random House, 2000), which treats lies as tools of identity-construction in such a way that the reader can't be sure the writer isn't lying about it; Elena Lappin, "The Man with Two Heads," in *Granta* 66 (1999): 7–65, on the strange case of Benjamin Wilkomirski's lying autobiography; and, of course, Mark Twain's story, "My First Lie and How I Got Out of It," published first in 1899, and now to be found in just about every Twain anthology in print.

Among general works of a broadly scholarly sort (not less mendacious than the ones mentioned in the last paragraph, but usually less entertaining), I've had much help from the following: Eberhard Schockenhoff, *Zur Lüge verdammt? Politik, Medien, Medizin, Justiz, Wissenschaft und die Ethik der Wahrheit* (Freiburg, Germany: Herder, 2000), which is is lively and accurate, and contains especially good treatments of the theological tradition, as well as of the evidence about habits and norms available from professional codes of ethics; Sissela Bok, *Lying: Moral Choice in Public and Private Life* (New York: Pantheon, 1978, with frequent reprints and updates), which, though dated and in some particulars inaccurate, is still useful for the careful conceptual distinctions it makes and for the range of material it covers. There are some recent surveys, such as those by Jeremy Campbell, *The Liar's Tale: A History of Falsehood* (New York & London: W. W. Norton, 2001), and Evelin Sullivan, *The Concise Book of Lying* (New York: Farrar, Strauss & Giroux, 2001), which are evidence of a growth of interest in the subject, but are not, so far as I can see, of any independent value.

Among conceptual treatments I recommend: Alasdair MacIntyre, "Truthfulness, Lies, and Moral Philosophers: What Can We Learn from Mill and Kant?" in Grethe B. Anderson, ed., *The Tanner Lectures on Human Values* (Salt Lake City: University of Utah Press, 1995), 16:307–61; Jacques Derrida, "History of the Lie: Prolegomena," trans. Peggy Kamuf, in Richard Rand, ed., *Futures: Of Jacques Derrida* (Stanford, Calif.: Stanford University Press, 2001), pp. 65–98. I endorse the conclusions of neither of these essays, but each in its own way provides much stimulus. Michel Foucault's *Fearless Speech* (Los Angeles: Semiotext[e], 2001) is useful on the history and meaning of the kind of truth-telling connected with the Greek term *parrhesia*. On the difficult question of self-deception (which I don't touch in this book), Herbert Fingarette, *Self-Deception* (Berkeley & Los Angeles: University of California Press, 2000; first published 1969) is the best place to start, to be followed by Donald Davidson's "Deception and Division," in Jon Elster, ed., *The Multiple Self* (Cambridge, U.K.: Cambridge University Press, 1985), pp. 79–92, and "Who Is Fooled?" in Jean-Pierre Dupuy, ed., *Self-Deception and Paradoxes of Rationality* (Stanford, Calif.: Center for the Study of Language and Interpretation, 1998), pp. 1–18; see also Annette Barnes, *Seeing through Self-Deception* (Cambridge, U.K.: Cambridge University Press, 1997). There is an enormous periodical literature on this subject. On definitional questions and associated topics I've profited from: Roderick Chisholm & Thomas D.

Feehan, "The Intent to Deceive," *Journal of Philosophy* 74 (1977): 143–59; Mary Mothersill, "Some Questions About Truthfulness and Lying," *Social Research* 63 (1996): 913–29; and Jonathan E. Adler, "Lying, Deceiving, or Falsely Implicating," *Journal of Philosophy* 94 (1997): 435–52.

Empirical study of lies and liars can be found in: Bella M. DePaulo et al., "Sex Differences in Lying: How Women and Men Deal with the Dilemma of Deceit," in Michael Lewis & Carolyn Saarni, eds., *Lying and Deception in Everyday Life* (New York & London: Guilford Press, 1993), pp. 126–47; Bella M. DePaulo et al., "Lying in Everyday Life," *Journal of Personality and Social Psychology* 70 (1996): 979–95; Deborah A. Kashy & Bella M. DePaulo, "Who Lies?" *Journal of Personality and Social Psychology* 70 (1996): 1037–51. These essays can be supplemented by the more theoretical sociological work of J. A. Barnes, *A Pack of Lies: Towards a Sociology of Lying* (Cambridge, U.K.: Cambridge University Press, 1994), and David Nyberg, *The Varnished Truth: Truth Telling and Deceiving in Ordinary Life* (Chicago: University of Chicago Press, 1993).

On lying and politics: Hannah Arendt, "Lying in Politics: Reflections on the Pentagon Papers," in *Crises of the Republic* (New York: Harcourt Brace Jovanovitch, 1972), pp. 1–47, and "Truth and Politics," in Arendt, *Between Past and Future* (New York: Penguin, 1993), pp. 227–64, still repay attention, as does Alexander Koyré, "The Political Function of the Modern Lie," *Contemporary Jewish Record* 8/3 (June 1945): 290–300. Glen Newey, "Political Lying: A Defense," *Public Affairs Quarterly* 11/2 (1997): 93–116, is representative of a recent trend to argue (rightly) that democracy cannot be practiced without public lying, and (wrongly) that there's nothing much wrong with this. On this see also John Rist, "Democracy and Religious Values: Augustine on Locke, Lying, and Individualism," *Augustinian Studies* 29 (1998): 7–24.

Further Reading on Augustine

If you'd like to read more about Augustine, you can begin with the two best biographies: Peter Brown, *Augustine of Hippo: A New Edition with an Epilogue* (Berkeley & Los Angeles: University of California Press, 2000); Serge Lancel, *Saint Augustine*, trans. (from French) by Antonia Nevill (London: SCM Press, 2002). Indispensable works of reference and guidance include: Allan D. Fitzgerald, ed., *Augustine through the Ages: An Encyclopedia* (Grand Rapids: Eerdmans, 1999); Eleonore Stump

& Norman Kretzmann, eds., *The Cambridge Companion to Augustine* (Cambridge, U.K.: Cambridge University Press, 2001). Both of these have substantial bibliographic guides of their own. Interpretive literature on Augustine and Augustinian themes is an ocean.

For a review of new contributions to this ocean you can consult the annual *Bulletin Augustinien* published in the *Revue des Études Augustiniennes*. Some idea of the depth of the ocean can be had by the fact that the yearly bulletin often signals as many as four hundred contributions (books and essays). You'd have to read, minimally, forty thousand words a day to keep even a foothold on this mountain. I make no attempt to do so, but in the notes to each chapter I do indicate the works I've found most useful for the topics treated in that chapter.

If you'd like to read more of Augustine's own works and you'd rather read him in English, I recommend the complete Augustine being produced by the Augustinian Heritage Institute under the editorship of John Rotelle with the general title *The Works of St. Augustine: A Translation for the Twenty-First Century*. Some thirty volumes in this series had appeared by the spring of 2003, and there seems every chance that the project will be completed before the century is out. If you like beautiful books and can benefit from Latin or Italian, I recommend the bilingual *Opere di Sant'Agostino* published in Rome by Città Nuova Editrice in the Nuova Biblioteca Agostiniana under the general editorship of Remo Piccolomini. This proceeds apace and may beat the English edition to the finish line. And if you can benefit from Latin or French and like pocket-sized editions, I recommend the bilingual *Oeuvres de Saint Augustin,* published by the Institut des Études Augustiniennes as part of the Bibliothèque Augustinienne. This series has been under way since 1936, and is the most nearly complete of the three I've mentioned. These three series all (or eventually will) contain editions and/or translations of the sermons and letters by Augustine uncovered since 1970 in the archives of Europe. If you prefer your Latin unsullied by proximity to any modern language, there are more or less critical editions of many (though, again, not all) of Augustine's works in the *Corpus Christianorum, Series Latina,* published by Brepols since 1953; and in the older *Corpus Scriptorum Ecclesiasticorum Latinorum.* For completeness and ease of access (though not for the most accurate texts), it's still hard to beat the seventeenth-century edition of Augustine's Latin produced by the Maurists and reproduced by J.-P. Migne in volumes 32–45 of the *Patrologiae Cursus Completus Series Latina* published in Paris between 1844 and 1864.

Introduction

11 *Wittgenstein writes*: In *Culture and Value* (Chicago: University of Chicago Press, 1980), p. 60.

11 *Wittgenstein's own passion for honesty:* Discussed in Ray Monk, *Ludwig Wittgenstein: The Duty of Genius* (New York: Free Press, 1990), pp. 367–72.

12 *"The Serjeant no doubt":* Anthony Trollope, *Lady Anna* (1873–1874; Oxford, U.K.: World's Classics, 1950), p. 375.

15 *Isidore of Seville's lament:* Quoted in Allan D. Fitzgerald, ed., *Augustine through the Ages: An Encyclopedia* (Grand Rapids: Eerdmans, 1999), p. 457.

15 *two short treatises:* The most recent English versions of these treatises can be found in Roy J. Deferrari, ed., *Saint Augustine: Treatises on Various Subjects*, Fathers of the Church 16 (Washington, D.C.: Catholic University of America Press, 1952), pp. 145–79. For the Latin I've used Carlo Carena et al., ed. & trans., *Sant'Agostino: Morale e Ascetismo Cristiano*, Opere di Sant'Agostino 7/2 (Rome: Città Nuova Editrice, 2001), pp. 293–488.

21 *Pascal's prescription:* In Francis Kaplan, ed., *Les Pensées de Pascal* (Paris: Éditions du Cerf, 1988), p. 143.

Chapter 1: Lying

Useful work on Augustine's understanding of what it is to lie includes Thomas D. Feehan, "Augustine on Lying and Deception," *Augustinian Studies* 19 (1988): 131–39; idem, "Augustine's Own Examples of Lying," *Augustinian Studies* 22 (1991): 165–90; Boniface Ramsey, "Two Traditions on Lying and Deception in the Ancient Church," *The Thomist* 49 (1985): 504–33; Alan Brinton, "St. Augustine and the Problem of Deception in Religious Persuasion," *Religious Studies* 19 (1983): 437–50; Marcia Colish, "The Stoic Theory of Verbal Signification and the Problem of Lies and False Statements from Antiquity to St. Anselm," in Lucie Brind'Amour & Eugene Vance, eds., *Archéologie du signe*, Recueils d'études médiévales 3 (Toronto, Ontario, Canada: Pontifical Institute of Medieval Studies, 1982), pp. 17–43; Eberhard Schockenhoff, *Zur Lüge verdammt? Politik, Medien, Medizin, Justiz, Wissenschaft und die Ethik der Wahrheit* (Freiburg, Germany: Herder, 2000), pp. 41–62; Jean-Louis Chrétien, *Saint Augustin et les actes de parole* (Paris: Presses Universitaires de France, 2002), ch. 10; Julia A. Fleming, "The Helpful Lie: The Moral Reasoning of Augustine and John Cassian," Ph.D. dissertation, Catholic University of America, 1993.

25 *"No one, certainly, who says something false":* Translating *Enchiridion* 6.18 from J. Rivière, ed. & trans., *Exposés généraux de la foi*, Oeuvres de Saint Augustin 9 (Paris: Institut des Études Augustiniennes, 1988), p. 134.

26 *"If you don't pay attention":* Translating *Enchiridion* 6.18 from Rivière, p. 134.

26 *Homer, who has Achilles say: Iliad* 9.413.

26 *"Ambition led many to become false":* Translating Sallust, *Bellum Catilinae* 10, from John C. Rolfe, ed. & trans., *Sallust*, Loeb Classical Library 116 (Cambridge, Mass.: Harvard University Press, 1931), p. 18.

27 *"He lies who has one thing in his mind":* Translating *De mendacio* 3.3, from Carlo Carena et al., eds. & trans., *Sant'Agostino: Morale e Ascetismo Cristiano*, Opere di Sant'Agostino 7/2 (Rome: Città Nuova Editrice, 2001), p. 312.

27 *"In fact that which is without the double heart":* Translating *Enarrationes in psalmos* 5.7 from Migne, vol. 36, col. 86.

27 *"The lie is false signification":* Translating *Contra mendacium* 12.26 from Carena, p. 458.

28 *"No one doubts":* Translating *De mendacio* 4.5 from Carena, p. 318.

28 *"The question of whether":* Translating *De mendacio* 3.4 from Carena, p. 314.

28 *the case of the skeptical friend:* Discussed in *De mendacio* 4.4, in Carena, pp. 314–18.

29 *"the mind is thoroughly aware":* Translating *De mendacio* 4.4 from Carena, p. 318.

29 *speaking what's in the mind with a desire to deceive:* See *De mendacio* 3.3, in Carena, p. 314.

29 *jokes are not lies:* See *De mendacio* 2.2, in Carena, pp. 310–12.

29 *duplicity suffices for the lie:* See *Soliloquia* 2.9.16, in Migne, vol. 32, col. 892.

29 *he wrote of his first treatise:* In *Retractationes* 1.27, in Gustave Bardy, ed. & trans., *Les révisions,* Oeuvres de Saint Augustin 12 (Paris: Desclée de Brouwer, 1950), pp. 444–46.

30 *with sweetly pleasing speech:* On *suaviloquium* and the lie see *De mendacio* 11.18, in Carena, pp. 346–48.

34 *"Therefore, he [Abraham] has been silent":* Translating *Contra mendacium* 10.23 from Carena, p. 448. See also *De mendacio* 13.24, in Carena, pp. 356–58.

34 *Augustine reports a joker:* In *Confessiones* 11.12.14, in James J. O'Donnell, *Augustine: Confessions,* 3 vols. (Oxford, U.K.: Clarendon Press, 1992), 1:153.

35 *(in figura)* . . . *(in proprietate):* See *Sermo* 4.22–23, in Migne, vol. 38, cols. 45–46. Compare *Contra mendacium* 10.24, in Carena, pp. 448–53.

38 *eight kinds of lie:* discussed in *De mendacio* 14.25, in Carena, pp. 358–60.

39 *only internally:* Paraphrasing *De peccatorum meritis et remissione et de baptismo parvulorum* 2.7.9 from Migne, vol. 44, col. 137.

Chapter 2: Being

43 *Diagnostic and Statistical Manual of Mental Disorders:* This work, published by the American Psychiatric Association in Washington, D.C., is now in its 4th (2000) edition.

45 *"The things to be enjoyed":* Translating *De doctrina christiana* 1.5.5 from Vincenzo Tarulli, ed. & trans., *La Dottrina Cristiana,* Opere di Sant'Agostino 8 (Rome: Città Nuova Editrice, 1992), p. 16. On God as *res* see also *In epistulam iohannis ad parthos tractatus* 7.10, in Giovanni Reale, ed. & trans., *Agostino: Amore Assoluto e "Terza Navigazione"* (Milan: Edizione Bompiani, 2000), p. 350.

46 *predicated* secundum essentiam: See *De trinitate* 15.5.8, in Paul Agaësse, ed. & trans., *La trinité, livres VIII–XV,* Oeuvres de Saint Augustin 16 (Paris: Institut des Études Augustiniennes, 1997), pp. 438–40.

47 *"God is maximal being":* Translating *De civitate dei* 12.2 from Philip Levine, ed. & trans., *Saint Augustine: The City of God against the Pagans, Books XII–XV,* Loeb Classical Library 414 (Cambridge, Mass.: Harvard University Press, 1988), p. 10.

49 *"Among those things":* Translating *De civitate dei* 11.16 from David S. Wiesen, ed. & trans., *Saint Augustine: The City of God against the Pagans, Books VIII–XI,* Loeb Classical Library 413 (Cambridge, Mass.: Harvard University Press, 1988), p. 488.

49 *(sensibilia)* . . . *(intellegibilia):* For this distinction, see: *De magistro* 12.39, in F. J. Thonnard, ed. & trans., *Dialogues philosophiques,* Oeuvres de Saint Augustin 6 (Paris: Desclée de Brouwer, 1941), pp. 104–6; *De civitate dei* 8.6, in Wiesen, pp. 30–34.

49 *"Nothing touched by a physical sense":* Translating *Epistula* 2.1 from T. Alimonti & L. Carrozzi, ed. & trans., *Sant'Agostino: Le lettere/1 (1–70),* Opere di Sant'Agostino 1/1 (Rome: Città Nuova Editrice, 1969), p. 6.

51 *forms, species, and reasons:* See *De diversis quaestionibus 83* 46, in Gustave Bardy,
    J.-A. Beackaert & J. Boutet, eds. & trans., *Mélanges doctrinaux*, Oeuvres de Saint
    Augustin 10 (Paris: Desclée de Brouwer, 1952), pp. 122–28.

51 *"To approach* (propinquare) *him":* Translating *Enarrationes in psalmos* 34/2.6 from
    Migne, vol. 36, col. 337.

52 non sit aliquid: *De civitate dei* 11.10, in Wiesen, p. 464.

53 amore inhaerere: *De doctrina christiana* 1.3.4, in Tarulli, p. 14.

53 non cui supervolitet: *De trinitate* 8.3.4, in Agaësse, p. 34.

54 *"And so there are two cities":* Translating *De catechizandis rudibus* 19.31 from Carlo
    Carena et al., ed. & trans., *Sant'Agostino: Morale e Ascetismo Cristiano*, Opere di
    Sant'Agostino 7/2 (Rome: Città Nuova Editrice, 2001), p. 248.

Chapter 3: Sinning

On Augustine's understanding of sin I've profited especially from James Wetzel,
Augustine and the Limits of Virtue (Cambridge, U.K.: Cambridge University Press,
1992), in which the discussion of sin as entropy is especially suggestive; G. R.
Evans, *Augustine on Evil* (Cambridge, U.K.: Cambridge University Press, 1982),
whose discussion of Augustine on *malum* has many implications for Augustine
on *peccatum;* William E. Mann, "Augustine on Evil and Original Sin," in Eleonore
Stump & Norman Kretzmann, eds., *The Cambridge Companion to Augustine* (Cambridge, U.K.: Cambridge University Press, 2001), pp. 40–48; Scott MacDonald,
"Primal Sin," in Gareth B. Matthews, ed., *The Augustinian Tradition* (Berkeley:
University of California Press, 1999), pp. 100–139; Charles T. Mathewes, *Evil and
the Augustinian Tradition* (Cambridge, U.K.: Cambridge University Press, 2001),
which is more concerned with the reception-history of Augustine's thought than
with Augustine himself, but which nonetheless sheds much light on the structure
of Augustine's thought about sin; J. F. Procopé, "Initium omnis peccati superbia,"
Studia Patristica 22 (1989): 315–20, which treats Augustine's reliance on Sirach
for his understanding of the relation between pride and sin.

56 *"Sin," says Augustine, "is perversity":* Translating *Ad simplicianum* 1.2.18 from
    Migne, vol. 40, col. 122.

56 peccatum *is an* aversio: *De libero arbitrio* 2.20.54, in F. J. Thonnard, ed. & trans.,
    Dialogues philosophiques, Oeuvres de Saint Augustin 6 (Paris: Desclée de Brouwer,
    1941), pp. 318–20.

56 *"Our good lives always with you":* Translating *Confessiones* 4.16.31 from James J.
    O'Donnell, *Augustine: Confessions*, 3 vols. (Oxford, U.K.: Clarendon Press, 1992),
    1:45.

56 *"Sins," then, "are committed only voluntarily":* Translating *De duabus animabus*
    10.14 from Migne, vol. 42, col. 105.

56 *"The mind can be deposed":* Translating *De libero arbitrio* 1.16.34 from Thonnard,
    p. 204.

57 *"The definition of sin I once gave":* Translating *Retractationes* 1.15.4 from Gustave
    Bardy, ed. & trans., *Les révisions*, Oeuvres de Saint Augustin 12 (Paris: Desclée de
    Brouwer, 1950), p. 368. Augustine quotes his own earlier definition of sin from *De
    duabus animabus* 11.15, in Migne, vol. 42, col. 105.

59 *"Sin is not a desire for naturally evil things":* Translating *De natura boni* 36 from
    Giovanni Reale, ed. & trans., *Agostino: Natura del bene* (Milan: Edizione Bompiani,
    2001), pp. 176; see also *De vera religione* 20.38, in J. Pegon, ed. & trans., *La foi
    chrétienne*, Oeuvres de Saint Augustin 8 (Paris: Desclée de Brouwer, 1951), pp.
    72–74.

59 *"The soul is proud"*: Translating *Epistula* 118.15 from Migne, vol. 33, col. 439.

60 *the good shared by all*: See *De civitate dei* 12.1, in Philip Levine, ed. & trans., *Saint Augustine: The City of God against the Pagans, Books XII–XV*, Loeb Classical Library 414 (Cambridge, Mass.: Harvard University Press, 1988), pp. 2–8.

60 *He sought this lack spontaneously*: See *De genesi ad litteram* 11.14.18, in Paul Agaësse & A. Solignac, *La Genèse au sens littéral en douze livres, VIII–XII*, Oeuvres de Saint Augustin 49 (Paris: Desclée de Brouwer, 1972), pp. 256–58.

60 *many-symptomed sickness of the body*: For this metaphor see *In iohannis evangelium tractatus* 2.16, in M.-F. Berrouard, ed. & trans., *Homélies sur l'Évangile de Saint Jean I–XVI*, Oeuvres de Saint Augustin 71 (Paris: Institut des Études Augustiniennes, 1993), pp. 204–6.

60 *medicinal effects of Jesus' embrace of humility*: See *Enarrationes in psalmos* 70.2.7, in Migne, vol. 36, cols. 896–97.

60 *the attempt to be a self-pleaser*: "Self-pleaser" translates *sibi placere*, a phrase taken from 2 Peter 2:10 in the Latin version known to Augustine, one of Augustine's favorite scriptural verses.

61 *"Only a nature made out of nothing"*: Translating *De civitate dei* 14.13 from Levine, pp. 336–38.

61 *"What else can we call this lack than pride?"*: Translating *De civitate dei* 12.6 from Levine, p. 24. Augustine quotes Sir. 10:13 in this passage.

62 *"The soul, delighting in its own power"*: Translating *De trinitate* 12.9.14 from Paul Agaësse, ed. & trans., *La trinité, livres VIII–XV*, Oeuvres de Saint Augustin 16 (Paris: Institut des Études Augustiniennes, 1997), pp. 236–38.

62 *Augustine likes to connect* privatus *with* privatio: See, for example, *De genesi ad litteram* 11.15.19, in Agaësse & Solignac, pp. 258–60.

62 *"Truth* (veritas) *and wisdom* (sapientia) *are common to all"*: Translating *De libero arbitrio* 2.19.52 from Thonnard, p. 314.

63 *full causal account*: *De libero arbitrio* 2.20.54, in Thonnard, pp. 318–20. Compare *De civitate dei* 12.6, in Levine, p. 24.

64 *"Non solum non peccemus adorando"*: *Enarrationes in psalmos* 98.9, in Migne, vol. 37, col. 1264.

64 *"This is the water"*: Translating *Enarrationes in psalmos* 31/2.18 from Migne, vol. 36, col. 270.

65 *loss of being that is produced by sin*: See *Sermo* 290.4–5, in Migne, vol. 38, cols. 1314–15; *Sermo* 291.3–5, in Migne, vol. 38, cols. 1317–19.

65 *"[In the conception of Jesus]"*: Translating *De trinitate* 13.18.23 from Agaësse, p. 330.

65–66 *to wiggle their ears and to fart musically*: See *De civitate dei* 14.24, in Levine, p. 388.

66 *transparent before God*: On transparency see *De genesi ad litteram* 8.12.26, in Agaësse & Solignac, pp. 48–50; *De bono coniugali* 18.21, in P. G. Walsh, ed. & trans., *Augustine: De bono coniugali, De sancta virginitate* (Oxford, U.K.: Clarendon Press, 2001), p. 38.

66 *adolescent theft of pears*: The account, together with analysis of its meaning, is found in *Confessiones* 2.3.5–2.10.18, in O'Donnell, 1:16–22. All Augustine quotations from this point to the end of the chapter are translated from these pages. My interpretation of the pear-theft has been greatly influenced by Jean-Luc Marion's analysis of Luke 15 in *God without Being: Hors-Texte* (Chicago: University of Chicago Press, 1991), pp. 95–102. I've also profited from the commentary in O'Donnell, 2:119–44; Danuta Shanzer, "Pears Before Swine: Augustine *Confessions*, 2.4.9," *Revue des Études Augustiniennes* 42 (1996): 45–55; H. Derycke, "Le vol des poires, parabole du péché originel," *Bulletin de Littérature Ecclesiastique* 88 (1987): 337–48.

66 *Nietzsche, for example:* I translate the Nietzsche and Brecht quotations from the
     German given in O'Donnell, *Confessions*, 2:227.
66 *the throne of lies: Confessiones* 9.2.4, in O'Donnell, 1:104.
70 *Catiline is the figure of importance here:* On Augustine and Catiline see Pierre
     Courcelle, *Opuscula selecta: bibliographie et recueil d'articles publiés entre 1938 et
     1980* (Paris: Institut des Études Augustiniennes, 1984), pp. 319–28.
70 *the Calabrian host:* The story is given by Horace in *Epistula* 1.7.14–31, in H. Rushton
     Fairclough, ed. & trans., *Horace: Satires, Epistles, and Ars Poetica*, Loeb Classical
     Library 194 (Cambridge, Mass.: Harvard University Press, 1991), pp. 294–96.

Chapter 4: Speaking

On Augustine's understanding of speech and thought I've been helped by Clif-
ford Ando, "Augustine on Language," *Revue des Études Augustiniennes* 40 (1994),
45–78; Marcia Colish, "The Stoic Theory of Verbal Signification and the Problem
of Lies and False Statements from Antiquity to St. Anselm," in Lucie Brind'Amour
& Eugene Vance, eds., *Archéologie du signe*, Recueils d'études médiévales 3 (To-
ronto, Ontario, Canada: Pontifical Institute of Medieval Studies, 1982), pp. 17–43;
B. Darrell Jackson, "The Theory of Signs in Augustine's *De Doctrina Christiana*,"
Revue des Études Augustiniennes 15 (1969): 9–49; Christopher Kirwan, *Augustine*
(London & New York: Routledge, 1989), pp. 35–59; Andrew Louth, "Augustine on
Language," *Journal of Literature and Theology* 3/2 (1989): 151–58; R. A. Markus,
"St. Augustine on Signs," in R. A. Markus, ed., *Augustine: A Collection of Critical
Essays* (New York: Anchor Books, 1972), pp. 61–91; John M. Rist, *Augustine: Ancient
Thought Baptized* (Cambridge, U.K.: Cambridge University Press, 1994), pp. 23–40;
Alfred Schindler, *Wort und Analogie in Augustins Trinitätslehre* (Tübingen, Germany:
Mohr/Siebeck, 1965), pp. 75–118; Brian Stock, *Augustine the Reader: Meditation,
Self-Knowledge, and the Ethics of Interpretation* (Cambridge, Mass.: Belknap Press,
1996), pp. 138–73; Rowan Williams, "Language, Reality, and Desire in Augustine's
De Doctrina Christiana," *Journal of Literature and Theology* 3 (1989): 138–50.
73 *Words, for Augustine, are signs:* In the next several paragraphs I draw principally on
     De doctrina christiana 2.2.3, in Vincenzo Tarulli, ed. & trans., *La Dottrina Cristiana*,
     Opere di Sant'Agostino 8 (Rome: Città Nuova Editrice, 1992), p. 62.
74 *Recalling (or, better, imagining) his own preverbal babyhood:* See *Confessiones* 1.6.8,
     in James J. O'Donnell, *Augustine: Confessions*, 3 vols. (Oxford, U.K.: Clarendon
     Press, 1992), 1:5.
75 *"Observe your own heart":* Translating *In iohannis evangelium tractatus* 14.7 from
     M.-F. Berrouard, ed. & trans., *Homélies sur l'Évangile de Saint Jean I–XVI*, Oeuvres de
     Saint Augustin 71 (Paris: Institut des Études Augustiniennes, 1993), pp. 734–36.
76 *"naked to the intelligence":* Translating *Sermo* 187.3.3 from Migne, vol. 38, col.
     1002.
76 *no need of language in heaven:* On this topic see *De civitate dei* 22.29, in William
     M. Green, ed. & trans., *Saint Augustine: The City of God against the Pagans*, Books
     XXI–XXII, Loeb Classical Library 417 (Cambridge, Mass.: Harvard University
     Press, 1972), pp. 370–72 ("patebunt etiam cogitationes nostrae invicem nobis");
     De genesi ad litteram 1.9.15, in Paul Agaësse & A. Solignac, eds. & trans., *La Genèse
     au sens littéral en douze livres, I–VII*, Oeuvres de Saint Augustin 48 (Paris: Desclée
     de Brouwer, 1972), pp. 100–102; *De musica* 6.13.41, in Guy Finaert & F.-J. Thon-
     nard, eds. & trans., *La musique*, Oeuvres de Saint Augustin 7 (Paris: Desclée de
     Brouwer, 1947), pp. 446–48; *De genesi adversus manicheos* 2.4.5–2.4.6, in Migne,
     vol. 34 , cols. 198–99.

77 *"It's also true for me":* Translating *De catechizandis rudibus* 2.3 from Carlo Carena et
    al., eds. & trans., *Sant'Agostino: Morale e Ascetismo Cristiano,* Opere di Sant'Agostino
    7/2 (Rome: Città Nuova Editrice, 2001), pp. 182–84. Compare *De trinitate* 15.7.13,
    in Paul Agaësse, ed. & trans., *La trinité, livres VIII–XV,* Oeuvres de Saint Augustin
    16 (Paris: Institut des Études Augustiniennes, 1997), pp. 452–56; *Confessiones*
    11.8.10, in O'Donnell, 1:151–52.

77 *"not by sounding words":* Translating *De civitate dei* 11.29, from David S. Wiesen,
    ed. & trans., *Saint Augustine: The City of God against the Pagans, Books VIII–XI,*
    Loeb Classical Library 413 (Cambridge, Mass.: Harvard University Press, 1988),
    p. 546.

78 *daylight knowledge is of something "in* ea ratione: Quoting and summarizing *De
    civitate dei* 11.29 from Wiesen, pp. 546–50.

80 *"hidden notions* (arcana notitia): Translating *De trinitate* 4.6.10 from M. Mellet &
    T. Camelot, eds. & trans., *La trinité, livres I–VIII,* Oeuvres de Saint Augustin 15
    (Paris: Institut d'Études Augustiniennes, 1997), p. 364.

82 *"Everything, therefore, that human consciousness knows":* Translating *De trinitate*
    15.12.22, from Agaësse, p. 484.

83 *"And so the word vocalized externally":* Translating *De trinitate* 15.11.20 from Agaësse,
    pp. 470–72.

83 *"When the [inner] word is vocalized":* Translating *De trinitate* 15.11.20 from Agaësse,
    p. 474.

83 *the latter is physical and the former is not:* On the dissimilarity between the embod-
    ied Son and the invisible second person of the Trinity, see *De civitate dei* 10.13, in
    Wiesen, p. 310.

83 *"But when that which is found in the judgment":* Translating *De trinitate* 15.11.20
    from Agaësse, p. 474.

Chapter 5: Disowning

I've found much in Jean-Louis Chrétien's *Saint Augustin et les actes de parole* (Paris:
Presses Universitaires de France, 2002) useful for this chapter. There are many
echoes of his thought (and probably some of his elegant phrase-making) in it.

85 *"It is not only that we avoid sin when we adore":* Translating *Enarrationes in psalmos*
    98.9 from Migne, vol. 37, col. 1264.

86 *"He [Diabolus] chose to live according to himself":* Translating *De civitate dei* 14.3,
    from Philip Levine, ed. & trans., *Saint Augustine: The City of God against the Pagans,
    Books XII–XV,* Loeb Classical Library 414 (Cambridge, Mass.: Harvard University
    Press, 1988), pp. 272–74.

86 *"And so, when human beings live according to humanity":* Translating *De civitate
    dei* 14.4 from Levine, p. 274.

87 *"We clearly want to be happy":* Translating *De civitate dei* 14.4 from Levine, pp.
    274–76.

87 *"every sin is a lie":* Translating *Enarrationes in psalmos* 91.6 from Migne, vol. 37,
    col. 1174.

88 *told for the sheer joy of telling it:* Discussed in *De mendacio* 14.25, in Carlo Carena et
    al., eds. & trans., *Sant'Agostino: Morale e Ascetismo Cristiano,* Opere di Sant'Agostino
    7/2 (Rome: Città Nuova Editrice, 2001), pp. 358–60.

88 *twist and corrupt our speech:* For metaphors of twisting and corrupting see: *In
    iohannis evangelium tractatus* 5.1 & 8.5, in M.-F. Berrouard, ed. & trans., *Homélies
    sur l'Évangile de Saint Jean I–XVI,* Oeuvres de Saint Augustin 71 (Paris: Institut
    des Études Augustiniennes, 1993), pp. 290–92, 476–78.

88 *"drink from the truth"*: Translating *Enarrationes in psalmos* 91.6 from Migne, vol. 37, cols. 1174–75.

88 *"God alone is a truth-teller"*: Translating *Sermo* 28A.2 from François Dolbeau, ed., *Vingt-six sermons au peuple d'Afrique*, Collection des Études Augustiniennes, Série Antiquité 147 (Paris: Institut des Études Augustiniennes, 1996), p. 31. The quotation from Ps. 116 follows Augustine's Latin rather than NAB.

89 *"So what do they [the Donatists] say?"*: Translating *In iohannis evangelium tractatus* 13.16 from Berrouard, pp. 706–8.

90 *cathedra mendacii*: *Confessiones* 9.2.4, in James J. O'Donnell, *Augustine: Confessions*, 3 vols. (Oxford, U.K.: Clarendon Press, 1992), 1:104.

91 *The only coherent speech-act, therefore, is confession:* On Augustine's understanding of *confessio* I've benefited from Joseph Ratzinger, "Originalität und Überlieferung in Augustins Begriff der *confessio*," *Revue des Études Augustiniennes* 3/1 (1957): 375–92; Pierre Courcelle, *Recherches sur les confessions de Saint Augustin* (Paris: Boccard, 1950), pp. 13–29. Augustine's lengthiest discussion of the term is in *Confessiones* 10.1.1–10.2.2, in O'Donnell, vol. 1, p. 119.

91 *the performative contradiction, that opposes itself to God:* Summarizing and elaborating upon *Enarrationes in psalmos* 137.2, in Migne, vol. 37, cols. 1774–75.

92 *"Confession of evil actions is the beginning of good actions"*: Translating *In iohannis evangelium tractatus* 12.13 from Berrouard, pp. 660–62. Compare *Enarrationes in psalmos* 68/1.19, in Migne, vol. 36, cols. 853–54.

93 *something intrinsically evil:* For this point see *Contra mendacium* 7.18, in Carena, pp. 434–38.

93 *"so that each person may transfer his thoughts"*: Translating *Enchiridion* 7.22 from J. Rivière, ed. & trans., *Exposés généraux de la foi*, Oeuvres de Saint Augustin 9 (Paris: Institut des Études Augustiniennes, 1988), p. 146.

96 *the wise judge:* Discussed in *De civitate dei* 19.6, in William M. Greene, ed. & trans., *Saint Augustine: The City of God against the Pagans, Book XVIII, Chapter XXXVI— Book XX*, Loeb Classical Library 416 (Cambridge, Mass.: Harvard University Press, 1972), pp. 142–46.

96 *"On the end of temporal life"*: Translating the chapter title to *De civitate dei* 1.11 from George E. McCracken, ed. & trans., *The City of God against the Pagans, Books I–III*, Loeb Classical Library 411 (Cambridge, Mass.: Harvard University Press, 1995), p. 56.

97 *Augustine preached a sermon on a text from Matthew 18:* This is *Sermo* 81, in Migne, vol. 38, cols. 499–506; the next several paragraphs summarize and elaborate upon this sermon. All translations, including those from Scripture, are made from Augustine's Latin.

100 *"When I place before the eyes of my heart"*: Translating *Contra mendacium* 18.36 from Carena, p. 476.

100 *You are the truth, presiding over everything:* Translating *Confessiones* 10.41.66 from O'Donnell, 1:145.

Chapter 6: Storytelling

Augustine read widely in pagan and Christian literature, but arriving at clarity about what he read and when he read it is not easy. On this see Harald Hagendahl, *Augustine and the Latin Classics*, Studia Graeca et Latina Gothoburgensia XX:1–2 (Stockholm: Almqvist & Wiksell, 1967), which is a painstaking review and collation of the evidence of this reading. James J. O'Donnell's "Augustine's Classical Readings," *Recherches Augustiniennes* 15 (1980): 144–75, usefully complements and extends Hagendahl's study. Sabine MacCormack, *The Shadows of Poetry: Vergil in the Mind of Augustine* (Berkeley: University of California Press, 1998), is excellent on Augustine's use and understanding of Vergil. On Augustine as reader and theorizer about reading, see Brian Stock, *Augustine the Reader: Meditation, Self-Knowledge, and the Ethics of Interpretation* (Cambridge, Mass.: Belknap Press, 1996).

101 *"The aim of science":* A. E. Housman, *The Confines of Criticism: The Cambridge Inaugural 1911* (Cambridge, U.K.: Cambridge University Press, 1969), p. 31.

101 suaviloquium, *sweetly elegant speech:* On *suaviloquium* and associated matters see: *De mendacio* 11.18, in Carlo Carena et al., eds. & trans., *Sant'Agostino: Morale e Ascetismo Cristiano*, Opere di Sant'Agostino 7/2 (Rome: Città Nuova Editrice, 2001), pp. 346–48; *De trinitate* 14.11.14, in Paul Agaësse, ed. & trans., *La trinité, livres VIII–XV*, Oeuvres de Saint Augustin 16 (Paris: Institut des Études Augustiniennes, 1997), pp. 384–86.

102 *"For mimes and comedies and many poems are full of lies":* Translating *Soliloquia* 2.9.16 from Migne, vol. 32, col. 892.

102 *"a story (fabula) is a lie":* Translating *Soliloquia* 2.11.19 from Migne, vol. 32, col. 894.

102 *what Vergil wrote about these events must be understood as a poetical falsehood:* Summarizing *De cura pro mortuis* 10.12 from Migne, vol. 40, cols. 600–601.

102 *the difficulties of knowing what a particular writer took to be the case:* This is discussed in *Confessiones* 12.18.27, in James J. O'Donnell, *Augustine: Confessions*, 3 vols. (Oxford, U.K.: Clarendon Press, 1992), 1:174.

102 *Vergil as the transmitter of false ideas:* On Vergil so understood, see *De civitate dei* 10.30, in David S. Wiesen, ed. & trans., *Saint Augustine: The City of God against the Pagans, Books VIII–XI*, Loeb Classical Library 413 (Cambridge, Mass.: Harvard University Press, 1988), pp. 392–98; *De civitate dei* 13.19, in Philip Levine, ed. & trans., *Saint Augustine: The City of God against the Pagans, Books XII–XV*, Loeb Classical Library 414 (Cambridge, Mass.: Harvard University Press, 1988), pp. 204–10; *De civitate dei* 14.3, in Levine, pp. 268–74; *Sermo* 105.7.10, in Migne, vol. 38, cols. 622–23.

103 *"After his resurrection":* Translating *Contra mendacium* 13.28, from Carena, p. 460.

104 *reasons to worry about reading pagan fictions:* Such reasons are discussed in *De utilitate credendi* 4.10–5.11, in J. Pegon, ed. & trans., *La foi chrétienne*, Oeuvres de Saint Augustin 8 (Paris: Desclée de Brouwer, 1951), pp. 228–34.

104 *grief aroused in him by reading Vergil's account:* See *Confessiones* 1.13.21, in O'Donnell, 1:11.

104 *he notes on reconsidering that book:* For Augustine's thoughts on the effects of the *Confessiones* on its readers, see *Retractationes* 2.6.1, in Gustave Bardy, ed. & trans., *Les révisions*, Oeuvres de Saint Augustin 12 (Paris: Desclée de Brouwer, 1950), p. 460.

104 *the passions . . . of the* pius animus: Summarizing *De civitate dei* 9.5, from Wiesen, pp. 166–70.

105 *he praises the polished and elegant style of a correspondent:* In *Epistula* 231.1, in Migne, vol. 33, col. 1023.

105 *the greater its ordered harmony:* Augustine develops this view most fully in *De musica*.

106 *Sophocles' play* Philoctetes: I've read the Greek text in Hugh Lloyd-Jones, ed. & trans., *Sophocles*, Loeb Classical Library 21 (Cambridge, Mass.: Harvard University Press, 1994).

109 *obsessive loquaciousness of the author:* I'm indebted here and in the paragraphs
     that follow to Jean-Louis Chrétien, *Corps à corps: à l'écoute de l'oeuvre d'art* (Paris:
     Éditions de Minuit, 1997), esp. pp. 91–121.
109 *"I desire so not to deny desire's":* Geoffrey Hill, *The Orchards of Syon* (Washington,
     D.C.: Counterpoint, 2002), p. 55.
109 *its own self-consuming recursivity:* Stanley Fish has understood this better than anyone
     else. See his *Self-Consuming Artifacts: The Experience of Seventeenth-Century Literature*
     (Berkeley & Los Angeles: University of California Press, 1972); *The Living Temple:
     George Herbert and Catechizing* (Berkeley & Los Angeles: University of California
     Press, 1978).
109 *"Sorrie I am, my God, sorrie I am":* George Herbert, "Sinnes Round," in Helen
     Gardner, ed., *The Poems of George Herbert,* Oxford World's Classics (London: Oxford
     University Press, 1961), p. 112. Compare John Donne, "La Corona," in Arthur L.
     Clements, ed., *John Donne's Poetry,* Norton Critical Editions, 2d ed. (London &
     New York: Norton, 1992), pp. 109–111.

Chapter 7: Plato

I've used the Greek text of the *Hippias ellatōn* given in Harold N. Fowler, ed. & trans.,
Plato: Cratylus, Parmenides, Greater Hippias, Lesser Hippias, Loeb Classical Library
167 (Cambridge, Mass.: Harvard University Press, 1939), pp. 428–74. All translations
and paraphrases in this chapter are based upon the text in these pages, unless other-
wise noted. Translations are mine, though I've consulted with profit the translation
in Fowler, which appears to be a close lineal descendant of the Victorian version by
Benjamin Jowett. Useful commentary upon the dialogue can be found in Robert G.
Hoerber, "Plato's *Lesser Hippias*," *Phronesis* 7/2 (1962): 121–31; Roslyn Weiss, "*Ho
Agathos* as *Ho Dunatos* in the *Hippias Minor,*" *Classical Quarterly* 31/2 (1981): 287–304.
(Weiss provides a detailed analysis of the dialogue's argument, whose main goal is
to save it from equivocation and fallacy; she does not, in my judgment, succeed, but
her analysis is nonetheless helpful, and I've drawn upon it gratefully. She also cites
and discusses most of the pre-1981 discussions of the dialogue's argument.) See
also Jean-François Balaudé, "Que veut montrer Socrate dans l'*Hippias Mineur?*" in
Gabriele Giannantoni & Michael Narcy, eds., *Lezioni Socratiche* (Rome: Bibliopolis,
1997), pp. 259–77; Gregory Vlastos, *Socrates, Ironist and Moral Philosopher* (Ithaca,
N.Y.: Cornell University Press, 1991), pp. 275–80. There are some stimulating comments on the dialogue scattered broadside through Jacques Derrida, "History of the
Lie: Prolegomena," trans. Peggy Kamuf, in Richard Rand, ed., *Futures: Of Jacques
Derrida* (Stanford, Calif.: Stanford University Press, 2001), pp. 65–98.

There's a very large literature on Plato and the lie in general, most of which
doesn't attend to the *Hippias Minor.* I've found the following substantively helpful
(each opens new paths into the trackless wastes of the secondary literature): Arno
Baruzzi, *Philosophie der Lüge* (Darmstadt, Germany: Wissenschaftliche Buchge-
sellschaft, 1996), pp. 151–60; Thomas Brickhouse & Nicholas D. Smith, "Justice
and Dishonesty in Plato's *Republic,*" *Southern Journal of Philosophy* 21/1 (1983):
79–95; Christopher Gill, "Plato on Falsehood, Not Fiction," in Christopher Gill & T.
P. Wiseman, eds., *Lies and Fiction in the Ancient World* (Austin, Tex.: University of
Texas Press, 1993), pp. 38–87; Martha Nussbaum, " 'This Story Isn't True': Poetry,
Goodness, and Understanding in Plato's *Phaedrus,*" in Julius Moravcsik & Philip
Temko, eds., *Plato on Beauty, Wisdom, and the Arts* (Totawa, N.J.: Rowman &
Littlefield, 1982), pp. 79–124; Jane Zembaty, "Plato's *Republic* and Greek Morality
on Lying," *Journal of the History of Philosophy* 26 (1988): 517–45.

115 *The task of the presenter of the* elenchus: On the *elenchus* see Gregory Vlastos, "The Socratic Elenchus," *Oxford Studies in Ancient Philosophy* 1 (1983): 27–58; Jean-François Balaudé, "La finalité de l'*elenchos* d'après les premiers dialogues de Platon," in Gabriele Giannantoni & Michael Narcy, eds., *Lezioni Socratiche* (Rome: Bibliopolis, 1997), pp. 235–58.

116 *he then goes on to quote episodes:* Socrates quotes or mentions *Iliad* 9:308, 1:169ff., 9:357ff.

119 *Socrates in fact means what he says:* But Xenophon, in *Memorabilia* 4.2, in Amy L. Bonette, trans., *Xenophon: Memorabilia* (Ithaca, N.Y.: Cornell University Press, 1994), pp. 113–24, represents Socrates as arguing for just the same view as that expressed in the *Hippias Minor,* and Aristotle (see ch. 8) seems to have assumed that the conclusion of the *Hippias Minor* reflects what Socrates (and Plato) thought. Many modern scholars have doubted it: see Weiss, pp. 303–4; Vlastos, *Socrates,* pp. 275–80, for different views.

121 *Odysseus really is the man who thinks one thing and says another:* In *Iliad* 9:308.

121 *the distinction appears to have been either unavailable or uninteresting to him:* I leave aside the question of whether the distinction between falsehood and duplicity is made, and if made used, in Plato's other works. So far as Socrates is concerned, it's worth consulting Xenophon, *Memorabilia* 4.2.14–29, in Bonette, pp. 113–24, in which Socrates' discussion with Euthydemus about justice takes the example of the lie and follows largely the same track as the *Hippias Minor.* See also *Republic* 327A–332B, on lying and justice, where it's concluded that justice does not always require truth-telling; *Republic* 376A–392C, where the discussion shows that what really worries Plato about the lie is not knowing what's the case (again, this accords with the *Hippias Minor*); *Republic* 414B–415D, on the noble lie necessary to good government; *Republic* 459A–462D, on lying and eugenics; and *Republic* 595A–608B, on truth and falsehood in poetry.

Chapter 8: Aristotle

My text for this chapter is Aristotle's *Metaphysics*, 1024b17–1025a13. I've used the Greek text and commentary in W. D. Ross, *Aristotle's Metaphysics: A Revised Text with Introduction and Commentary,* 2 vols. (Oxford, U.K.: Clarendon Press, 1958), 1:344–48. All quotations or paraphrases in the chapter are based upon these pages; it would be superfluous to provide page or paragraph references because of the brevity of the text. Translations are mine, but I've derived much profit from Ross's translation in Jonathan Barnes, ed., *The Complete Works of Aristotle,* 2 vols. (Princeton, N.J.: Princeton University Press, 1984), 2:1618–19. This section of the *Metaphysics* has attracted less commentary than most. Among what there is I have found useful Jane S. Zembaty's "Aristotle on Lying," *Journal of the History of Philosophy* 31 (1993): 7–29.

126 "*I said the thing which was not*": Jonathan Swift, *Gulliver's Travels,* ed. John Hayward (1726; London: Cresset Press, 1949), pt. 4, ch. 3, p. 326.

131 *he thinks of duplicity as sometimes acceptable:* Some important Aristotelian discussion of the lie can be found in the *Nicomachean Ethics* (1107A–1108B; 1124B; 1127AB), where truth is presented as the mean between boastfulness and mock modesty (this will be taken up by Aquinas, for discussion of which see ch. 12), and these latter, by implication, presented as examples of the lie. Aristotle also says that false-speaking is intrinsically contemptible, but permits the magnanimous man lies of self-depreciation because these show his freedom from need for praise and affirmation—they show, in fact, precisely his magnanimity. In general, for Aristotle

there is an initial presupposition against the lie's acceptability, but one that is based either upon its negative effects upon the social and political order, or upon the character defects of which it is evidence. But, as the example of the magnanimous man shows, he also allows that some lies may not be evidence of any character defect but rather of the opposite; and that some lies may not offend against the well-being of the city. There is not to be found in Aristotle any systematic critique of duplicity.

Chapter 9: Chrysostom

My text for this chapter is the first book of John Chrysostom's *Peri hierōsunēs*, often referred to by its Latin title, *De sacerdotio*, which in English is *Priesthood*. I've read and translated from the Greek text found in Anne-Marie Malingrey, ed. & trans., *Jean Chrysostome: sur le sacerdoce*, Sources Chrétiennes 272 (Paris: Éditions du Cerf, 1980), pp. 60–98. All quotations or paraphrases in this chapter are based upon the text in these pages. Translations are mine. Malingrey's edition also contains a French translation, which has been useful. In English, the most recent version I've come across is W. A. Jurgens, trans., *The Priesthood* (New York: Macmillan, 1955). This is of some use, though it's too free to be an accurate guide to Chrysostom's vocabulary and style. It does contain (pp. xiii–xiv) guidance to and details of previous English translations. Biographical studies of Chrysostom include: J. N. D. Kelly, *Golden Mouth: The Story of John Chrysostom, Ascetic, Preacher, Bishop* (Ithaca, N.Y.: Cornell University Press, 1995); Wendy Mayer & Pauline Allen, *John Chrysostom* (London & New York: Routledge, 2000), pp. 3–16 (a useful supplement to and modification of Kelly). Malingrey's edition also contains (pp. 9–11) a lucid and blessedly brief biographical summary.

142 *Augustine discusses a case of this kind:* In *Contra mendacium* 18.36–37, in Carlo Carena et al., eds. & trans., *Sant'Agostino: Morale e Ascetismo Cristiano*, Opere di Sant'Agostino 7/2 (Rome: Città Nuova Editrice, 2001), pp. 474–78.

Chapter 10: Jerome

For the Latin text of the letters between Jerome and Augustine I've used Migne, vol. 33. There are more up-to-date critical editions of the letters, but the libraries available to me at the time of writing this chapter lacked them. I give letter numbers according to the enumeration in the collection of Augustine's correspondence (they are also found, of course, in the collection of Jerome's correspondence, where they are given different numbers). Translations are my own, but I've consulted with great profit the annotated translation of the complete correspondence by Carolinne White, *The Correspondence (394–419) Between Jerome and Augustine of Hippo*, Studies in Bible and Early Christianity 23 (Lewiston-Queenston-Lampeter, U.K.: Edwin Mellen, 1990). Among the recently reviewed sermons by Augustine, found in 1990 in the Mainz municipal library, is one that addresses the topic of his disagreement with Jerome. See François Dolbeau, ed. and trans., *Vingt-six sermons au peuple d'Afrique* (Paris: Institut des Etuses Augustiniennes, 1996), pp. 45–56.

Work on the correspondence that I've found useful includes: Ronald Cole-Turner, "Anti-Heretical Issues and the Debate over Galatians 2:11–14 in the Letters of St. Augustine to St. Jerome," *Augustinian Studies* 11 (1980): 155–66; Julia A. Fleming, "The Helpful Lie: The Moral Reasoning of Augustine and John Cassian," Ph.D. dissertation, Catholic University of America, 1993, pp. 206–19, which provides a helpful overview; Ralph Hennings, *Der Briefwechsel zwischen Augustinus und Hieronymus*

*und ihre Streit um den Kanon des Alten Testaments und die Auslegung von Gal.
2,11–14,* Supplements to Vigiliae Christianae 21 (Leiden, Netherlands: Brill, 1994),
which is a comprehensive though pedestrian study, both textual and theological;
Frank Morgenstern, *Die Briefpartner des Augustinus von Hippo: Prosopographische,
sozial- und ideologie-geschichtliche Untersuchungen,* Bochumer historische Studien,
Alte Geschichte 11 (Bochum, Germany: Brockmeyer, 1993), which treats Augustine's
letters in general (there is an especially useful bibliography at pp. 311–15); Robert J.
O'Connell, "When Saintly Fathers Feuded: The Correspondence Between Augustine
and Jerome," *Thought* 54/215 (1979): 344–64, which is an elegant but overexcited
summary of the content and context of the correspondence.

146 *his commentary on Galatians:* Jerome's commentary on Galatians, the *Commentarius in Epistolam S. Pauli ad Galatas,* is found in Migne, vol. 26, cols. 331–468.
His comments on Gal. 2:11–14 are in Migne, vol. 26, cols. 363–67.

147 *figmentorum poeticorum vestigia: Confessiones* 1.17.27, in James J. O'Donnell,
Augustine: Confessions, 3 vols. (Oxford, U.K.: Clarendon Press, 1992), 1:13.

147 *"Once any useful lie is admitted": Epistula* 28.3.3, translated from Migne, vol. 33,
cols. 112–13.

148 *the propriety of the patriarchs' polygamous habits:* Discussed by Augustine in *De
bono coniugali* 15.17, in P. G. Walsh, ed. & trans., *Augustine: De bono coniugali,
De sancta virginitate* (Oxford, U.K.: Clarendon Press, 2001), p. 34.

148 *Augustine therefore asked Jerome to write a palinode:* In *Epistula* 40.4.7, Migne, vol.
33, col. 157. See also *Epistula* 82.33, Migne, vol. 44, col. 290.

148 *claiming that Galatians 2 is a tissue of* simulatio: *Epistula* 75.4, in Migne, vol. 33,
cols. 252–53.

149 *Augustine thought that at the time of Paul and Peter: Epistula* 82.9, Migne vol. 33,
col. 279.

149 honesta dispensatio *rather than* officiosum mendacium: For more on these terms,
see J. Reumann, "*Oikonomia* as Ethical Acommodation in the Fathers," *Studia
Patristica* 3 (1961): 370–79; Michèle Sinapi, "La question du mensonge officieux
dans la correspondance Jérôme-Augustin," *Rue Descartes* 8/9 (1993): 63–83.

150 *"I'd like to know": Epistula* 82.21, Migne, vol. 33, col. 285.

150 *refers to a phrase used by Jerome in an earlier letter: Epistula* 75.14, Migne, vol. 33,
col. 259.

150 *"Either this is what I'd label a useful lie": Epistula* 82.21, Migne, vol. 33, col. 285.

150 *frequently calling it* carnis dispensatio: For example, in *In iohannis evangelium
tractatus* 36.2, in M.-F. Berrouard, ed. & trans., *Homélies sur l'Évangile de Saint
Jean XXXIV–XLII,* Oeuvres de Saint Augustin 73A (Paris: Institut des Études Augustiniennes, 1988), p. 178.

150 *"Is it the case that those who lie usefully": Epistula* 82.21, Migne, vol. 33, cols.
285–86.

152 *Augustine does not think so:* On Augustine's readings of the apparent lies in Exod. 1
and Josh. 2 see *De mendacio* 5.5, in Carlo Carena et al., eds. & trans., *Sant'Agostino:
Morale e Ascetismo Cristiano,* Opere di Sant'Agostino 7/2 (Rome: Città Nuova Editrice, 2001), p. 320; *Contra mendacium* 15.32, in Carena, pp. 466–68.

Chapter 11: Cassian

My text for this chapter is the seventeenth of John Cassian's *Conlationes.* I refer
to and translate from the Latin given in E. Pichery, ed. & trans., *Jean Cassien:
Conférences VIII–XVII,* Sources Chrétiennes 54 (Paris: Éditions du Cerf, 1958), pp.
248–84. All quotations and paraphrases of Cassian are based upon these pages.

Translations are mine, though I've consulted with great profit the translation and notes in Boniface Ramsey's *John Cassian: The Conferences*, Ancient Christian Writers 57 (New York: Paulist Press, 1997). The French translation in Pichery has also been useful. Adalbert de Vogüé's "Understanding Cassian: A Survey of the Conferences," *Cistercian Studies Quarterly* 19 (1984): 101–21, is helpful on the literary genre and structure of the work.

The two best treatments of Cassian's life in English are Owen Chadwick, *John Cassian*, 2d ed. (Cambridge, U.K.: Cambridge University Press, 1968); Columba Stewart, *Cassian the Monk* (New York: Oxford University Press, 1998). The latter, in particular, gives detailed guidance to scholarship on the life, and to much of that on the work.

156 *There is no doubt that Cassian knew about Augustine:* On the question of Cassian's knowledge of and degree of explicit response to Augustine I've used (though I disagree with) Julia Fleming's "By Coincidence or Design? Cassian's Disagreement with Augustine Concerning the Ethics of Falsehood," *Augustinian Studies* 29/2 (1998): 19–34. See also Boniface Ramsey, "John Cassian: Student of Augustine," *Cistercian Studies Quarterly* 28 (1993a): 5–15; 28 (1993b): 199–200.

167 *"one thing by way of another, so that a truth might be understood":* Translating *Contra mendacium* 10.24 from Carlo Carena et al., eds. & trans., *Sant'Agostino: Morale e Ascetismo Cristiano*, Opere di Sant'Agostino 7/2 (Rome: Città Nuova Editrice, 2001), p. 448.

167 *Jacob was quite right to say, "I am Esau":* Augustine argues this line in *Sermo* 4.23, in Migne, vol. 38, cols. 45–46.

Chapter 12: Aquinas

My text for this chapter is Question 110 of the second part of the second part of the *Summa Theologiae* (ST). I cite, quote, and translate this from the manual edition of the *Summa* in vol. 81 of the *Biblioteca de Autores Cristianos*, 3d ed. (Madrid: Biblioteca de Autores Cristianos, 1963), pp. 678–86. Otherwise unlocated quotations of, references to, and summaries of Aquinas are to this question. The two most easily available English translations of the *Summa* are (1) *The Summa Theologica, literally translated by Fathers of the English Dominican Province*, 22 vols. (New York: Benziger, 1911–1925, with frequent reprints & revisions). This version is accurate and literal, sometimes to the point of incomprehensibility. (2) T. Gilby & T. C. O'Brien, eds., *Summa Theologiae*, 60 vols. (New York & London: Blackfriars, 1964–1973). This edition contains Latin and English on facing pages; the translations are sometimes sufficiently free as to be questionable.

On the structure of ST, and on the times and places of its composition, I follow Jean-Pierre Torrell, *The Person and His Work*, vol. 1 of *Saint Thomas Aquinas*, trans. (from French) by Robert Royal (Washington, D.C.: Catholic University of America Press, 1996), pp. 153–56. Torrell is also excellent on the life.

Among discussions of Aquinas's treatment of *mendacium*, I've benefited especially from Joseph Boyle, "The Absolute Prohibition of Lying and the Origins of the Casuistry of Mental Reservation: Augustinian Arguments and Thomistic Developments," *American Journal of Jurisprudence* (1999): 43–65; Lawrence Dewan, "St. Thomas, Lying, and Venial Sin," *The Thomist* 61/2 (1997): 279–99; and Gérard Courtois, "Mensonge et parjure selon saint Thomas d'Aquin," *Rue Descartes* 8/9 (1993): 85–97.

173 *These seven virtues:* Treated in ST IIaIIae, qq. 1–170.

173 *"establishes a certain equality among things":* Translating from ST IIaIIae, q. 109, a. 3.

174 *they fail in one way or another in the sphere of external interpersonal actions:* This
     is the upshot of the definitions and analyses of *iustitia* in ST IIaIIae, qq. 58–60.
177 *"de se supra se aliquid dicit":* ST IIaIIae, q. 112, a. 1.
178 *houses built for them:* Most Contemporary English versions read "families" for
     "houses." I follow Aquinas's Latin (and compare the version given by King James's
     translators).
179 *hiding the truth* (occultare veritatem) *isn't the same as lying:* On this see: *Contra
     mendacium* 10.23, in Carlo Carena et al., eds. & trans., *Sant'Agostino: Morale e As-
     cetismo Cristiano,* Opere di Sant'Agostino 7/2 (Rome: Città Nuova Editrice, 2001),
     pp. 446–48; *De mendacio* 10.17, in Carena, p. 346.
179 *"someone signifies by [nonverbal] signs of things":* Translating from ST IIaIIae, q.
     111, a. 1.
180 *what Aquinas means by distinguishing mortal from venial sins:* On this distinction
     see ST IaIIae, qq. 88–89; *De malo,* q. 7, translated in John A. Oesterle & Jean T.
     Oesterle, *On Evil* (Notre Dame, Ind.: University of Notre Dame Press, 2001), pp.
     248–306.
181 *Sin in general is, for Aquinas, any disordered act:* See ST IaIIae, q. 71, a. 1.
181 *anything said, done, or desired against the eternal law:* See ST IaIIae, q. 71, a. 6.
181–182 *what Aquinas calls* verba otiosa: On *verba otiosa* and mortal sin, see *De malo,* q.
     2, a. 8, q. 7, a. 3, translated in Oesterle & Oesterle, pp. 81, 269. Compare ST IaIIae,
     q. 88, a. 5.
182 *"increase gravity infinitely":* Oesterle & Oesterle, p. 81 (*De malo,* q. 2, a. 8).
182 propter imperfectionem actus: ST IaIIae, q. 88, a. 6.

Chapter 13: Kant

I've used the text of Kant's lying essay ("Über ein vermeintes Recht aus Menschenliebe zu lügen"—"On a Supposed Philanthropic Right to Lie") in *Kant's Werke,*
ed. Königlich Preussischen Akademie der Wissenschaften, (Berlin & Leipzig,
Germany: de Gruyter, 1923), 8:425–30. All quotations or paraphrases are based
upon these pages unless otherwise noted. Translations are mine, though I've
consulted with profit the English versions in James W. Ellington, *Immanuel
Kant: Grounding for the Metaphysics of Morals* (Indianapolis: Hackett, 1993), pp.
63–67; and in Lewis White Beck, trans., *Critique of Practical Reason and Other
Writings in Moral Philosophy* (Chicago: University of Chicago Press, 1949), pp.
346–50.

There's a good deal of secondary scholarship on the lying essay and matters aris-
ing from it. I've found the following especially helpful: Robert J. Benton, "Political
Expedience and Lying: Kant vs. Benjamin Constant," *Journal of the History of Ideas*
43/1 (1982): 135–44; Christine M. Korsgaard, *Creating the Kingdom of Ends* (Cam-
bridge, U.K.: Cambridge University Press, 1996), chs. 5, 12; Alasdair MacIntyre,
"Truthfulness, Lies, and Moral Philosophers: What Can We Learn from Mill and
Kant?" in Grethe B. Peterson, ed., *The Tanner Lectures on Human Values* (Salt Lake
City: University of Utah Press, 1995), 16:307–61; H. J. Paton, "An Alleged Right to
Lie: A Problem in Kantian Ethics," *Kant-Studien* 45 (1953–1954): 190–203; Sally
Sedgwick, "On Lying and the Role of Content in Kant's Ethics," *Kant-Studien* 82
(1991): 42–62; Jules Vuillemin, "On Lying: Kant and Benjamin Constant," *Kant-
Studien* 73 (1982): 413–24.

186 *"so as to make it possible":* Karl Ameriks, "Kant," in Robert Audi, ed., *The Cambridge
     Dictionary of Philosophy,* 2d ed. (Cambridge, U.K.: Cambridge University Press,
     1999), p. 461.

186 *applied as a universal law:* This is a paraphrase of the formulation in Kant's *Grundlegung zur Metaphysik der Sitten*, in *Kant's Werke*, ed. Königlich Preussischen Akademie der Wissenschaften (Berlin & Leipzig, Germany: de Gruyter, 1903), 4:421.

186 *"Act in such a way that you treat humanity* (Menschheit)": Translating from *Grundlegung zur Metaphysik der Sitten*, p. 429.

189 *enter the "doctrine of virtue":* Kant's mature understanding of the difference between *Rechtslehre* and *Tugendlehre* shapes the *Metaphysik der Sitten*, which should be consulted for a detailed presentation. Vuillemin has helpful remarks to make about Kant's restriction of the question about the lie to the doctrine of right.

192 *interpreters of Kant's thought have not, in general, been very happy:* Paton, for example (p. 202), holds that the doctrine of the lying essay is not consistent with that of Kant's mature philosophy, and that the problems with the essay should be attributed to the petulance and forgetfulness of an old man.

195 *He does think of himself as a Christian thinker:* For Kant's understanding of religion, Christianity, and his relation to both, see his *Religion innerhalb der Grenzen der bloßen Vernunft*, and *Vorlesungen über die philosophische Religionslehre*, both available in English in Allen W. Wood & George di Giovanni, eds. & trans., *Immanuel Kant: Religion and Rational Theology* (Cambridge, U.K.: Cambridge University Press, 1997).

197 *"taught to listen to the divine Scriptures.":* Translating *De catechizandis rudibus* from Carlo Carena et al., eds. & trans., *Sant'Agostino: Morale e Ascetismo Cristiano*, Opere di Sant'Agostino 7/2 (Rome: Città Nuova Editrice, 2001), p. 208.

Chapter 14: Newman

My text for this chapter is notes F and G to the 1865 edition of Newman's *Apologia Pro Vita Sua*. I've used for this Martin J. Svaglic's edition, *Apologia Pro Vita Sua: Being a History of His Religious Opinions*, by *John Henry Cardinal Newman* (Oxford, U.K.: Clarendon Press, 1967), pp. 299–311. All quotations from or paraphrases of Newman are to these pages unless otherwise indicated. Svaglic's edition has the best text of the *Apologia*, and also contains much of the background material relevant to understanding Newman's text—especially Kingsley's pamphlet, "What, Then, Does Dr. Newman Mean?"

The argument between Newman and Kingsley has attracted a good deal of attention and prompted much writing one way and another. In addition to the accounts in the standard biographies—among which Ian Ker's *John Henry Newman: A Biography* (New York: Oxford University Press, 1995) is by far the best; his lucid account may be found at pp. 533–59—there is P. J. Fitzpatrick's *Apologia pro Charles Kingsley* (London: Sheed & Ward, 1969), published under the nom de plume "G. Egner" ("opponent" in German), which is entertainingly, though obsessively, anti-Newman (the same author has written several other essays on the question). Not much of the Kingsley-Newman literature, however, has to do with Newman on the lie: this is a relatively understudied topic.

199 *"Truth, for its own sake":* Svaglic, p. 341.

200 *"the slave and puppet":* Svaglic, p. 366.

200 *"more materialist than the dreams of any bone-worshipping Buddhist":* Svaglic, p. 368.

200 *"a treacherous ape":* Svaglic, p. xlviii.

200 *"[T]here are people":* Svaglic, p. 387.

202 *"various Economies or Dispensations of the Eternal":* Svaglic, p. 36.

202 *"I understood these passages":* Svaglic, p. 36.

202 *"thoughts beyond their thought to those high bards were given":* Newman here quotes Keble's *Christian Year,* one of the most popular (Anglican) devotional works of the nineteenth century.

202 *"In the fulness of time both Judaism and Paganism had come to nought":* It's interesting to observe here the matter-of-course assumption on Newman's part of the end of Judaism. In this supersessionist judgment he is like most of his contemporaries, but this is of course no longer (if it ever was) the teaching of the Catholic church.

202 *his book about the Arians of the fourth century:* On the composition of this book see Ker, pp. 44–53; the third edition (of 1871) of the book was recently (2001) republished by the University of Notre Dame Press with a useful introduction by Rowan Williams, installed as (Anglican) Archbishop of Canterbury in 2002. Especially useful (for the topic of this book) are Williams's comments (pp. xxviii–xxxvi) on Newman's treatment of the *disciplina arcani.*

202 *the phrase* carnis dispensatio: Used by Augustine in, for example, *In iohannis evangelium tractatus* 36.2, in M.-F. Berrouard, ed. & trans., *Homélies sur l'Évangile de Saint Jean XXXIV–XLII,* Oeuvres de Saint Augustin 73A (Paris: Institut des Études Augustiniennes, 1988), p. 178.

204 *Newman's thought on the lie is framed by the question of justice, as Aquinas's also was:* Newman nowhere mentions Aquinas in his discussion of the lie. For an English nineteenth-century Protestant audience Aquinas would have been the opposite of an authority, which is a partial explanation of his absence from Newman's text. But even in the Catholic world of the 1860s Aquinas did not have the importance he would have after the First Vatican Council in 1870, and still more after Leo XIII's encyclical *Aeterni Patris* in 1879. Newman's principal authority—the bête noire of hyper-Protestants like Kingsley—was Alphonsus Liguori, whose anti-Jansenist *Theologia Moralis* of the mid–eighteenth century dominated Catholic moral theology until the Second Vatican Council.

207 *"saying the thing that is not":* This is (almost) Jonathan Swift's phrase: when the Houyhnhnm who is teaching Gulliver to speak the Houyhnhnm language doubts something Gulliver tells him, the Houyhnhnm says, "That I must needs be mistaken, or that I *said the thing which was not.* (For they have no Word in their language to express Lying or Falsehood.)" Jonathan Swift, *Gulliver's Travels,* ed. John Hayward (1726; London: Cresset Press, 1949), pt. 4, ch. 3, p. 326 (and often thereafter). Newman probably assumes knowledge of Swift on the part of his readers (though the change of pronoun from "which" to "that" is interesting, and may indicate that the words are a half-remembered and unattributed echo in Newman's mind). See also ch. 8, on Aristotle, and notes thereto.

209 *the ethic of the English gentleman (in this matter at least) trumps that of the Christian:* A similar point can be made—though disputably—about Newman's view of the university (in *The Idea of a University*) and the ideal of education that goes with it. If the point can be made to stick (and I think it can), it goes a good way toward explaining why so many Catholic theorists of education in the United States have been captivated by the idea of a liberal arts education. In fact, this idea has distinctively non-Christian roots, and (often) non-Christian purposes and results.

Chapter 15: Nietzsche

My text for this chapter is Nietzsche's "Über Wahrheit und Lüge in aussermoralischen Sinne" ("On Truth and Lie in an Extramoral Sense"). I cite and translate from the text in Giorgio Colli & Mazzino Montinari, eds., *Friedrich Nietzsche: Nachgelassene*

Schriften 1870–1873, Nietzsche Werke Kritische Gesamtausgabe 3/1 (Berlin & New York: de Gruyter, 1973), pp. 369–84. All translations, quotations, and paraphrases are based on these pages unless otherwise noted. An excellent English translation may be found in Daniel Breazeale, *Philosophy and Truth: Selections from Nietzsche's Notebooks of the Early 1870s* (Atlantic City, N.J.: Humanities Press, 1997), pp. 79–91.

The best book on Nietzsche known to me is Alexander Nehamas, *Nietzsche: Life as Literature* (Cambridge, Mass.: Harvard University Press, 1985)—in its careful distinction between what Nietzsche writes about and how he writes about it, and his constant fruitful connection of the two, it provides a model for interpreting a philosopher's oeuvre. A useful biography is Rudiger Safranski, *Nietzsche: A Philosophical Biography,* trans. Shelley Frisch (New York: Norton, 2002)—ch. 4 is most relevant to the topic of this chapter. Christoph Cox, *Nietzsche: Naturalism and Interpretation* (Berkeley: University of California Press, 1999), pp. 63–68, is good on Nietzsche and art; Tim Murphy, *Nietzsche, Metaphor, Religion* (Albany: State University of New York Press, 2001), is helpful on metaphor; Richard Schacht, *Nietzsche* (London & New York: Routledge, 1983), is a synoptic and helpful exploration of Nietzsche's entire philosophical edifice—chs. 2 and 8 are the most helpful for the purposes of this book.

214 *"sound figures":* For more on these see Richard T. Gray, trans., *Friedrich Nietszche: Unpublished Writings from the Period of Unfashionable Observations,* Collected Works of Friedrich Nietzsche 11 (Stanford, Calif.: Stanford University Press, 1999), p. 30.

214 *"[a] movable host of metaphors":* I follow here Breazeale's translation (p. 84).

216 *"art's mastery over life":* Nietzsche's view on this point is given elegant and witty form by Oscar Wilde in "The Decay of Lying: An Observation," in Edgar Saltus, ed., *Intentions,* Complete Works of Oscar Wilde (Garden City, N.Y.: Doubleday, 1923), 5:5–63.

216 *quest for nonmetaphorical truth as pathetic:* See, for example, "Über das Pathos der Wahrheit," in Colli & Montinari, pp. 249–54, translated in Breazeale, pp. 61–66.

217 *"Our salvation does not lie in* knowing": Gray, p. 42.

217 *"What psychological falsity!":* Nietzsche to Franz Overbeck, 31 March 1885, trans. Christopher Middleton, *Selected Letters of Friedrich Nietzsche* (Indianapolis: Hackett, 1996), pp. 139–40. Nietzsche is quoting (or rather paraphrasing) *Confessiones* 4.9.14.